IMPERIAL
DREAMS

Scan to see the only images
ever taken of a living imperial woodpecker.

Previous works by Tim Gallagher

Falcon Fever: A Falconer in the Twenty-first Century

The Grail Bird: Hot on the Trail of the Ivory-billed Woodpecker

*Parts Unknown: A Naturalist's Journey
in Search of Birds and Wild Places*

Wild Bird Photography

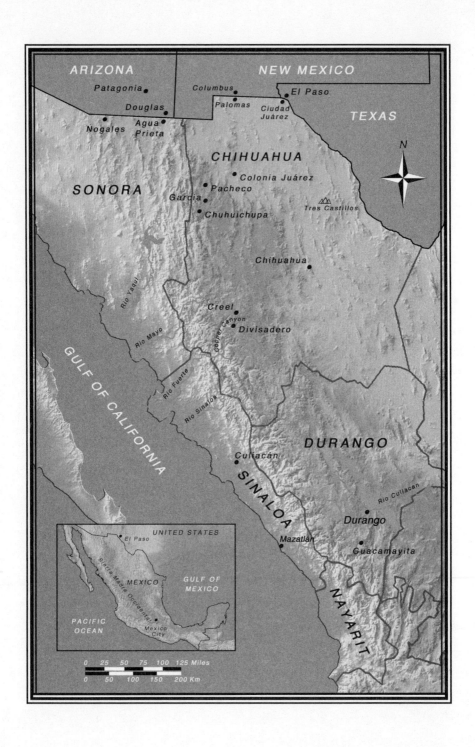

IMPERIAL
DREAMS

Tracking the
Imperial Woodpecker
Through the Wild
Sierra Madre

TIM GALLAGHER

ATRIA BOOKS

NEW YORK   LONDON   TORONTO   SYDNEY   NEW DELHI

ATRIA BOOKS
Atria Books
A Division of Simon & Schuster, Inc.
1230 Avenue of the Americas
New York, NY 10020

First Atria Books hardcover edition April 2013

ATRIA BOOKS and colophon are trademarks of Simon & Schuster, Inc.

Frontispiece map by Bobby Harrison

For information about special discounts for bulk purchases, please contact Simon
& Schuster Special Sales at 1-866-506-1949 or business@simonandschuster.com.

The Simon & Schuster Speakers Bureau can bring authors to your live event.
For more information or to book an event contact the Simon & Schuster Speakers
Bureau at 1-866-248-3049 or visit our website at www.simonspeakers.com.

Designed by Maura Fadden Rosenthal

Manufactured in the United States of America

10   9   8   7   6   5   4   3   2   1

Library of Congress Cataloging-in-Publication Data is available.

ISBN 978-1-4391-9152-1
ISBN 978-1-4391-9153-8 (ebook)

598.72 Gal

FOR MY SON,
JACK O'BANNON GALLAGHER
1994–2012

The beauty and genius of a work of art may be reconceived, though its first material expression be destroyed; a vanished harmony may yet again inspire the composer, but when the last individual of a race of living things breathes no more, another heaven and another earth must pass before such a one can be again.

—WILLIAM BEEBE

CONTENTS

DOWN MEXICO WAY

IN THE HIGH MOUNTAINS of Mexico's rugged Sierra Madre Occidental there once lived a woodpecker unlike any other—a giant, largest of its clan in the world, whose pounding drumbeat echoed through the primeval forests as it bored into massive pines, hammering on them powerfully for weeks at a time until they groaned, shuddered, and finally toppled with an impact that shook the ground. Victorian explorers dubbed the bird *Campephilus imperialis*—the imperial woodpecker. But it had already been named long before. To the Aztecs, it was *cuauhtotomomi* in Nahuatl; to the Tarahumaras, *cumecócari*; to the Tepehuanes, *uagam*; and to the Spanish speakers, the *pitoreal*.

Two feet in length from beak to tail, the imperial woodpecker stood out. It had deep black plumage, except for a white shield on its lower back formed by brilliant snow-white flight feathers, and a big crest (red on the males, black on the females) that curled forward to a shaggy point. Its eyes glowed golden yellow; its long, chisellike bill shone white as polished ivory. And it was noisy, blaring a loud trumpetlike toot as it hitched up a pine trunk, foraging for beetle grubs as big as a man's thumb. Its showy splendor was its undoing—that and the fact that it stayed in tight family groups, often hanging around when one of its group was wounded or killed.

The Huichol, who believe they made the sun themselves, say that the only animals who protected the sun during his first journey across the sky were the gray squirrel and the giant woodpecker.

Because of this, the giant woodpecker carries the color of the sun on his scarlet crest.

Norwegian explorer Carl Lumholtz, who spent eight years traveling on muleback down the 900-mile length of the Sierra Madre Occidental in the 1890s, declared that the birds would soon be exterminated. Indigenous people relished the bird's taste and believed their feathers and bills held curative powers; curious shooters killed them as a novelty; insatiable loggers moved into their vast forest empire and felled most of the great trees across their range. All played a role in decimating the bird's population. By 1956, when amateur ornithologist William L. Rhein from Pennsylvania filmed a lone female imperial woodpecker near a logging camp in the mountains of Durango, the birds were already dangling over the abyss. That single *pitoreal* was the last of its kind ever documented by a birder, naturalist, or scientist.

Yet it's difficult to say for certain that the imperial woodpecker is extinct. Many biologists have already written the bird's epitaph, a sad tale of massive habitat destruction and wanton killing. But among the mountain villagers, stories persist of lone *pitoreales* still flying over the most remote pine forests of the Sierra Madre. Perhaps a handful of the birds do exist and the species could still be saved—if someone would just travel through the mountains of northwestern Mexico and talk to people, follow up on leads, and locate a pair of imperial woodpeckers.

Spurring me on my quest was my inheritance of a treasure map—not for gold or a lost Dutchman's mine, but a cherished topographical map handed to me by a dying man, a noted photographer and naturalist who had himself been given it and had not been able to return to Mexico to explore the areas marked in red on the chart. Carefully preserved for nearly forty years, it showed where imperial woodpeckers had nested in the Sierra Madre as recently as the early 1970s.

The more I thought about this potential discovery, the more I saw myself in the role of the bird's tracker. Rediscovering a lost bird as magnificent as the imperial woodpecker, I hoped, would rally scientists, birders, and nature enthusiasts around the world to save this unique species and the habitat it needs to survive. I postponed my search for several years on the advice of Mexican friends, who cautioned, "It's far too dangerous now because of all the drug growing and violence in the mountains; better wait till next year." But each year the situation only got worse, and we did not have the luxury of waiting years for things to simmer down. By 2008, I had an overwhelming belief that the imperial woodpecker could be saved—but only if we acted immediately.

The Sierra Madre has always been wild, from the time of the Aztecs to the rule of the Spanish to present-day Mexico. It has always been impossible to govern. Although the mountain range starts less than a hundred miles south of the United States border, it seems worlds away, locked in a distant time. Rugged, remote, and dangerous, it is haunted by the ghosts of martyrs and outlaws, ancient and modern, by legends of lost treasures—and by the imminent loss of its natural treasures, found nowhere else.

The mountains are high, nearly ten thousand feet above sea level along much of their length with even higher peaks, and cut through with deep *barrancas*, or canyons, one of which is deeper than the Grand Canyon. There the Tarahumara (or Rarámuri)—those magnificent long-distance runners who think nothing of racing 150 miles or more nonstop through the mountains—resisted all efforts to colonize them and maintained their stone-age existence well into the twentieth century. And there the last free Apaches (who had fled to the Sierra Madre after Geronimo surrendered to US Brigadier General Nelson A. Miles in 1886) held on into the 1930s, in roving bands, attacking settlers who encroached on their land. And there legendary Mexican revolutionary Pancho Villa fled after his daring 1916 raid into New Mexico, successfully evading capture by ten thousand US troops sent on a punitive mission by President Woodrow Wilson. No doubt Villa and his men saw the dust of the American cavalry billowing up from fifty miles away, like a dirty cumulus cloud, into the dry, clear air of the high-mountain plateaus, giving the rebels plenty of time to disappear without a trace into the deep *barrancas* of the Sierra Madre.

Although the Sierra Madre has always been dangerous, it has gotten far worse recently. An unofficial truce of sorts, which had existed for years between the Mexican government and the *narcotraficantes* in the area, ended when Presidente Felipe Calderón (at the urging of the United States) cracked down on drug growers; open rebellion has since broken out in northern Mexico. After the arrest of several major drug kingpins, many lesser *narcotraficantes* are now battling to replace them. Several other measures Calderón attempted also backfired. Some of the numerous crooked cops Calderón fired have since become full-time professional criminals without any of the restraints they might have had when they were civil servants. And worse, dozens of elite Mexican troops who received Special Forces training from the United States have crossed to the dark side, selling their deadly skills to the very drug traffickers they were recruited to fight.

On almost any given day, shootouts erupt between rival drug gangs, who spray each other (and anyone else who might get in the way) with bullets from their AK-47s or blast rocket-propelled grenades. Nearly fifty thousand people have been killed since 2006 in the conflict, including hundreds of police and soldiers, and the death toll keeps rising. In one outrageous incident, the governor of Chihuahua was attacked by armed men and had to speed away in his bulletproof SUV in a hail of bullets, leaving one of his bodyguards dead on the ground. Huge gun battles have erupted in the middle of major cities such as Durango and Chihuahua as well as

Ciudad Juárez, directly across the border from El Paso, Texas. The governors of Texas and New Mexico have asked for federal troops to be sent to the border area to ensure that the violence won't spill over into the United States, and the US State Department is warning at the time of this writing that the entire nation of Mexico is in danger of becoming a failed state.

So why would anyone go looking in such a terrifyingly dangerous place for a bird that might not even exist? I've heard this question many times from family, friends, and acquaintances, and it is difficult to answer. The road to the Sierra Madre has been a long one for me and began with a different species—a tiny falcon rather than a giant woodpecker. As a young boy, the first time I gazed at a wild kestrel perched on a tree in the field near my home, something about the exquisite beauty of the bird touched me deeply, and I was never the same again. Later, at the age of twelve, I took a young male kestrel from a nest and trained him to circle around high above me as I ran through the field. When I blew a whistle, he would return to me.*

I've been a devoted falconer ever since. For thirteen years, I've been flying a captive-bred peregrine falcon called Macduff. On some brisk autumn days, he flies so high that I lose sight of him straight overhead—a tiny speck disappearing in and out of the cumulus clouds.

My love for peregrine falcons drove me to become a staunch, determined conservationist. The species had been nearly pushed to extinction in much of North America by the late 1960s due

---

*The possession of birds of prey is now much more restricted in the United States. People aspiring to train raptors must apply for state and federal licenses, get an experienced falconer to sponsor them, take a detailed written exam, and have their hawk house inspected and approved. They must also serve an apprenticeship with their sponsor for at least two years, during which time they can own only one wild-trapped kestrel or a red-tailed hawk.

to DDT contamination in its environment. Although DDT was banned in the United States in 1972, the damage to the peregrine had largely already been done; the birds were no longer breeding in the contiguous United States east of the Mississippi, and most of the nests to the west had also been abandoned. It took a series of bold steps to bring the peregrine falcon back. First, researchers had to figure out how to breed the birds in captivity—no small effort for a species used to nesting on lofty cliffs and engaging in high-speed courtship displays, soaring and diving across the entire sky. Cornell professor and falconer Tom Cade led the effort, forming the Peregrine Fund, a group dedicated to reversing the falcon's decline. He persuaded other falconers to donate their birds to his breeding project, which ultimately became a colossal success, producing thousands of young peregrines for release.

Fresh out of college I went to work at the Santa Cruz Predatory Bird Research Group, an affiliate of the Peregrine Fund in California, and helped them build their breeding chambers, care for the captive falcons, and study wild peregrines. The job did not pay well, but it answered a fundamental need of mine: to try to do some good in the world—especially helping sensitive wildlife species, so many of which are being pushed toward extinction.

Things have worked out extremely well for the peregrine falcon. Thousands of captive-bred young were released across the continent, and now their wild populations are booming. I'm proud to have been part of that effort. But as the peregrine falcon population recovered, I started looking for other ways to help in wildlife conservation.

In many ways, I've built my life around birds. In the mid-1980s, I was on the start-up crew of *WildBird*, a magazine for birdwatchers, and became its first managing editor. And for more than twenty years, I've been editor in chief of *Living Bird* magazine, the flagship publication of the Cornell Lab of Ornithology. But for me, it has never been enough just to write; I've frequently felt the need to get down on the ground in threatened habitats, from the Arctic to the tropics, to participate in field research.

Before looking for the imperial woodpecker, I had searched for the presumably extinct ivory-billed woodpecker, the closest relative of the imperial and very similar in appearance (it's not unusual even now for the Anglo-Mexicans who remember the imperial to call it an ivory-billed woodpecker), in the vast swamps and bayous of the South. I was drawn to these large, beautiful woodpeckers in the same way I was to the raptors I've trained. Although I didn't run into any *narcotraficantes* in the southern swamps, searching for the ivory-bill had presented its own problems: the stifling heat of the place, getting lost in the trackless bayous where every direction looks the same, and deadly water moccasins rearing up from the murky water as I drifted past in my canoe.

I spent several years interviewing people who had seen ivory-bills in the 1930s and '40s in their last known stronghold, an 81,000-acre chunk of virgin Louisiana swamp forest called the Singer Tract. After the woods were clear cut, the birds dropped from the scientific radar screen for more than sixty years. But I kept finding people—mostly hunters and fishermen who routinely spent entire days hunkered down in swamps, clad head-to-foot in camouflage clothes—who claimed more recent sightings of birds that fit the description of an ivory-bill. Some of them seemed honest and capable, so I started following up on their observations, visiting the very places where they had seen these mystery birds. In many cases, their sightings were more than thirty years old, and sometimes the woods had already been cut, but in other places, the habitat still seemed excellent.

Then I interviewed a kayaker named Gene Sparling who had sighted a likely looking bird less than a week earlier in a remote swamp in the backwoods of Arkansas. A few days later, I hit the bayou with Bobby Harrison—an old friend and longtime ivory-bill chaser from Alabama. We planned to spend twenty-four hours a day for a week in Bayou de View, where Sparling's sighting took place, floating the length of it and camping out at night. But in the early afternoon of the second day, an unmistakable ivory-bill flew across the bayou less than seventy feet in front of our canoe and swung up to land on the trunk of a large tupelo. "Ivory-bill!" we cried out simultaneously, and the bird veered off through the woods.

That was the start of a vast search led by the Cornell Lab of Ornithology. Our team had several follow-up sightings, and one of the searchers, David Luneau of the University of Arkansas at Little Rock, managed to take a blurry video of the bird, which we analyzed in an article that appeared in the journal *Science*. The rediscovery announcement led to intensive coverage by the international media. Later, the *60 Minutes* television crew and Ed Bradley spent almost a week with us in the swamp and documentary filmmaker George Butler spent months filming *The Lord God Bird*. Naysayers inevitably emerged who didn't believe we'd really found the bird, and a huge scientific debate ensued.

Looking back, it had seemed so dangerous traveling through those southern backwoods and swamps, sometimes alone, sometimes with Bobby. But the level of danger in the Sierra Madre is exponentially higher than that in any southern swamp.

From the start, my search for the imperial woodpecker would be an entirely different kind of quest. On expeditions to Iceland and Greenland I had rappelled down sheer cliffs to reach the nest ledges of gyrfalcons, the world's largest falcon, as the parents hurtled past my head like howitzer shells in sizzling power dives. I had gone on two open-boat voyages along the storm-torn coast of northern Greenland, surveying nesting colonies of seabirds and helping to gather data on the Earth's changing climate patterns and how they affect bird populations. But I would face a far different kind of danger in the mountains of Mexico—a human danger that hung like a malevolent cloud over everything I did.

Soon after I launched my search for the imperial woodpecker, I began having a terrifying recurrent nightmare. It always went something like this: I am traveling alone on a rough footpath through the high country of the Sierra Madre. As I trudge ever deeper into the forest, the pines become larger and larger, lofty old-growth giants with trunks several feet across, towering into the sky. Then I hear the deafening raps of a foraging woodpecker, far louder than I ever imagined, each blow like an explosion echoing through the forest, again and again and again, like nothing I have ever heard. What else could it be but an imperial woodpecker? And then I'm racing as fast as I can after the sound, flying across the ground as fleet as a deer, hoping to catch a glimpse of this elusive ghost. But suddenly a dark-haired man dressed in black and holding an AK-47 steps out in front of me from behind a tree, and I cry out in shock.

On the good nights, I'd wake with a jolt right then, shivering in a cold sweat. But other times, the dream continued, with the man shouting at me in a tongue I can't decipher, like some strange mountain dialect of Spanish or the ancient Nahuatl of the Aztecs. I try speaking to him in broken Spanish, in English, and even in sign language, but he doesn't understand and glares at me with dark, burning eyes—pitiless and menacing. Pulling out my wallet, I try to show him my identification . . . some pictures of my kids . . . some American money. He knocks them to the ground and shoves me hard with the butt of his rifle, driving me away from the trail, deeper into the woods. I walk ahead of him, sick with dread. Finally he stops and points the rifle at me. I glance down and see his finger tightening on the trigger.

Then I hear it . . . a loud noise like a toy trumpet, ringing out high above me. Looking up, I see an imperial woodpecker hitching up the trunk of a lofty pine, and the bird is huge, two feet long, like a big white-billed raven with gleaming white on its lower back. The bird pauses and lifts its head, gazing at me with a yellow eye, its brilliant red crest blowing shaggily in the wind. And it is the most beautiful sight imaginable—so vivid, so real, I could reach out and touch it, and I choke up.

An instant later, a powerful explosion rips my vision and all is darkness.

Sometimes I would cry out loudly, which frightened my wife. One night I thrashed in terror so wildly, I struck her on the back with my hands. And yet I continued on. The project had taken over my life. Everything about it fascinated me: the imperial woodpecker, the landscape—endless blue ridges of pine forest, filling my mind both night and day. And the people . . . like no others I had met in all of my world travels.

Mexico's hold on me had begun years before I started searching for the imperial woodpecker. I first went there shortly after my family immigrated to the United States from England, by way of Canada, in the early 1960s. I was ten years old, and we were living in San Diego. My father and I drove into Mexico on a Saturday morning to try out one of the cheap barbershops we'd heard about that lay just across the border in Tijuana.

Everywhere we walked on the tight little city streets, throngs of lively people pushed past us speaking rapid-fire Spanish. The pungent delicious aroma of tacos, enchiladas, chile rellenos, and frijoles filled the air. Music belted out everywhere—mariachi bands with brassy trumpets and guitars, singers performing classic Mexican folk ballads. Brightly colored serapes and sombreros adorned the walls of shopping stalls that spilled onto the grimy sidewalks. Street vendors led white donkeys—painted with black stripes to resemble zebras—laden with trinkets for tourists. A middle-aged man with a bushy black moustache stopped us and pulled up the sleeve of his coat to reveal twenty wristwatches, with shiny golden and silver bands, adorning the length of his arm, all of them for sale—cheap. Sleaze merchants beckoned from blind alleyways, enticing visiting gringos to watch various illicit entertainments.

We got lost trying to drive out of the city, and my dad had to make a U-turn with his tiny beige Renault Dauphine so we could retrace our steps. Just as he finally got the car turned around, after many back-and-forth movements in the narrow street, a policeman who had been standing in front of an outdoor taco stand came running over and stood in front of the Renault, blocking our way. Clad in a tan uniform with a policeman hat, he looked like a Mexican Barney Fife. He told my father he had made an illegal turn and would have to pay a $2 fine. After Dad handed him the two bills, the policeman opened his wallet, put the money inside, and strode slowly back to the taco stand.

Mexico was so bright, so colorful, so unlike the United States. I loved it.

My interest in the country continued into my teens, and I would go camping there—first with my Boy Scout troop, later as a young hippie wearing a leather-fringed jacket, which I bought there, and sleeping under the stars on a beach in Baja California. I once sailed down the coast in a 36-foot sloop and in the 1970s camped with friends in the Sierra Madre Occidental. I actually hoped I might stumble across an imperial woodpecker in the pinewoods or perhaps hear its tooting call while cooking breakfast coffee. But at that time, I was more interested in finding a peregrine falcon nest on a rocky cliffside than seeing a woodpecker, even a giant and incredibly rare one. I just didn't know how imperative it would soon be to search for them. When I think back to how much easier it might have been to find one in the 1970s, when there must have been small remnant populations in several areas in the Sierra, I can't help kicking myself. But maybe it wasn't too late to make amends and through hard work I could still find one.

Then, one quiet afternoon in May 2009, I was off, ready to search the farthest reaches of the Sierra Madre, traveling to remote villages, seeking out people who had known this bird. My trail took many surprising twists and turns as I scoured the historical records, sought out others who had looked for this bird before me, and launched my own expeditions into the Sierra Madre, seeking evidence that the great imperial woodpecker might still exist. The trail sometimes led me on tangents away from the bird as I delved into the fascinating history of these mountains and the people— Geronimo's Apaches, Pancho Villa's raiders—who found sanctuary there. But all trails in the Sierra Madre tend to converge, and I found many parallels between the fates of the people and wildlife of the mountains. I was fortunate enough to meet many remarkable men and women who told me vivid stories of seeing imperial woodpeckers, which I recount here. Whether I found a living imperial woodpecker or not, I wanted to help fill in the pitifully small scientific record of this bird's existence with their recollections. I desperately hoped that, if things went just right, I might find a pair of these birds still hanging on, still raising young in some forgotten corner seldom visited by people. That thought kept me going.

But a rival thought also constantly nagged at my mind: that in some ways, imperial woodpecker chasers have much in common with all of the other Sierra Madre seekers who spend their lives scouring the mountains for lost Spanish mines, buried hoards of stolen gold, or the lure of long-vanished native tribes. Whatever they seek seems always to be looming just over the next ridge, barely out of reach. And now I had become one of them.

PART I

TREASURES AND TRAGEDIES OF THE SIERRA MADRE

In Palomas, Mexico, just across the border from Columbus, New Mexico, which Pancho Villa's troops attacked in 1916, stands a statue of the rebel leader galloping with his gun raised. (*Photo by Tim Gallagher*)

1 ✦ In Pancho Villa's Land

 The stretch of highway from El Paso, Texas, to Columbus, New Mexico, is lonely—flat, desolate country where about the only people you see are the Border Patrol agents, sitting sullenly along the roadside in their pale-green-and-white SUVs, peering intently at every passerby. Just a stone's throw to the south is the Mexican border, marked by the crisscrossed metal barriers laid across the desert to prevent vehicles from entering or leaving the country unofficially. The directions I got from Mapquest.com tried to steer me northward to Interstate 10 before going west, which would have added an hour to my time. Perhaps they were trying to tell me that it might be dangerous traveling on Highway 9, a tiny, two-lane state road. I decided to take it anyway.

I was on my way to meet Paul Salopek, a Pulitzer Prize–winning foreign correspondent who had recently returned from Johannesburg, South Africa, where he ran the Africa bureau for the *Chicago Tribune*. Now he lives with his wife, artist Linda Lynch, in an old adobe building on the town's main road. Paul is best known for being the journalist who was arrested as a spy in Darfur in 2006 and held for more than a month, a harrowing experience. On assignment for *National Geographic*, he had hired a driver and a translator and tried to cross the lawless border country of Chad to reach Darfur but was nabbed by a pro-government militia. After the three were severely beaten, the militia leader told his men to take them out and shoot them but then changed his mind. A few days later, they were swapped to the Sudanese government in exchange for some military uniforms.

En route by helicopter to El Fasher, the capital of the Sudanese state of North Darfur, Paul suddenly heard the explosive bursts of automatic weapons far below as rebels opened fire. Tiny beams of daylight appeared inside the helicopter's dim interior as the bullets broke through the fuselage, and a bespectacled officer sitting on the seat right across from Paul slumped over and fell to the floor, bleeding. Although the helicopter made it safely the rest of the way to El Fasher, Paul's ordeal continued. He was charged with espionage and two other criminal counts, and a trial date was set for a month later. He was looking at a twenty-year sentence or perhaps a firing squad. Anything was possible.

His arrest stoked a storm of controversy back home from fellow journalists as well as politicians, a handful of whom—including Barack Obama, at that time a junior senator from Illinois—actually visited him in his cell in the stark, maximum-security prison in El Fasher. But it was Governor Bill Richardson of New Mexico who finally got Paul and the other two men released, traveling to North Darfur in person and negotiating on his behalf. Afterwards, Paul went back to Africa and completed the article for *National Geographic*.

I had sought out Paul because, in the late 1990s, he had traveled the length of the Sierra Madre Occidental from north to south on a mule for *National Geographic*, re-creating an epic 1890s journey by Norwegian ethnologist Carl Lumholtz, who had gone there searching for the lost Anasazi tribe who had built the spectacular cliff dwellings in the American Southwest. Paul took nine months to complete the trek; Lumholtz had taken several years. Paul had heard about the imperial woodpecker and had even spoken with several people about the bird during his journey through the Sierra Madre. I hoped he could point out the best-looking habitat he had seen and suggest people I might contact to help me in my own explorations.

◆　◆　◆

Looking down the dusty main street of tiny Columbus—a handful of small shops and buildings without much charm, surrounded by nothing but blue sky and empty desert—you'd never know the place has any historical significance. But right here, in 1916, for the first time since the War of 1812, a hostile foreign army had invaded the United States, led by legendary Mexican rebel Francisco "Pancho" Villa.

With his wide sombrero, full walrus moustache, and cartridge belts crisscrossed bandolero-style on his chest, Pancho Villa in many ways established the stereotypical image of the Mexican revolutionary/bandito, later immortalized in figures of ridicule such as the Frito Bandito of corn chips fame. But he was anything but a joke as he battled the Mexican government during the bloody revolution that terrorized the country from 1910 to 1920—with additional sporadic outbursts of mayhem for several years thereafter. More than a million Mexicans were killed in this struggle (which is far more people than died in the American Civil War), yet it has been largely forgotten in the United States.

At the height of the violence, Villa's ragtag army attacked the Mexican army in the city of Juárez, while Americans across the border in El Paso sat on the hillsides in the evening to watch the horrendous spectacle unfold as thunderous artillery barrages and explosions lit up the night.

Villa's victory at Juárez led directly to the overthrow of Presidente Porfirio Díaz and brought Francisco Madero to power for a short time, until he was deposed and executed in 1913. This was the beginning of a long parade of presidents who came to power at the front of a mob only to fall into disfavor later and be assassinated. Villa helped Venustiano Carranza become president after the assassinations of Madero and his successor Victoriano Huerta, but Villa quickly turned against him.

Most Americans had viewed Villa favorably at the beginning of the Mexican Revolution. A romantic hero, he had risen from poverty to become a powerful rebel leader, and the US government supplied him with guns and ammunition. But when Villa tried to overthrow Presidente Carranza, the United States sided with Carranza. President Woodrow Wilson saw Carranza as the best hope for peace in Mexico and actively supported him, even allowing Mexican federal troops to cross the border and ride on US trains so they could flank Villa's army. Villa was so outraged that, when some Americans who worked in Mexico were found traveling on a train that his men had stopped near Santa Isabel, Chihuahua, all seventeen were taken out, stripped of their clothes, and shot—though one American played dead and survived, taking his story to the press.

Just a couple of months later, on March 9, 1916, Pancho Villa launched his predawn attack on Columbus, New Mexico, storming through the town with some five hundred armed men. They ran inside houses and other buildings and shot town residents; they set fires and stormed the nearby military encampment, killing several soldiers. Some people fled into the desert to avoid being shot, while others hid inside the two-story Hoover Hotel—its thick adobe walls protecting them from the raiders' bullets. The only building left standing in the central part of the town by the time the fires burned out, the hotel is now a private residence—coincidentally, the home of Paul Salopek and his wife.

After the initial shock of the surprise attack, the small force of American troops managed to regroup and set up a machine gun in front of the Hoover Hotel and another down the street, catching Villa's raiders in a deadly crossfire. The rebels fled south, pursued by a detachment of US cavalry, who chased them fifteen miles into Mexico.

Columbus was a smoking ruin, with eighteen Americans dead and eight wounded—of these, eight of the dead and six of the wounded were US soldiers. But Villa's losses were far greater, with at least sixty-seven dead in Columbus and an untold number shot by the pursuing cavalrymen, who dismounted and fired at them with rifles whenever they got within range.

It's hard to say exactly what Villa's objective was. Of course, he needed the weaponry and ammunition he plundered, but many believe the attack was an act of vengeance against a Columbus arms merchant named Samuel Ravel, who Villa believed had swindled him. Unfortunately for Villa, Ravel was away having dental work in El Paso at the time of the attack.

Within a week, President Woodrow Wilson had dispatched General John J. Pershing and an army of ten thousand troops on a punitive expedition into Mexico to capture Pancho Villa, transforming Columbus overnight into a staging area for the vast military campaign. But the "Punitive Expedition" quickly became a fiasco. Villa and his army vanished into the hinterlands of the Sierra Madre and, despite the US Army's immense technological advantages— including four Curtiss JN-4 "Jenny" biplanes—Pershing was unable to locate him. The airplanes had a number of disadvantages in the Sierra Madre, including the fact that the fuel required to operate them had to be carried 150 miles by mule across rugged terrain.

One of the few successful skirmishes in the campaign was led by George S. Patton, then a twenty-six-year-old lieutenant and later one of the most famous (and controversial) generals in World War II. Having heard a rumor that Julio Cárdenas, one of Villa's right-hand men, would sometimes visit a ranch in the area, Patton and several of his men staked out the place, and when they saw three armed men leave the ranch house and mount their horses, hid near the entrance gates and waited for them to approach. Young Patton stepped out in the center of the road, his pistol drawn, and ordered them to halt. The lead rider galloped toward him, pulling a rifle from a saddle scabbard and firing. Patton coolly aimed his pistol and fired five times, breaking the man's arm and knocking him off his horse. He ran into a shed and hid. Patton shot the horse out from under the second rider, who then came up from the ground shooting his rifle but was quickly cut down by Patton and his men. A soldier killed the third rider with a rifle shot. At that point, the first man—who turned out to be Cárdenas—burst from his hiding place, shooting wildly, and was killed by a bullet through his head. According to reports, Patton filed two notches on the ivory handle of his pistol, one for each of the men he had personally killed. The Americans then drove back to their encampment. Each of their three automobiles bore a dead Villista tied across its hood like a game trophy.

Heaton Lunt, the great-uncle of my friend John Hatch—a Mexican Mormon whose family has lived in Mexico since the late nineteenth century—went along as a scout on Patton's raid. At the end of it, Patton asked Lunt why he hadn't taken part in the shoot-out, to which he replied that he didn't have a gun. So Patton gave him one of his own pistols, an ivory-handled beauty, which is still one of the prized possessions of John's family.

After almost a year of chasing Pancho Villa, the expedition was suspended. Publicly, General Pershing called it a success, but to his family and friends he was more candid: he had been "outwitted and out-bluffed at every turn," he wrote in a letter. "When the true history is written, it will not be a very inspiring chapter for schoolchildren, or even grownups to contemplate. Having dashed into Mexico with the intention of eating the Mexicans raw, we . . . are now sneaking home under cover, like a whipped cur with its tail between its legs."

Perhaps most interesting about this whole episode is that it was aided, abetted, and encouraged by the German government, which was then fully engaged in World War I and hoped that, if it could get the United States bogged down in a Mexican war, it would not be able to come to the aid of Britain and France against Germany. Most of Villa's fighters, in fact, carried Mauser carbines from Germany. But the ploy backfired. The grim experience in Mexico hardened Woodrow Wilson, who largely turned away from his original pacifist leanings. And this, along with the infamous Zimmermann Telegram—an intercepted message sent from the German government to the Mexican government offering to cede much of the American Southwest to Mexico if they would declare war on the United States—finally pushed this country into World War I, which meant inevitable defeat for Germany.

In 1920, Pancho Villa made a deal with the Mexican presidente to disband his army. In exchange, the national government gave him a palatial hacienda near Parral, Chihuahua, where he lived for three years. But on July 20, 1923, riflemen attacked Villa as he rode in his automobile during a visit to town. Villa staggered from the car, riddled with bullets, but was able to kill one of his assailants with a pistol before falling to the ground.

"Don't let it end like this," said Pancho Villa in his last words. "Tell them I said something."

Pulitzer Prize–winning journalist Paul Salopek holds a photograph of the old Hoover Hotel (now his home), taken around the time of Pancho Villa's 1916 attack on Columbus, New Mexico. (*Photo by Tim Gallagher*)

◆ ◆ ◆

When I arrived at the former Hoover Hotel in Columbus, New Mexico, Paul Salopek was standing outside, clad in a white T-shirt, faded blue jeans, and flip-flops. Thin, with short brown hair combed back and slightly unkempt, he looked younger than his forty-seven years. We shook hands warmly, and I followed him inside, out of the blazing desert sun. With its thick adobe walls and two large fans turning slowly overhead, the house was surprisingly cool and pleasant inside. Abstract paintings by Paul's wife, Linda Lynch, who has exhibited across the United States as well as in Mexico, hung on the walls. Most of the upstairs serves as her art studio.

"So, this is the old Hoover Hotel," I said. "Amazing."

"Yes," he said, grinning. "This is where people took shelter during Pancho Villa's raid, because the walls were thick enough to stop Mauser bullets. At least one person bled to death in the bedroom upstairs."

He showed me a framed photograph of the hotel in its heyday, before the raid. Out the front window, the area looks as desolate today as it had after most of the buildings were burned down in 1916. A pile of adobe rubble and part of a wall still lies across the road, with a small historical plaque in front to commemorate the raid.

After giving me a quick tour of his home, Paul and I sat together at the dining room table, drinking lemonade and eating chocolate chip cookies his wife had made that morning. I had just missed her: she was flying to New York. We started talking about Mexico, and Paul asked if I'd like to have dinner with him at a cantina just across the border in the Mexican town of Palomas.

"Sure, that'd be great," I said. "Has there been much violence there?"

He smiled. "Well, some bad things have happened in the past few months," he said. "But it's pretty much only the *narcos* killing each other or murdering police. They're not targeting Americans. You're okay as long as you don't get caught in a crossfire."

"That's ironic," I said. "I came all the way to Columbus because I thought it would be safer than crossing at Juárez."

We got into his old pickup truck and drove a couple of miles south to the border where he parked in a bare-dirt field that serves as a parking lot. The late afternoon sun beat down fiercely as we walked to the border crossing, but the heat was so dry it felt pleasant, and I didn't even break a sweat.

It's amazing how easy it is to cross the border. We just walked through without anyone even asking us what we were doing or making us show any documents. Of course, it would have been much different if we had been crossing the border in a car.

Palomas was much more bustling and alive than Columbus. Street vendors lined the main road, hawking straw cowboy hats and serapes, various trinkets and folk art. The side of one building is covered with murals of Pancho Villa. A huge bronze statue of him galloping on a horse, wildly firing a pistol, adorns a nearby plaza—a not-so-subtle taunt to the gringos who visit this border town. Lately, though, tourism has slowed to a bare trickle, and now even residents of Columbus, who have always come here to shop or to get less expensive haircuts and dental work, are mostly staying away.

Palomas has about seventy-five hundred residents (compared with fewer than eighteen hundred in Columbus) and gets its name from the Spanish word for *doves*—a peaceful moniker for a town that had seen such horrendous violence lately, often in broad daylight. Stray bullets occasionally come whizzing past the border station as people try to escape their attackers by fleeing into America. Sometimes gunshot-wounded people are dropped off at the border crossing to be treated by American paramedics. In one of the wildest examples, a van came racing up to the border crossing and crashed into a concrete barricade. The driver had been shot dead and was slumped over in the front seat. A passenger, also wounded, was hiding on the floor, steering the van blindly and pushing the gas pedal down with his hand.

In March 2008, the police chief of Palomas showed up at the border crossing seeking political asylum in the United States. He and his men had found some murder victims just outside town and received telephoned death threats. All of his deputies had quit their jobs and fled, leaving him alone to face the criminals. After the chief left for the United States, the Mexican Army moved in to keep order in Palomas. Corruption is found on the American side, too; in March 2011, the US government indicted the mayor of Columbus and several other local officials for gunrunning.

Paul and I walked into a small cantina and ordered some Mexican entrees. As we waited for our food, we drank beer and talked about the Sierra Madre Occidental.

"It's become much dicier since my trip in the 1990s," said Paul. "Back then people carried old Winchester rifles on their saddles as a ranching tool. But, now everyone has AK-47s, and it's become much more violent. You have to be very careful."

I'd been trying to set up this trip for a long time, and the situation only seemed to get worse each year. "All of these elderly people I want to talk to are starting to die, and the bird is getting closer to extinction, if it's not extinct already."

He nodded and took another swig from his beer. He told me that the men he would run into in the drug fields used to be just local farmers and ranchers who hired themselves out to make some extra money.

"They were okay," he said. "I ran into them dozens of times and survived. But now, strangers from Sinaloa have moved in, and they're much more prone to shoot. You have to rely on local intelligence—someone to say 'Don't go up this river' or 'Stay away from that plateau.'"

Paul also knows my Mexican Mormon friend John Hatch, whom I planned to meet the following morning, and recommended that I always travel with him on my journeys through Mexico. A former schoolteacher in Colonia Juárez—a pretty little town in the foothills of the Sierra, not to be confused with Ciudad Juárez, the center of recent drug violence—John had left that career to run his own fruit orchard and sometimes hires himself out as a translator and guide.

Although I had some knowledge of Spanish, my language skills were not good enough for the kind of in-depth interviews I had in mind. To brush up, I had spent hours practicing Latin American Spanish with my then nine-year-old daughter, Gwen, using Rosetta Stone language CDs, but it seemed to be taking forever for me to become capable of meaningful conversation. I didn't want to repeat my Italian adventure of four years earlier when I'd traveled alone to some remote areas of the country, barely knowing any Italian, and gotten robbed, returning home with only the clothes on my back, a passport, and a single credit card I had kept in a zipped pocket in my shirt. In Mexico, my fate might be much worse.

John had found some passages about the imperial woodpecker in a family history written by his great-uncle Broughton Lunt: "The Ivory Billed Wood Pecker, a very rare and beautiful bird, weighing 2 or 3 pounds each, was also found in abundance. They were very shy and known to the natives as 'pito real.'"

Another of John's ancestors, his grandfather, Clarence Lunt, guided famed essayist and pioneering ecologist Aldo Leopold on his 1936 journey through the Sierra Madre, about which he wrote glowingly in his essay "Song of the Gavilan," in *A Sand County Almanac*, as a place with a pristine ecosystem, "still in perfect aboriginal health."

As we sat in the cantina drinking our beer, Paul pointed out that, since the North American Free Trade Agreement was signed, many of the *ejidos*—the communal landholdings that were parceled out to groups of peasants after the revolution—had been broken up and sold to people with money to burn, who were all too often drug growers: the *narcotraficantes*. They have fenced in their land, making it difficult to get around in some parts of the Sierra Madre. Paul doubts he could even make his mule journey south today.

"In some ways it's like the American West in the 1890s," he said. "The range wars are over and one faction has won, and now they're putting fences up everywhere."

"You think the war is over?" I asked. "You'd never know it, considering how many people are getting killed."

"Yeah, I know," he said. "I was raised in Mexico and . . . well . . . I'm pessimistic. I'm afraid the government has basically lost, and what we're seeing is the Colombianization of Mexico."

"So all this effort and bloodshed is for nothing?" I said. "The war is already lost?"

"Not necessarily," said Paul. "But the *narcos* have been in power for so long, it'll take another ten to twenty years of this kind of violence before they can get them under control."

"Depressing," I said.

"Yes, it is," he said. He lifted his glass of beer and drank it down, then signaled the waiter for another. He looked back at me.

"You should try to stay away from the hot spots," he said. "You're going there when the crop is in. It'll be growing. There are guys with guns up there guarding it, and you don't want to bump into them."

He paused, perhaps noticing the look of terror in my eyes. "Well, if you do bump into them, it's not necessarily the end of the world," he said. "Just put your arms in the air and explain what you're doing. Show them your bird books. You might be okay."

A minute later, the waiter brought us plates of enchiladas, beans, and chile rellenos, and we dug into them. "This is great food," I said. "You can't get any decent Mexican food in Ithaca, New York.

"So, you grew up in Mexico?" I asked.

"Yeah," he said. "But not in the Sierra Madre. Much farther south in the Altiplano, in Jalisco state."

I nodded. "I actually came very close to moving to Mexico as a kid," I said. My father had been a sailor in the Royal Navy and was constantly uprooting our family. "We moved from England to Canada, and then after a few years he got bored with that. It was like, 'Well, we're either moving to Mexico or the United States.' And he did the paperwork for both places. We were accepted by the United States first. I've often thought it might've been nice if we had gone to Mexico. At least I'd be a really great Spanish speaker now."

"My story is very similar," said Paul. His father, a veteran of the US Navy, was restless and depressed over the assassination of Robert F. Kennedy, and he decided to take his family and leave the United States. "I don't think my family even knows how he picked Mexico," said Paul. "None of us spoke Spanish when we moved there. By the time I was a teenager, he was ready to move on again and go back to the Balkans where his people were from. He was very much a nomad."

Paul loves Mexico and laments how much it has been Americanized. "In most cities, people have Sam's Club cards and shop at Wal-Mart. The Sierra Madre is one of the last places where the rural Mexican culture is intact and there are still remnant wildlife populations."

I pointed out that the Sierra Madre Occidental had always been wild, unmanageable.

"Yes, a lot of people have laid their bones there," said Paul. "Even the dialect in the mountains sounds rough. When the mountain people go down to a big city like Chihuahua or Ciudad

Juárez, people can pick them out instantly, because they talk like they're angry." He added that this kind of forceful, aggressive way of speaking seems to be true of mountain people just about anywhere. "Whether it's the Pashtu of eastern Afghanistan, the hill people of Ethiopia, or the Scots-Irish of the Appalachians, mountains seem to breed a toughness, an aggressiveness into people."

We sat quietly eating our food, the only diners in the cantina, and then I turned the conversation toward the imperial woodpecker. "Anything you can tell me about the bird?" I asked.

"A few times I did hear some old-timers who recalled the imperial woodpecker when they were young," he said. "A couple of guys I met in a sawmill town near Parral told me what a great racket the birds made when they were pecking. Everyone up there is armed, and they would take potshots at the birds. That was a decade ago when I spoke with those men, and even then they said they hadn't seen any in years."

Another man Paul met lived in a town called Guachochi—a big logging center south of Creel—and was involved in preserving the old-growth forest for the native Tarahumaras and Tepehuanes near Barranca Sinforosa. "He would spend time with the Tarahumara in the most remote areas, where roads had not yet penetrated and the people were the most traditional culturally," he said. "He asked them about animals like the wolf, the grizzly bear, and the imperial woodpecker. He was of the opinion that all of these animals were gone. But, of course, the mountains are big."

That area had one of the best remnants of old-growth forest left in the Sierra Madre, but most of the wildlife had reportedly vanished from the area decades earlier. "Supposedly, it's hard to find even a lizard or a squirrel there, let alone a large bird," I said.

Paul nodded and started talking about the area in the northern part of the Sierra Madre, where the Apaches had held sway for more than two centuries, creating a giant no-man's-land that lasted into the twentieth century. "Actually, on my mule trip through the Sierra, I just missed meeting an old man who had a scar on his hand from an Apache arrowhead," said Paul. "He died a couple of days before I went through his village and was being buried the day I got there. So I came that close to meeting a man who had lived through the Apache wars.

"That area is still very desolate," he said. "It's my favorite part of the whole mountain range."

The Apache area was the part of the Sierra Madre I was most interested in exploring. The imperial woodpecker would have vanished much sooner if not for the Apaches. With their constant raids and ferocious reputation, they kept away settlers—who would have quickly killed off the imperial woodpeckers or at least destroyed their old-growth forest habitat—from those mountains for more than two centuries. In many ways, the Apaches had been the saviors of the imperial woodpecker. Its extinction only became possible after the Sierra Madre Apaches vanished in the late 1930s.

"If any of these birds are still alive, I bet it'll be in the Apache country," I said.

"That makes a lot of sense," said Paul. "Probably the most unpopulated, wild swath of the mountains I know of is in the northern sector along the Rio Aros, which is where some of the Apaches lived. It's very desolate. I rode there for four days and didn't see anybody. And it's also the stronghold of the jaguar, so you know it's pretty unpopulated."

"That's exactly the kind of place I'm looking for," I told him. "The fact that it still has jaguars means it was never hit hard like these other places."

The vast majority of forest in the Sierra Madre has been logged extensively. Forestry has not been regulated well in Mexico, and many places now have only small pines barely large enough to make good fence posts. By the 1980s, logging had become closely associated with the narcotics trade. Wherever logging moved in, the drug growers soon followed. People made huge amounts of money clear-cutting forests and opening up fields for planting opium poppies.

Paul told me I should interview a ninety-nine-year-old man named Benito Parra, who was living on a farm in the Copper Canyon area, about a dozen miles north of Creel. Paul was very fond of old Benito and viewed him as a grandfather figure. He got to know him well during his mule trek through the Sierra Madre and had visited him many times since.

"He's a remarkable person—like a Mexican Zorba," said Paul. "He has great old stories. He was a mule driver in the 1930s, carrying supplies to all the mines. He knows the northern mountain river systems like the back of his hand. And I remember speaking with him about the imperial woodpecker."

Paul also suggested I explore a small outlier range called the Sierra Tasahuinora, just across the Great Divide in Sonora. It still had conifers on top and bears when he last visited it in the late 1990s. Paul had met a mountain lion hunter named Rene, who knows the place well and lives in the remote mountain village of Altamirano.

"The only problem is, dope is being grown right now at the base of the mountains," said Paul. "You'll have to find a way to get around those plantations. Rene would be the guy to talk to if you go up there. And even if he is growing dope himself, he'd be someone who could take you through his plantation.

"Really, though, Rene is one of the best people I met on the whole trip," said Paul. "He just loves being outside. He'd be up there even if he wasn't hunting mountain lions."

"So, how can I get in touch with these people?" I asked.

"Well, you really just have to go there," said Paul. "The last time I went through Altamirano it was still not electrified and didn't have telephone service. It probably still doesn't. But everyone knows everyone else, so it's usually not hard to find someone."

◆ ◆ ◆

It was past sunset when we finished eating and walked back to the border crossing. I passed through with no problems, but the border guard did a double take on Paul's passport—a thick, weather-beaten wad, jam-packed with visas and stamps from various trouble spots like Afghanistan, Iran, Iraq, and the Congo. He looked sternly at Paul.

"Why do you go to all these places?" he asked.

"I'm a foreign correspondent," said Paul.

"Who do you work for?"

"The *Chicago Tribune.*"

The man finally shrugged and waved us through. A short time later, I bade Paul farewell.

"I envy you your quest," he said. "It sounds great."

With that, I was on my way, driving back along the lonely border highway to my motel room in El Paso. Early the next morning, John Hatch would pick me up, and I'd drop off my rental car. Then I'd be on my way—into the surreal Cormac McCarthy borderlands of Old Mexico.

2 ◆ High Sierra

The rumble of a distant truck clawing its way slowly up the mountain at dusk caught our attention. Who could it possibly be, and why were they coming here at this hour? It couldn't be good. It had taken hours of tough four-wheeling—grinding our way through dry, rocky arroyos and along treacherous mountainsides with sheer drops just inches from our tires—for John Hatch and me to reach the Continental Divide, more than eighty-five hundred feet up in the Sierra Madre, along the border between the Mexican states of Chihuahua and Sonora. We'd expected to be alone on that early spring evening in 2009, exploring the high plateau forests of pine and oak—favorite haunt of the imperial woodpecker.

But we'd already seen the first grim evidence of drug growing earlier in the day, partway up the mountain: three-inch black-plastic tubing emerging from a spring and disappearing over the edge into a wooded canyon. This is how opium and marijuana crops are typically irrigated in these remote mountains. The *narcotraficantes* usually leave one or two helpers to guard and water the crop and often don't come back until harvesttime.

We'd steered clear of that canyon—not even peeking over the edge to see what might be down there—and headed up as far as we could drive on the mountain, frequently stopping to let our overheated truck cool down. One rough track went even higher, up a perilously steep incline through the trees. John had never seen this trail before. At first we tried to drive up it, but our truck's tires spun uselessly in the black topsoil less than a hundred feet up, and we started sliding sideways. We finally gave up and set off on foot, eventually emerging on top of the mountain, gasping in the thin air.

A small, whitewashed cinder-block hovel—about eight feet by ten feet in size—sat on the highest spot, practically hanging off the precipice, with a jaw-dropping view of the vast Sierra Madre stretching for miles: ridge after ridge of pine-clad mountains, pastel purple in the warm afternoon light. A plume of smoke rose from a tiny metal stovepipe on top of this rustic abode, as though someone was cooking a midday meal, but when we peeked through the open door, no one was around. The interior was stark: a metal stove at one end, a wooden platform with a bedroll at the other, and the ubiquitous small framed painting of the Virgin Mary gazing down from the far wall. But we also saw something that seemed out of place—a boat-style VHS radio with wires clamped to an old truck battery. From this lofty, unimpeded vantage point, the radio could broadcast to receivers a hundred miles or more away. This might be some kind of lookout station, and the person who stayed here had obviously just left, perhaps minutes earlier, leaving the fire still smoldering in the stove.

A few minutes later, after we'd looked into the hovel, a dark-haired, deeply tanned man stepped out of the trees beneath us, walking quickly up from the direction opposite from where we had come. He was middle-aged and chubby, wearing torn jeans, an old blue work shirt, and a dirty, sweat-stained baseball cap, and he almost jumped out of his skin when he saw us standing in front of his shack.

"*Hola, señor,*" said John, cheerfully. "*¿Qué tal?*" And he walked toward the man with his hand held out to shake hands. The man seemed spooked at first, but he quickly warmed as John told him all about himself—that he grew up in Colonia Juárez and knew many of the local people in the tiny mountain villages. John also showed great interest in the man, asking him about his life and his family and where he came from. In a few minutes, the man seemed completely at ease. He told us he spent months alone in the mountains, and he knew the local birds well, giving accurate descriptions of trogons, thick-billed parrots, and other species found there. When we asked him about *carpinteros*, he said yes, he had seen woodpeckers, but mostly the *poquito* (tiny) ones—obviously acorn woodpeckers.

I pulled out my eight-by-ten-inch color woodpecker illustrations, showing artists' conceptions of the acorn woodpecker, as well as the pale-billed, lineated, and imperial woodpeckers—all species found in Mexico. I always kept the imperial woodpecker illustration at the bottom of the stack so people would have to go through the other ones first. The man stopped at the illustration of the acorn woodpecker and smiled. He told us how these tiny birds—smaller than a robin—would bore hundreds of shallow holes in the trunks and large limbs of trees and stash an acorn in each hole. I nodded. These are the communal granary trees for which these birds are famous.

He turned to the next page, which showed the pale-billed woodpecker, a bird that shouldn't occur at this altitude. He stared at it blankly for a moment, then flipped to the lineated woodpecker—still no change in his expression. I held my breath as he removed the lineated woodpecker illustration, exposing the imperial woodpecker below. His eyes lit up instantly. I could feel my heart pounding. I hoped the man was about to tell me he knew this bird well and perhaps that it even nested on this very mountain. The habitat was great, with towering old pines and firs and numerous snags, some with huge cavities bored in them that could easily have been roost holes or even nests of these giant woodpeckers. But as I watched, the man's expression turned wistful, and my heart sank.

No, he'd never seen this bird, but an old man he'd known long ago in the village of Creel, far to the south, used to talk to him about the *pitoreal*, how spectacular it was, like nothing else he had ever seen. The old man had described it so well to him that he knew the instant he saw the illustration that this was the bird. The old man had died years earlier, and he didn't know exactly when or where he had seen the great woodpeckers or whether they might still be there.

As I traveled through Mexico, no one under the age of about seventy-five seemed to know the imperial woodpecker. A few people, like this man (who was probably in his midforties), had heard stories of the bird from elderly friends and relatives. But as with most young people I encountered in Mexico, I might as well have been asking about the mythical phoenix.

These encounters only made my quest seem all the more imperative. If the imperial woodpecker were indeed already extinct, then we were quickly losing our living connection with the species as the people with intimate knowledge of the bird became more elderly and died. We know so little about this species, its natural history and behavior, and why its numbers plummeted so quickly and drastically. This might be my best—perhaps only—chance to find the imperial woodpecker, while at least a few elderly people who knew it were still alive, with their memories intact, in the mountain villages. Maybe one of them would point me to a place where the last imperial woodpeckers still hang on to a precarious existence. As long as I was out there trying, I thought, hope of finding the bird existed.

After a while, having learned everything I could in our short interview, I closed my small notebook and put it back in my shirt pocket. Nothing earthshaking, but he did point me once more in the direction of Creel, near where Paul Salopek's elderly friend, Benito Parra, lived on a farm in the Choguita Valley. "His house has a red roof and sits on the right side of the road to Creel, at the far end of the valley on the drive south. People will know the place," Paul had told me.

Of course, if old Benito happened to be away from home the

day we arrived, I'd be out of luck—after having driven for more than seven hours to reach Creel. I'd already experienced that kind of missed opportunity twice in the course of my quest. First when I went to visit Elvin Whetten, a ninety-five-year-old Mormon rancher who spends a lot of his time at his daughter's old red-brick house in Colonia Juárez. I'd spoken to several of his friends who told me he had seen imperial woodpeckers in the old days while driving cattle or hunting in the high country. But when I arrived to interview him, Whetten was visiting one of his ranches on the far side of the state of Chihuahua. Even at his age, he was still an active rancher. Just five years earlier, at the age of ninety, Whetten had been stomped by a bull that nearly killed him. I did get to interview Whetten's daughter, Nelda Villa, who is in her sixties, and she told me some of the stories about imperial woodpeckers she'd heard from her father, including that he'd had most of his sightings in the Sierra Azul, or Blue Mountains. I said I definitely wanted to travel there, and she blanched.

"The area is full of drug growers now and much too dangerous," she said.

Still, I added the place to a mental list I was developing of the most important sites to visit. I would also have to come back again to interview Elvin, because, although everything Nelda told me about the natural history and behavior of the imperial woodpecker was fascinating, it was secondhand.

I'd also missed seeing Rene, the mountain lion hunter who lived in the tiny village of Altamirano, out on the road to nowhere in the high Sierra Madre. What Rene did for a living was a grim business. Ranchers would hire him to go up into the high country for weeks at a time and employ any means necessary to kill the mountain lions that threatened their cattle. Using baited jaw traps, teams of dogs, and sometimes poison, Rene usually got the big cats he was after. That's the way it is in the Sierra Madre and the way it has always been—livestock comes first, wildlife last. Rene had spent years in the surrounding wilderness and knew the area intimately. If anyone knew about the bird and could lead me deep into its haunts, it was him. But tracking the tracker was a problem. Altamirano is one of those tiny Sierra Madre villages where people live the same as they did more than a century ago—no electricity, no phone service, no running water. We'd have to drop in on the village and ask whomever we ran into where Rene lived.

It had taken us hours to travel just thirty miles on that treacherous dirt track; *road* is too good a word for it. We drove endlessly through rock-filled arroyos and up and over ridges, our truck bouncing up and down, this way and that, slamming us against the dashboard, windows, and doors with every foot we advanced. Before we were even halfway to Altamirano, I was bruised and aching and felt like I'd been thrown down a rocky hillside. According to my handheld GPS, for much of the trip we'd moved less than two miles per hour—slower than most people walk—and we could not have gone any faster.

Right at the Continental Divide, en route to Altamirano, stood an enclosed cinder-block shrine with a framed painting of Jesus on the wall inside. Passersby had placed numerous small votive candles in glass holders inside, some of which still flickered in the dim light.

We would pass other shrines on our journey. Another one was set deep in a natural cave in a canyon where an Apache attack had taken place in 1929. Five members of the Molina family of Altamirano had been riding their horse-drawn wagon to Casas Grandes. (Their wagon could not have been any slower than our four-wheel-drive truck.) They passed through the narrow canyon right where we stood, a place called Piedra Volada, or Flying Rock. Lofty cliffs rise high on both sides, with many creases and boulders to hide behind as well as the cave: a perfect place for an ambush. Gazing at the canyon, I could picture the whole scene—the sudden rifle fire, the screams, the blood and dying. Two Apaches hiding in the cave opened fire on the wagon at close range, mortally wounding Leonardo Molina, his daughter Isabel, and his niece Tacha Chaparo. The horses bolted, overturning the wagon, spilling Leonardo's infant nephew Jose Corral to the ground. Molina's thirteen-year-old son, Nacho, jumped clear. The Apaches shot him twice—in the hip and the hand—as he fled, but he managed to plunge into a deep pool in the nearby stream and burrow into the thick overhanging brush on the other side, where he hid until the attackers left.

Nacho remembered the Apache raiders for the rest of his life, until his death in his fifties in 1968: their long, straight black hair, their bright red headbands, and one of them lifting his infant cousin Jose by the feet to swing him like a baseball bat, smashing his head against a wagon wheel, before riding away with the stolen horses.

When we finally drove along the dusty road into the village of Altamirano, it felt otherwordly, as if we were stepping back into the nineteenth-century American West. A ramshackle collection of old adobe structures and log cabins, built from timber harvested in the surrounding pine forests, Altamirano had no telephone poles—and no wires or pipes of any kind leading into or out of the houses. It was so quiet, just the lonely *whoosh* of an afternoon breeze blowing through town, sending up a cloud of dust from the road. We walked up to a couple of houses and knocked on their doors, but no one was around. I had an eerie *Twilight Zone* feeling that the entire populace of the village had vanished an instant before we arrived.

We finally stumbled upon a man in his early thirties, sitting in front of his tiny adobe home, who welcomed us with a broad grin and a handshake and told us his name was Jesús. He invited us inside his home, which had freshly whitewashed walls and scrupulously swept dirt floors. Colorful wall hangings and knickknacks had been carefully placed everywhere: various saints and other religious icons, multihued blankets, and pottery. Several clocks also hung on the walls, though all displayed different times and none worked.

Jesús wanted to show us the beautiful old relics from the Paquimé culture, which had thrived in the Casas Grandes area a thousand years ago. He had taken them from somewhere in the hills; one dirt-encrusted pot in the shape of an owl was especially nice. We'd already told him we weren't interested in buying anything like that, which would have been illegal, but he seemed happy enough to let us look at the pieces and admire them.

We finally got around to asking him about the imperial woodpecker and showing him the illustrations. He was fascinated by the story, genuinely sad to hear that this one-of-a-kind Mexican bird might be gone forever, but he had never heard of it. He gave us the names of a couple of old men who might be able to tell us about it.

Jesús knew Rene, though he hadn't seen him recently, because Rene now owned a ranch somewhere outside of town and a home in Casas Grandes, where he was most likely to be—which was somewhat ironic: we'd just spent hours driving to Altamirano from Casas Grandes. He suggested we ask some other people around town if they knew Rene's address and whether he had a telephone. Everyone (except Jesús) was celebrating the arrival of a statue of the Virgin Mary, a gift from another mountain village.

Up the main street, remarkably peaceful for a celebration day, several old beater pickup trucks were parked along the road, alongside a dozen or more horses and mules, which are the principal mode of transportation in most of the Sierra Madre. They stood tied to various fences and hitching posts everywhere we looked. A horse culture—like that of nineteenth-century America before the birth of the automobile—still thrives in the Sierra Madre. Most men, women, and children there know how to shoe horses and mules themselves and can perform basic veterinary care. They have to. There's no one else around to do it, and even if there were, no one could afford it. Every *ejido* and village has a tiny general store where people can buy the basics—from canned goods and flour to warm bottles of soda pop to hardware and nails—and at all of them I visited, sets of horseshoes and tiny mule shoes for sale hung prominently on the wall.

Up the road stood a ten-by-twelve log cabin with *SE VENDE GASOLINA* chalked in big white letters on the dark logs in front. No one was there, but I peeked inside and saw a couple of battered old oil drums full of low-octane gas, one of which had a hand pump screwed into the top.

A small procession came into view, walking up the dusty road to the church, led by a white pickup truck with a dozen or more white balloons tied to the top of its cab. Behind, in the truck bed, rode the statue of the Virgin Mary and two young children. The boy and girl, both about eight years old, were well scrubbed and clad in their best clothes—the girl in a long white dress with her black curly hair pulled up on her head; the boy in a white shirt and dark pants, with his dark hair slicked down and parted on the side.

Stopping in front of the little white church, the boy and girl jumped out as the townspeople unloaded the truck's precious cargo and carried it inside. The throng of people followed after, and then the streets were silent again. We noticed a few young hombres sitting in the shade up the street, sipping cans of Tecate beer, and walked over to talk with them. John is always at his best in this kind of situation: friendly, gregarious, and talkative. Although they were drunk, they were friendly and enthusiastic, and each of them got up and shook hands with us. We all briefly shared our life stories, and then I pulled out the woodpecker illustrations. But these guys were probably in their midtwenties and knew nothing about the *pitoreal*.

While we were there, another man rode up on a mule, holding a tin cup of tequila in his hand. Amazingly, he spoke perfect English and said he had worked in Denver for seven years. He came back, he said, because there was no work there anymore.

John asked the guys why they were not in church like all the other people in the village. They laughed and said they had too much of the devil in them. As we finally said good-bye, each of them shook hands with us again. We drove past the church, pondering what to do next. We obviously couldn't go inside and start asking questions in the middle of their ceremony. But we'd come so far. We parked in the shade of a tree and waited for about an hour. These kind of celebrations tend to last all day and into the night and eventually can devolve into bouts of heavy drinking and violence. This would not be a good place to be when it got dark. So we decided to drive on and try to get in touch with Rene some other time.

◆ ◆ ◆

A week later, as we stood on the lip of the cliff beside the white cinder-block hovel, the man pointed out various places on distant ridges, some more than fifty miles in the distance: the high country above the old Mormon colonies of Garcia and Chuhuichupa; the Apache stronghold above Tres Rios; the Sierra Tabaco; and, of course, the Sierra Azul—all places I wanted desperately to visit and all potentially dangerous. I felt as though I was looking out on the landscape of my life for the next year, but I had no idea how I would navigate it. John would go with me to the Sierra Azul and along the Rio Gavilan, but he wasn't eager to visit the Sierra Tabaco—the location of one of the most recent credible sightings of an imperial woodpecker, in the 1990s, but also a notoriously violent drug-growing area. He aimed to find some local Mexicans who would set me up with mules and guide me through the area.

We said our good-byes to the man, shaking hands and bidding each other "*Vaya con Dios*," and set off back down the steep trail to our truck. John had parked the truck in an out-of-the-way place we had found, where a very old logging trail dropped steeply away from the main trail and was quickly obscured by trees and thick foliage. A tall pine tree grew right in the center of the trail less than a hundred yards away, so it was obvious no one ever drove there. We pitched our camp right on the old logging trail, between our truck and the big pine, and were invisible from the main trail.

After we'd finished making camp, we went off exploring, listening closely for the sounds of foraging imperial woodpeckers—the loud hammering or their nasal trumpeting—but we heard only the scolding calls of Steller's jays and the occasional songs of migrant warblers, working their way north. We did spot a mountain trogon, a spectacular bird about the size of a pigeon, glossy green above with a black face, crimson breast, and long black-and-white patterned tail. It was near dusk when we got back to our campsite and started gathering wood for a fire. As we stood beside the pile of wood we'd gathered, we heard the rumble of a truck driving past on a trail above us. It was moving slowly, as though the driver were searching for something. When it finally passed us, we felt relieved. But just five or ten minutes later, it came back again . . . and then again. Had the man in the shack called on his radio to announce that some gringos were nosing around in the high country? Someone was clearly looking for us. As we heard the truck approaching yet again, John looked at me and said, "We better see what they want."

John is the kind of person who will head into a potentially difficult situation and try to brazen it out, relying on his natural skills as a talker and his friendliness to avoid trouble. I trusted his judgment and had no problem following his lead. Together we made our way back up to the main trail on foot.

In a few minutes, a black pickup truck appeared up ahead. When the driver saw us, he sped up, lurching and bouncing toward us on the rough dirt road, slamming on his brakes at the last instant. I could see the driver well—a slim, hard-faced Mexican in his late thirties, with a thin moustache, wearing a cowboy hat—and he was not happy. He lowered a window on the passenger side and motioned us over with a quick flick of his hand. John went immediately into full-friendship mode, walking toward the truck with a beaming smile, as though he had just run into a long-lost friend. He held out his hand to shake, but the man ignored it. "What are you doing up here?" he wanted to know.

I started babbling in broken Spanish about *pitoreales* and held out my woodpecker paintings, but he stared straight ahead, clenching and unclenching his hands on the steering wheel, his neck muscles taut. "We don't care about anything else but the birds here," I said, nervously, but he didn't seem to be listening. John started talking about all the people he knows in the area—various ranchers and other landowners—hoping he might come up with someone they both know.

The man didn't respond to anything we said. His mind seemed miles away—like he was going through some elaborate mental exercise, considering every possible course of action and following each one through separately, projecting every possible outcome. He finally opened his hands wide, still resting them on the steering wheel, and exhaled deeply, the tension fading from his face. But he still didn't smile. He said simply that it would be okay for us to sleep there that night, then drove off into the darkening gloom.

John and I were quiet as we turned back to our campsite and continued collecting firewood. We'd gathered oak for the initial fire, so we could cook our dinner in the slow-burning coals, and pine for later, when we would need a bright, hot fire to keep warm in the chilly mountain night. An hour or so later as we sat eating our chicken breasts, baked potatoes, beans, and tortillas, we started talking about what happened.

"You know, I probably haven't been as worried about the danger in the mountains as much as I should be," said John. "I've been coming here all my life, and I take a lot of things for granted. But it's changed so much. It used to be I'd know just about everyone I ran into up here."

John's family was among the first Mormon settlers who came to Mexico in 1885 to set up colonies in the Sierra Madre, at the invitation of Mexican Presidente Porfirio Díaz. To look at him and hear him talk you might think him a middle-aged American from Cincinnati; he certainly looks the part with his blue eyes, gray hair, and sunburned Anglo skin, short-sleeved plaid shirt, metal-framed eyeglasses, and baseball cap. But John is a Mexican national.

John is a great model to follow when it comes to getting along in Mexico. He is friendly, outgoing, and optimistic; everyone likes him. His father always taught him to treat everyone as an equal, from the poorest peasant to the leader of the nation, and everyone he encounters picks up on that. It's quite common for the mountain Mexicans to dislike visitors from Mexico City and other urban areas, because they sense their disdain. With John, there is none of that.

John's father was a rural doctor who would drive miles through the treacherous mountains in the middle of the night to tend to someone who was injured, ailing, or having a baby. The few pesos the peasants could give him wasn't even enough to pay for the gas he burned to get there, but he considered it part of his duties as a physician. John drove with him on a few of these missions of mercy when he was in grade school. Many of the people he runs into—at least the ones in their forties or older—were delivered by his father, and he used to be able to travel anywhere in the mountains with complete safety. But not since the drug kingpins from the state of Sinaloa moved in during the 1980s.

The *narcotraficantes* arrived in droves, with guns and drugs and money to burn. They started buying up property all through the mountains—and the people who owned the land often didn't have a choice about selling. At that time, John's uncle owned a large ranch near the old Mormon colony of Garcia, high in the Sierra. It had been in the family since the 1880s and had a fine brick house his forebears had built. A stocky man in his early thirties named Héctor—a drug lord from Sinaloa with slicked-back hair, a thin moustache, and wraparound sunglasses—paid a visit one day. Héctor admired the ranch and wanted to buy it, quoting John's uncle a price about twice what it was worth.

"That's a more than fair offer," John's uncle said, "but the place has been in my family for a hundred years. I really can't sell it."

"*No hay problema*," the man said. "I'll come back next month and buy it from your widow." The rancher looked at Héctor, whose face was blank, expressionless behind his dark glasses. A few days later, they drew up the papers, and the Mormon walked sadly away from his family home.

A few people from a local *ejido* had been squatting on part of Héctor's land, running their cattle there. This had been going on for several years at the ranch and is not unusual in Mexico. On many of the *ejidos*, the people keep too many cattle, which destroy the land, and they're fairly aggressive about spreading out onto other people's property. One day, Héctor dropped in on some vaqueros from the *ejido* as they tended their cattle.

"I want to introduce you to a friend of mine," he said, smirking grimly as he held up an AK-47. With that, he swung the gun around and let off a burst of gunfire right above their heads, splattering bullets into the nearby pine trees, bringing bark and branches raining down as the men cringed in terror. "My friend doesn't like it when people trespass on this land," he said. The men took the hint, packing up and leaving immediately.

Besides buying land, many of the newly arrived drug lords also went shopping for new cars and trucks. They always paid in cash, and whatever item they wanted, they had to have right away.

"I want that black truck with the tinted windows over there," the *narco* would say.

In some cases, the car dealer would answer, "I'm sorry, but that one has already been bought and paid for."

"No. You're wrong. That truck is mine." And he would lay down the cash, often two or three times what it was worth, and drive away with the new truck. The *narcos* would refuse to fill out any paperwork or give their names, leaving the salesmen in a quandary about how to account officially for the sold vehicles. But the car dealers could not say no. And so a lot of big, brand-new trucks with darkened windows were being driven around the Sierra Madre without license plates or paperwork. No one ever stopped them. The police were either in cahoots with the *narcotraficantes* or afraid to stand up to them.

Shortly after his election in 2006, Presidente Felipe Calderón directed the Mexican military to set up numerous roadblocks in the foothills and high desert surrounding the Sierra Madre, manned by soldiers from other parts of the country who don't have any local ties and are less likely to be corrupted. Many of these soldiers appear to be indigenous people from the far south of the country who don't look anything like the local Mexicans. They often have walls of piled sandbags next to their checkpoints, which they can easily jump behind if someone starts shooting. They stop every vehicle and require people to show their paperwork, and they also search for guns and drugs. Of course, all the *narcotraficantes* know where the army checkpoints are, but the soldiers still make business more difficult for those involved in the drug trade.

◆ ◆ ◆

As we came down off the mountain and made our way eastward through the rolling foothills, it was nearly dusk again. John suggested stopping at Meredith Romney's ranch and perhaps camping somewhere on his vast property, more than seventy thousand acres of prime ranchland. John likes to joke about how people in Colonia Juárez have to struggle to keep up with the Romneys, one of the wealthiest, most prominent Mormon families in the area. Indeed, the Romneys own a spectacular mansion on a hill adjacent to the Colonia's Mormon Temple. Their family had come to Mexico in 1885, too, in the first wave of Mormon immigrants to the country.

George W. Romney—who served as governor of Michigan in the 1960s and ran unsuccessfully against Richard Nixon to be the Republican presidential candidate in 1968—was part of this family and born not far from Colonia Juárez in 1907. Some questioned at the time whether Romney would be eligible to be president, because the US Constitution requires presidents to be "natural-born citizens." The first Congress in 1790 passed legislation stating that "The children of citizens of the United States that may be born beyond the sea, or outside the limits of the United States, shall be considered as natural-born citizens of the United States." Five years later, however, the Naturalization Act of 1795 removed the reference about the children of citizens of the United States being natural-born citizens, so there is still a question whether George Romney would have been eligible to be president. (His son, Mitt Romney, followed in his footsteps, vying for the Republican presidential nomination in 2008, but then went further, actually running for president against Barack Obama in 2012.) But like most of the Mormons in Mexico, the Romneys fled to the United States in 1912, at the height of the violence of the Mexican Revolution. George Romney's family chose to remain in the United States when the fighting subsided, whereas Meredith's branch of the family returned to Mexico.

I was looking forward to meeting Meredith, and also Felipe, an older man who runs the ranch. John said he spends a lot of time in the high country and might know something about the imperial woodpecker. When we got to the rancho, a young vaquero rode up, clad in a dark-blue long-sleeved shirt, leather chaps, and cowboy hat with a lariat attached to his saddle. He told us Don Felipe had taken ill with a serious respiratory infection and was in the hospital.

Right before I had left for Texas, the president of Cornell University sent an email campus-wide strongly advising faculty and staff to avoid traveling in Mexico because of the swine flu pandemic. I had arrived here at the peak of the swine flu scare, just a few days after the first deaths were reported. John assured me that the closest case of swine flu was more than a thousand miles away, even as he joked that I was the only tourist in Mexico; the ones who hadn't already been scared off by the violence had canceled their trips to avoid the flu. The day before my plane was to take off, my wife had said, "All you need now is for a big earthquake to hit Mexico." As if on cue, later that day a major quake hit near Mexico City.

Meredith Romney is a big robust cowboy, then in his late sixties, who still works side by side with the vaqueros on his vast ranch: roping and branding cattle, riding the range, and performing other duties that would tax a man half his age. Usually friendly and outgoing, he had neglected a cold that had become so severe his family feared he might develop pneumonia, so he couldn't visit with us.

John and I laid our bedrolls on Meredith's back veranda and spent the night listening to the yip of coyotes as a soft wind blew across the dry hills. We left the next morning at dawn. I opened the gate for John and closed it behind him after he drove through.

Just a couple of weeks later, at that very spot, a team of three kidnappers abducted Meredith Romney at gunpoint as he drove his pickup truck through the same gate. His wife and teenage grandson were with him, hauling a big cattle trailer behind them containing half a dozen steers. Meredith's grandson had gotten out to open the gate and stood there as the truck and trailer drove through. At that instant, three men with balaclavas covering their faces sped toward them in an old Willys four-wheel-drive wagon. Slamming on the brakes, the men burst from the vehicle brandishing 9mm automatic pistols. One man held a gun to Meredith's grandson's head as he trembled in fear with his arms held up. The other two ran up to each of the two side doors and pointed pistols at Meredith and his wife. The man on Meredith's side dragged him from the truck, roughing him up as he pushed him toward the other car. When Meredith glanced up to see if his grandson was okay, the thug hit him in the back of the head with his pistol and cursed at him. When the other attacker shot out the tires in his truck, Meredith jumped at the sound and looked behind him, so the thug struck him again in the back of the head with his pistol, making him stagger. Then he pulled Meredith's arms behind his back, clamped handcuffs tightly on his wrists, put a dark cloth bag over his head, and shoved him down onto the floorboards in the back of their vehicle. Just as quickly as they had appeared, they left, speeding away on the dusty dirt road, leaving Romney's wife and grandson in stunned silence.

This was just the beginning of Meredith Romney's ordeal, which he recounted to me several months later. The kidnappers seemed in a panic, driving much too fast for the rough mountain road they were on, swerving wildly on every turn. Several times the vehicle bounced up, becoming airborne for an instant only to come crashing down, the undercarriage bottoming out on the wheels. At that point, Meredith was more concerned about dying in a car crash than being shot by the men.

The driver finally stopped on a high promontory, where the men knew they had cell phone coverage, and called an associate to let him know that the kidnapping was successful. One of the thugs stuck his index fingers in each of Meredith's ears to prevent him hearing the conversation, but he could still make out the voices. They were speaking to someone called Pancho, who was working out the details of his ransom.

The kidnappers drove miles into the Sierra Madre, going higher and higher until long after the sun went down. When they reached the edge of a remote canyon, they pulled to the side of the road where a steep rocky trail ran downward, winding treacherously to a cave far below. When they switched off the headlights, the world turned instantly black, which even Meredith could tell with the cloth hood over his head. One of the kidnappers spread a blanket on the ground behind the car, told Meredith to lie down on it, and said if he tried to escape, or if anything went wrong and they didn't get the ransom money, they would kill him.

An hour later as the moon rose, casting a cold blue light over the rugged landscape, the kidnappers put their balaclavas back on, roused Meredith, and removed his hood so he could watch his step as he hiked down the trail. (This was the first time he'd been bare-headed since the kidnapping began.) The descent down the steep slope was terrifying, with rocks sometimes shifting underfoot and falling over the edge. When they reached the cave, they took Meredith deep inside; he had to bend down to get through a narrow spot before it opened into a larger cavern. There they made him sit down and once again put the cloth bag over his head.

Meanwhile, the kidnappers' accomplice in town had telephoned Meredith's brother, Leighton, demanding a six-figure ransom, to be delivered by the next day. Leighton told the man there was no way he could possibly come up with that much cash in such a short time. He also warned the kidnapper that Meredith has diabetes and would become seriously ill and possibly die if they didn't feed him soon.

After further negotiations the kidnappers finally lowered their ransom price to $30,000, which they told Leighton to put in a bag and throw out his car window as he drove past a particular corner in Casas Grandes. The plan was that, as soon as the pickup person had gotten safely away with the money, he would get in touch with the men holding Meredith, and they would release him. If Leighton tried anything funny, his brother would be killed immediately. Before he would agree to it, Leighton insisted that they prove Meredith was still alive by getting him to answer several questions that only he would know. When they called back later with correct answers to the questions, Leighton took the money to the drop-off place as instructed.

Meredith had been abducted about two o'clock in the afternoon and spent all of the first night and the following day as well as most of the next night in the cave. In that time, they had given him only a few small snacks and a couple of Diet Cokes. His blood sugar was low and he felt terrible.

It was about 3:00 a.m. on a chilly mountain night when the men guarding him received word to release him. They took him out of the cave and made him trudge in the dark back up the trail. Meredith said it was the toughest thing he had ever done. He had to sit down several times, each time doubting he could take another step. When they finally got close to the drop-off point, the men removed his handcuffs and left him there alone with a granola bar, a flashlight, and a cigarette lighter so he could build a fire to stay warm. The search party, which included John Hatch, didn't find him until noon the next day.

Shortly after his rescue, Meredith said, in his understated cowboy way, "They were pretty good to me—except for hitting me on the head a few times to get me into the car. But honestly, I was just glad they didn't take my grandson."

Meredith didn't find out until later that the same group that kidnapped him had killed fourteen of the eighteen people they had abducted, including an uncle of one of the kidnappers, who had recognized his nephew's voice. The kidnappers had even murdered some of the abductees for whom they had already received ransoms. Just a few weeks before Meredith was abducted, after several kidnappings had occurred in the area, he and his brother had talked about the danger of kidnapping. Meredith had told Leighton not to bother ransoming him if he were ever kidnapped. But he was very glad his brother had ignored his instructions.

A couple of weeks after Meredith's abduction, John Hatch telephoned me in Ithaca and brought me up to date on everything that had happened since I last saw him. Benjamin LeBaron, a thirty-two-year-old Mormon who lived in another community not far from Colonia Juárez, had organized a demonstration outside the governor's office in Chihuahua City to demand that the government do more to maintain law and order in the state of Chihuahua, and John and Meredith went along to support the protesters. Benjamin LeBaron's sixteen-year-old brother had been kidnapped before Meredith's abduction and held for a week before being released. Their June demonstration drew a lot of media attention to the cause *and* to Benjamin LeBaron—which is not a good idea in present-day Mexico.

Shortly after midnight on July 7, 2009, a group of heavily armed thugs dressed in camouflage fatigues surrounded LeBaron's home, breaking windows and hammering on the door, demanding to be let inside. They said they would throw a hand grenade inside if he didn't open the door. When he let them in, the men beat LeBaron severely. A neighbor who heard the attack called two of LeBaron's brothers-in-law, Luis Jose Widmar and Lawrence Widmar, but when Luis arrived minutes later, the attackers also beat him. Then they loaded Luis and LeBaron into their truck. As they were driving away, Lawrence Widmar arrived, and the gunmen strafed his truck with automatic weapons fire.

Searchers later found the bodies of Benjamin LeBaron and Luis Jose Widmar dumped on the highway about four miles away, near a cemetery. Both had been shot in the head.

◆ ◆ ◆

The next time I traveled through Mexico with John, we drove past Colonia LeBaron, where the murdered men had been abducted. The village looked about the same as any small, reasonably upscale desert community in the United States, except that it was eerily quiet. Nobody was standing outside in their yards and no children played in the street.

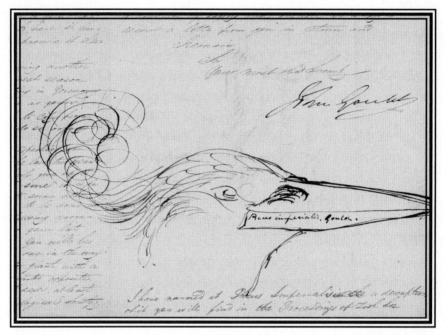

At the bottom of an 1833 letter to a friend, John Gould did a rough sketch of the bird he had named the imperial woodpecker. (*Courtesy of the National Museums of Scotland*)

3 ◆ A Natural History of the Imperial Woodpecker

 The scientific world first took note of the imperial woodpecker in 1832 on August 14—my birthday, as it turns out, but well over a century before I was born—when renowned English ornithologist and bird artist John Gould brought some specimens of this previously

undescribed bird, "remarkable for its extraordinary size," to a meeting of the Zoological Society of London. Gould gave the bird its regal appellation—*Picus imperialis*, which was later changed to *Campephilus imperialis*. (Another nineteenth-century English ornithologist, George Robert Gray, established the genus *Campephilus*, which means "lover of grubs," the primary diet of these birds, the larvae of wood-boring beetles.) What a bird. What a discovery.

Gould was vague about where the specimens were collected, saying they were obtained from "that little explored district of California which borders the territory of Mexico." The skins were actually collected by a mining engineer named Floresi, who had collected a number of birds at that time in the Sierra Madre near Bolaños, Jalisco, quite a long way from California. Because of the remoteness of the areas the species favored, the high-altitude pine-oak forests of northwestern Mexico, years went by before any other specimens showed up in museums.

The first scientific article of note with firsthand observations on the behavior and habitats of the imperial woodpecker was published more than fifty years later in 1898, a detailed piece titled simply "The Imperial Ivory-billed Woodpecker, *Campephilus Imperialis*," by Edward William Nelson, which appeared in *The Auk*, the esteemed journal of the American Ornithologists' Union.

When Nelson launched his Mexico expedition in January 1892, he had already achieved a measure of fame as an Arctic explorer who studied the wildlife and indigenous people of Alaska while serving as a weather observer for the US Army Signal Corps. Spencer F. Baird, the first curator of the Smithsonian Institution, had encouraged the young naturalist to join the Signal Corps and used his influence to get Nelson posted to extremely remote locations where he could collect specimens and gather data on little-known species. He was later the special field agent for a major expedition in Death Valley, California.

Shortly before leaving for Mexico, Nelson hired an eighteen-year-old named Edward A. Goldman to work as his field assistant, teamster, and camp man for what was supposed to be a trip of about three months but which "was lengthened to an indefinite period," as Goldman wrote years afterward. The two ended up spending fourteen years in Mexico, crossing the country from sea to sea six times and traversing the length of it twice, traveling to numerous places never before visited by any other scientist.

The natural history of the imperial woodpecker practically begins and ends with Nelson and Goldman. The only other person with comparable firsthand knowledge of the species, besides the indigenous people, was Norwegian explorer Carl Lumholtz, who never wrote an in-depth scientific article about the bird.

The passages in Nelson's article about riding on horseback through the high country of the Trans-Mexican Volcanic Belt above Pátzcuaro, Michoacán, provide some of the best descriptions of the imperial woodpecker's primary habitat: "our trail led through a beautiful upland country . . . overgrown with open pine forest, in which grassy parks opened here and there affording charming vistas . . . at an altitude of about 7000 feet." Here Nelson and Goldman had their first sighting of the species as "a pair of Imperial Ivory-bills swung up and alighted near the top of a large dead pine on the border of an Indian cornfield."

Nelson goes on to write: "Their range in this region appears to be restricted to the rather narrow belt along the top of the main central ridge of the Sierra Madre which lies above an altitude of 7000 feet. This belt is more like a rolling and irregular tableland than the summit of a great mountain chain, [with] open pine forest, broken by grassy parks."

This brief statement says a lot. Most mountain ranges tend to become more rugged toward their summits, whereas the Sierra Madre Occidental opens up into a gently rolling tableland with vast forests of pines and oaks. The mesa forests were open and parklike from the frequent fires set by lightning and from those deliberately set by the indigenous people. The higher elevations are also cooler and get far more rainfall than the arid lands below, which promotes the growth of larger pines.

In these classic old-growth forests, there were plenty of dead and dying trees, many infested with huge beetle grubs, which the birds used their chisellike bills to get at, prying off huge chunks of bark. The big snags also provided ready housing for these immense woodpeckers, where they could hollow out a space sufficiently large to roost or nest inside.

On this natal ground, the imperial woodpecker evolved through millennia into a specialist in a unique niche: pine-oak mesa forest above 6,500 feet in altitude. Unfortunately for the imperial wood-pecker, these stands of huge pines on the tablelands were the most desirable and easiest for modern loggers to exploit. In little more than a century, since only the 1890s, an astonishing amount of this habitat has been significantly altered or destroyed. Loggers even-tually even cut down the dead pines to take to pulp mills for paper production. The destruction of most of their primary habitat was a huge blow to the imperial woodpecker.

Nelson's article points out another quality of the birds that didn't help them: "They were surprisingly easy to stalk, even after being hunted and shot at for days." He and Goldman had heard a series of "queer, penny-trumpet-like notes from the summit of a rounded hill near by," which proved to be the calls of an imperial woodpecker. Goldman headed in the direction of the sound, shot-gun in hand, and located three of the birds foraging on the trunk of a pine. Goldman shot both barrels of his side-by-side shotgun simultaneously, hoping to increase his chances of getting a speci-men, but, according to Nelson, the recoil of the gun "almost kicked [Goldman] off the hillside and the birds flew away unscathed uttering cries of alarm." They later found five of them flying "to a neighboring park-like flat"—again, the birds' favorite habitat.

Nelson noticed that the birds seemed to be closely attached to each other: "When one was shot the other members of the flock remained scattered about on the trees for a short time calling to each other at intervals," a behavior similar to that of some tropical parrots, which is also exploited by trappers. This would prove to be the undoing of the flock Nelson and Goldman had encountered, as they followed the group and soon wiped them out. "The entire party fell victim to our guns . . . so long as any were left they showed strange persistence in returning to their haunt on the hill."

If the imperial woodpeckers had been solitary birds, living in isolated pairs, each pair defending its own limited and well-defined territory, a single shooter could not have killed four, five, or even ten birds at one time. Some researchers have suggested that these imperial woodpecker groups might have been made up of a pair with its current brood of young plus offspring from the previous season. This could be partly true, but I think eight or ten birds is too large a number to explain in this way. It seems more likely that these groups were made up of roving pairs or families brought together by a common food resource at the sites where Nelson and Goldman found them. But we don't know how mobile these birds were or how far they would travel to exploit a new food source or escape harsh weather. There's no evidence of any kind of seasonal migration, either moving to a lower elevation or flying south in the winter. Nelson wrote, "It is probable that they lead a more wandering life during the winter months and sometimes absent themselves from their summer haunts," but went on to add, "it is quite certain they are not in any sense migratory." And the explorer Carl Lumholtz reported seeing them in the high country in the dead of winter, when snow covered the ground.

Evidence suggests that imperial woodpeckers are remarkably

sedentary. The birds' entire known range is only about nine hundred miles long, reaching from about fifty miles below the United States border south to the state of Michoacán, and about a hundred miles wide. As far as we know, the imperial woodpecker never made it over to the eastern spur of these mountains, the Sierra Madre Oriental, or to the mountains of southern Arizona, some of which you can see with your naked eye from the northernmost parts of the Sierra Madre Occidental. Other Mexican mountain birds, such as thick-billed parrots and trogons, certainly made that leap, but perhaps the imperial woodpeckers had everything they needed right where they were—that is, until loggers in the late nineteenth and twentieth centuries cut down the old-growth forests.

Their calls, "queer, penny-trumpet-like notes [had] the peculiar nasal tone that is characteristic of the notes of Sapsuckers, but with a penetrating quality that renders them distinct for a long distance. I am certain they were frequently heard at a distance of a mile," wrote Nelson. A call that carried so far and was so distinctive could have been another characteristic that made them easy to hunt and decimate.

Carl Lumholtz described the bird's call in a similar though more poetic way: "The plaintive trumpet sound of a giant woodpecker about sunset—as far as we could make out, the only living being in the vicinity—did not detract from the gloominess of the prospect." The best evidence of what the imperial woodpecker sounds like came from Cornell ornithologist Arthur A. Allen, one of the few people to have heard the calls of both the ivory-billed and imperial woodpeckers, who said: "They seemed identical." Fortunately, Allen's colleague Peter Paul Kellogg made sound recordings of ivory-bills during their 1935 expedition to the Singer Tract of northeastern Louisiana, so we can listen to these calls and have an excellent idea what imperial woodpeckers sound like. (Listen to a clip of ivory-billed woodpecker *kent* calls from the 1935 expedition at www.birds.cornell.edu/ivory/multimedia/sounds/known sounds/document_view.)

Most birds will respond if you play a recording of their species' vocalizations. They may sing or call or even fly in aggressively, looking for the intruder on their territory. But it's not clear whether an imperial or even an ivory-billed woodpecker will respond to a playback of the signature nasal kent call. Ivory-bill researcher James T. Tanner was able to mimic the kent call of an ivory-bill fairly accurately using the mouthpiece of a clarinet, but he got no response from the birds in Louisiana's Singer Tract. They did, however, respond when he pounded on the trunk of a tree with an axe handle to imitate the characteristic double-knock drum shared by most *Campephilus* woodpeckers—a genus found primarily in Central and South America. (The imperial and ivory-billed woodpeckers are the northernmost representatives of this group.) The double knock is lightning fast, *BAM-bam*, the second *bam* fainter, almost like an echo of the first. The space between the two beats is only about 75 milliseconds and at times can sound like a single *bam*. But it's clearly visible on a sonogram, which provides a visual representation of a sound, showing its pitch and duration.

You'd think that mimicking this double-knock signal would be the perfect way to survey an area for imperial woodpeckers and to draw a response from any of the birds within hearing range of the sound. It may be, but we don't know for certain that imperial woodpeckers employ a double-knock signal. Of the eleven *Campephilus* species, seven definitely make a double knock; three of them (the crimson-bellied, crimson-crested, and guayaquil woodpeckers) definitely do not; and the imperial woodpecker we're not sure about—although my colleague, Cornell woodpecker researcher Martjan Lammertink, wonders whether the Tepehuán name for the bird, *uagam*, might be a description of the bird's *wack-wam* double-knock sound.

Still, researchers should probably assume that the imperials do perform double knocks and attempt this method whenever they are surveying potential areas for this bird. The ivory-billed and imperial woodpeckers are obviously close relatives, differing mostly in size and altitude preference—and only slightly in plumage: the white "suspenders" on the upper back of an imperial woodpecker do not continue up the neck as they do on the ivory-bill. If the birds do indeed respond to a double knock, it could greatly increase the likelihood of finding one—if they still exist.

The crucial question in any discussion of the imperial woodpecker is: why did the bird's population crash so catastrophically in the 1950s? Whether they were reduced in numbers by hunting or habitat destruction or a combination of the two, without knowing the answer we have no way of determining how to help the species recover if enough of them remain to provide a seed population.

The first person to predict the demise of the imperial woodpecker was Carl Lumholtz, writing in the 1890s. "The giant woodpecker is seen in the more remote parts, but it is on the point of being exterminated, because the Tarahumaras consider his one or two young such a delicacy that they do not hesitate to cut down even large trees to get at the nests," he wrote in his two-volume book *Unknown Mexico*. "The Mexicans shoot them because their plumage is thought to be beneficial to health. It is held close to the ears and the head in order to impart its supposed magnetism and keep out maleficent effects of the wind. In the pairing season these birds keep up a chattering noise, which to my ears was far from disagreeable, but very irritating to a Mexican whom I employed. He used to shoot the birds because they annoyed him." This paragraph is loaded with information, as Lumholtz tells us the number of young the birds usually raise (others have estimated from one to four), mentions several reasons why people kill them, and describes a different kind of vocalization the birds sometimes make.

Decades later, James Tanner addressed the imperial woodpecker's bleak situation in an article titled "The Decline and Present Status of the Imperial Woodpecker of Mexico," which appeared in the January 1964 issue of *The Auk*. One of my great regrets is that I never got to meet or interview Jim Tanner before he passed away in 1991. I have been interested in the ivory-billed woodpecker since the early 1970s, and it would have been so easy to pick up the telephone and call him. No one knew the ivory-bill as well as Tanner did. As a grad student, he had accompanied Cornell ornithologists Arthur Allen and Peter Paul Kellogg on their famed 1935 expedition, helping them take still photographs, motion pictures, and sound recordings of these spectacular birds in Louisiana's Singer Tract—an 81,000-acre remnant of old-growth southern swamp forest and the last area where the species could reliably be found. After receiving an Audubon Society fellowship, he returned and spent a total of twenty-one months in a three-year period completing the first and only in-depth study of the ivory-bill, which was the focus of his doctoral thesis at Cornell. Sadly, most of the Singer Tract was heavily logged during World War II.

Jim's widow, Nancy, and I have become good friends, however. We have spoken together many times about ivory-billed woodpeckers, which she saw on two trips to Louisiana that she took with Jim before the war. Nancy has the distinction of being the last person to see multiple ivory-bills right on their territory, and I treasure her insights into the birds.

In 1962, years after his studies in the Singer Tract, Jim Tanner headed south to Mexico with his teenage son David to search for the imperial woodpecker. "My primary objective was to compare this species with the American Ivory-bill, which I had studied intensively," he wrote.

Jim and David headed to the state of Durango, where Arthur Allen had seen an imperial woodpecker in 1946. It was an incredibly long drive, particularly in their vehicle, an aging Jeep that broke down twice en route. It was June, and David was fresh out of high school, on his last summer break before college. The roads going into the Sierra Madre were atrocious, just as they are now. "It took forever to make any distance," David told me. In some places they had to follow the deep ruts of logging trucks leading into the alpine areas, and they frequently bottomed out.

Jim had taken a crash course in Spanish before leaving his home in Tennessee, and he set about interviewing the people he met in the Sierra Madre, asking them what they knew about the giant woodpeckers—just as he had done in the South while searching for ivory-bills. He found numerous people who were familiar with the *pitoreal*. "When talking with natives of the Sierra in southern Durango, I found that almost all but the youngest adults knew the '*pitoreal*,'" he wrote.

Jim and David visited village after village in the Sierra, but it always turned out the same: no one had seen any *pitoreales* for five or six years, which in most cases was shortly after the logging companies had moved into a given area. They found out about another area of largely old-growth forest about a hundred miles away. Although a logging camp had been in operation there for a couple of years, the area supposedly still had a lot of excellent habitat.

When they got there, they hired some horses and a guide the logging manager had recommended. The man warned them how dangerous it was to travel around unarmed in the mountains. Some people would do anything to steal their horses and belongings— perhaps even murder them, he told Jim. The man loaned him a pistol and a gun belt, which he strapped to his waist. "I got this huge Bowie knife, and the guide carried a rifle," said David.

The guide told them he knew where a *pitoreal* nest was and had seen the birds just the previous summer. They rode deep into the high country. It was bitterly cold and windy up there, especially compared with the weather lower down in the mountains. "You could look down thousands of feet into the valley and see sunny little villages with no roads leading to them," he said. "The people had to ride horses or mules or walk to go there," said David.

It took them almost four days to reach the imperial woodpecker tree—a massive old pine with two good-sized cavities chiseled into it. But although they spent a couple more days in the area and explored the surrounding woods, they didn't see any of the birds or find any recent woodpecker workings. "That was the closest I ever came to an imperial woodpecker," said David, "one year after the last bird had been there."

Jim firmly believed that habitat destruction was the overriding factor in the crash of the American ivory-bill, but he had serious doubts that the imperial woodpecker's decline had similar roots. "In all three areas we visited there was adequate habitat for the woodpeckers, in uncut pine forest and even in the areas which had been logged, for the cutting is highly selective and many large pines are left standing . . . and I think enough of these are dead or will die from natural causes to supply adequate food," he wrote. Tanner believed that people who shot the birds to eat or for various other purposes were the primary culprit in the imperial woodpecker's crash. Of course, the logging camps had opened up the virgin forests to human exploitation, but he felt it was mostly a case of collateral damage and not the logging itself.

"[The] disappearance of the woodpeckers had followed by a year or so the establishment of a lumber camp or of ranchitos in each area," he wrote. "Lumber camps have brought people into the forest, opened areas to settlement, and provided employment and wages with which firearms can be purchased." He believed that the only way to save the species was to somehow get people to stop killing them.

The killing of imperial woodpeckers had to have been a major factor in the bird's massive population crash, but the destruction of the bird's primary habitat in subsequent years has been horrendous, and Jim Tanner would be appalled if he saw the state of the forest habitat in the Sierra Madre now.

The imperial woodpecker is a classic example of a species that is extremely habitat specific, having evolved to fill a very narrow niche. A pine specialist, it thrives in classic old-growth conditions—the largest trees with numerous dead snags available to provide foraging areas with enough large beetle grubs and places they could chisel out cavities for nighttime roosts and nest sites large enough to accommodate an incubating adult and young.

If you look at the Sierra Madre Occidental now—driving through it, flying above in an airplane, or viewing satellite images on Google Earth—you may think the forest so extensive that surely in that incredibly vast expanse places still exist where these birds can linger on, safe from humans, awaiting the day when conditions will improve and they can once more reinhabit their previous domain. That has certainly always been my hope. But the habitat has been drastically altered. For the most part, the pine forests remaining in the Sierra Madre are not the beautiful vast old-growth mesa forests where the species evolved: big trees, spaced widely apart, with less underbrush and numerous large dead trees both standing and fallen.

In a 1996 scientific article, Martjan Lammertink and his coauthors shattered the dreams of people who thought there was still plenty of old-growth mesa forest in the most remote areas of the Sierra Madre. In 1994, he and his colleagues launched an intensive expedition through the known range of the species. They began by analyzing topographical maps and satellite images, doing aerial surveys of the mountains, interviewing forestry technicians and local people, and studying the available literature. They then spent thirteen months working in the Sierra Madre Occidental from Jalisco to Chihuahua, following various leads to find old-growth forest remnants. The destruction they found was staggering. Although most of the tablelands where the biggest trees stood were still forested, they tended to be densely packed with small trees and few large snags, providing little prime habitat for imperial woodpeckers.

Even knowing this grim background, I had begun my search. I still believed that some imperial woodpeckers might be surviving, more than a decade after Martjan's expedition—but they wouldn't be in the easy-to-reach mesa pine-oak forests where they had thrived for millennia. If the species yet lingers on, I reasoned that the birds would have to be in far less optimal habitat, perhaps in a place with second-growth forest that has been growing back for decades, or on uncut ridgetops, or in difficult-to-reach high-altitude canyons that still contain huge pines. After my first forays into the Sierra Madre, I was still eager to continue my search, and as I shared my thoughts with Martjan, who was a colleague of mine at the Cornell Lab of Ornithology, and told him about some of the places I'd already explored, he became increasingly interested in going back again, trying one more time to crack the mystery of this remarkable bird.

4 ◆ Out of Norway

On a quiet summer morning in June, I drove eastward with my wife, Rachel, and my son, Jack, through the Adirondacks to the village of Saranac Lake, New York. We were on our way to Pine Ridge Cemetery to visit the final resting place of Carl Sofus Lumholtz, famed Norwegian explorer, ethnologist, and a personal hero of mine. He was one of the very few—besides the native peoples of the Sierra Madre—who came to know the imperial woodpecker well. His two-volume book *Unknown Mexico* (published in 1902) contains several in-depth passages about the species that provide fascinating insights into its natural history.

Lumholtz was one of thousands of people from New York City and other metropolitan areas who stayed at a "cure cottage" at Saranac Lake, seeking a remedy for the then-deadly disease of tuberculosis. In the late nineteenth and early twentieth centuries, many doctors believed it was beneficial for TB patients to escape the city and come here to breathe the clean air of the Adirondacks. Numerous pictures at the Adirondack Museum show sanitarium patients sitting in easy chairs on open porches in the dead of winter, wrapped head-to-foot in blankets or furs to keep warm as they breathed the chill mountain air.

Unfortunately, the treatment was unsuccessful for Lumholtz, and after a few months at a cure cottage, he passed away on May 5, 1922, at the age of seventy-one. But he has not been forgotten. On the day we visited his grave, a pot of flowers rested against the granite headstone, and a small Norwegian flag stood just to the side in front.

Although Lumholtz was pushed by his father, a Norwegian military officer, to become a cleric—and actually took a theological degree at the University of Christiana in Oslo, Norway—he eventually rebelled and become a zoological collector, traveling far to obtain specimens. When he went to Queensland, Australia, he lived with a tribe of Aborigines in the rugged outback in order to collect specimens more effectively. He returned to Norway four years later with a huge collection for the University of Christiana, but something far more profound had occurred: his experience living with the Aborigines had changed his life, and studying indigenous people—especially those barely touched by Western civilization—and their cultures had become his life's work. He became a great chronicler, recording not just different peoples' physical appearance and outward culture, as others had done, but exploring their attitudes, relationships, religions, languages, and music to get as complete a picture as he could.

By the time his book *Among Cannibals* was published in 1889, his life course as an ethnologist was firmly set. He would spend the rest of his days studying the barely known cultures before modern civilization pushed them aside. "Primitive people are becoming scarce on the globe," he lamented. "I hope that I shall have rendered them a service by setting them this modest monument, and that civilised man will be the better for knowing of them."

Carl Lumholtz next set his sights on the Sierra Madre of northwestern Mexico, where few outsiders had traveled. "I had heard . . . of the wonderful cliff-dwellings in the Southwest of the United States, of entire villages built in caverns on steep mountain-sides," he wrote. "Might there not, possibly, be descendants of the people yet in existence in the northwestern part of Mexico hitherto so little explored?"

A dynamo both in the field and in fund-raising, Lumholtz began his explorations of the Sierra Madre in the winter of 1890. Although his expedition was partially funded by the American Museum of Natural History and the American Geographical Society, and he traveled under their auspices, he raised the bulk of the money through private subscriptions. Twice during the eight years he spent on his Mexican explorations, when his money ran low, he had to return to New York. "I was so absolutely confident of the ultimate success of my efforts, in spite of discouragements, that I twice crossed the entire continent of North America, went down to the City of Mexico and came north again—a journey of over 20,000 miles—seeing prominent people and lecturing to arouse a public interest," he wrote.

Lumholtz launched his expedition after first traveling to Mexico City, where he met with Presidente Porfirio Díaz and several members of his cabinet to obtain the necessary credentials. For the first segment of the expedition, Lumholtz and the others would depart from the western side of the Sierra Madre in the state of Sonora, making their own trail east across the mountains to Casas Grandes, Chihuahua.

The expedition at first was huge—which must have been strange for Lumholtz, who was so used to working alone—and included a geographer, an archaeologist, a zoological collector, a mineralogist, and two botanists, most of whom brought along various assistants. Wrote Lumholtz: "We were, all in all, thirty men, counting the scientific corps, the guides, the cooks, and the muleteers, and we had with us nearly a hundred animals—mules, donkeys, and horses—as we crossed the sierra."

The pack animals did surprise Lumholtz a number of times, especially when they tripped and went tumbling down the mountainside. Because of the heavy packs they carried, when an animal slipped it could easily lose its balance and fall. On one such occasion, Lumholtz heard a noise coming from above him on the switchback trail and looked up to see a donkey tumbling down the steep mountainside toward him, "pack and all, turning over and over with astounding speed. It cleared a perpendicular rock some twenty feet high and landed at its base, rolling over twice." To Lumholtz's sheer amazement, it then rose to its feet in the middle of its scattered cargo. "And do you know what the cargo consisted of?" wrote an astounded Lumholtz. "A case of dynamite and our tool chest." He wrote of a mule that would sometimes fall like this as many as three times in a day, "tumbling 150 to 200 feet without, however, being seriously hurt." Miraculously, he did not lose a single pack animal to these mishaps on his entire first journey across the Sierra Madre.

As he made his way toward the foothills of the Sierra Madre, Lumholtz was astounded by how little most of the Mexicans he met knew about these magnificent mountains, which rose so closely in front of them. "The most prominent man in Opoto, a town hardly forty miles from the sierra, told me that he did not know how far it was to the sierra, nor was he able to say exactly where it was." Even in the village of Nácori in the foothills of the mountain range, few knew anything about the Sierra Madre, which he attributed to the centuries-long presence of the Apaches, which made the locals afraid to travel there. "From their mountain strongholds these marauders made raiding expeditions," he wrote, "sweeping down upon the farms, plundering the villages, driving off horses and herds of cattle, killing men and carrying off women and children into slavery. Mines became unworkable; farms had to be deserted; the churches, built by the Spanish, mouldered into decay. The raiders had made themselves absolute masters."

All that the local people knew about the region, wrote Lumholtz, was "that it is a vast wilderness of mountains most difficult of approach; that it would take eight days to climb to some of the high ridges; that it contains immense pine forests alive with deer, bear, and wonderfully large woodpeckers, able to cut down whole trees."

Those wonderfully large woodpeckers, of course, were the imperials, which Lumholtz found soon enough as he entered the realm of the old-growth pine forest. He made camp at an elevation of 6,300 feet, which provided a spectacular view of the country they had just come through. And there he had his first encounter with the *pitoreales*. "Large flocks of gray [band-tailed] pigeons of remarkable size squatted on the pine trees nearby, and two specimens of the gigantic woodpecker we here observed for the first time."

Lumholtz wrote a wonderful description of "that superb bird, *campephilus imperialis*, the largest woodpecker in the world. This splendid member of the feathered tribe is two feet long; its plumage is black and white, and the male is ornamented with a gorgeous scarlet crest, which seemed especially brilliant against the winter snow."

Carl Lumholtz brought several specimens of the imperial woodpecker back from his explorations of the Sierra Madre Occidental in the 1890s, including this one at the American Museum of Natural History in New York. (*Photo by Tim Gallagher*)

He would see many more imperial woodpeckers during his time in Mexico and collected seven specimens. I got a chance to examine and photograph several of the ones from the Lumholtz Expedition during a visit to the American Museum of Natural History, in New York City. More than a century old, the birds are still in remarkably good shape, and I'm always taken aback by how big they are. I had earlier compared some specimens of imperial, ivory-billed, and pileated woodpeckers side by side during a visit to Harvard. The difference in size among the three is astounding.

When I look at specimens of birds as rare and beautiful as an imperial woodpecker lying just inches away, I imagine vividly what they must have been like as living, breathing creatures. Each one tells a story, which itself can be fascinating, starting with their old specimen tags. As I write this chapter, I'm looking at a picture of imperial woodpecker specimen number 56903 from the Lumholtz Expedition. The tag, though browned with age, is easily readable. This and the other Lumholtz tags I've seen were preprinted with "American Museum of Natural History; Lumholtz Expedition; N. Chihuhua" and the name of the official zoological collector of the expedition, "F. Robinette." But on this and at least three other imperial woodpecker specimens collected on the expedition, Robinette's name is crossed out and the name Meeds is handwritten over it, as is the specimen number and the date and location where it was collected—in this case on January 29, 1892, in Chuhuichupa, where I went more than a century later.

On page 89 of *Unknown Mexico* (Part I), Lumholtz wrote: "The day after my arrival at Chuhuichupa I continued my journey, now accompanied by Mr. Taylor and Mr. Meeds."

I was very curious who this Mr. Meeds was and where he came from. An 1892 article by J. A. Allen in the *Bulletin of the American Museum of Natural History* detailed the results of the early part of the Lumholtz Expedition and mentioned that an A. D. Meeds of

Minneapolis, Minnesota, had joined the expedition in Mexico as a naturalist. After some searching, I found an article Meeds had written in the *Bulletin of the Minnesota Academy of Natural Sciences*.

"On October 4, 1891," wrote Meeds in the third person, "the writer having been granted a leave of absence from the University of Minnesota, left Minneapolis for EI Paso, Texas, where he joined Dr. Carl Lumholtz, the Norwegian explorer, who was about to continue his expedition in northern Mexico." I do not have a picture of A. D. Meeds, but I know more about him now, which makes the specimens he collected even more meaningful to me, since we traveled the same ground.

I interviewed several people who knew the high country above Chuhuichupa well, including Bill Martineau, a Mormon now in his early seventies, whose family was among those who founded Chuhuichupa in the 1880s, although most of the Mormons have now left the old mountain colonies such as Chuhuichupa and Pacheco.

"The Martineaus were one of the first Mormon families to settle in Chuhuichupa, and I was the last one to leave," he told me, laughing. "It was a paradise on Earth," he said of the old-growth pine forests he saw when he was a boy in the 1940s, and he described enormous sylvan giants rising high above the forest floor. When they were cut, it took an entire logging truck to carry each one out, one massive log at a time.

At Bill's home in Colonia Juárez, on the other side of town from John Hatch's home, we spent several hours digging through old picture albums and keepsakes. Few people have spent as much time in the old-growth forest of the Sierra Madre as Bill. When he was just three or four years old, his father would tie him to the saddle of a horse so he wouldn't fall off and take him along as he tended his cattle in the high country. Sometimes the elder Martineau would lose track of Bill, but apparently he never worried about

John Hatch (*at left*) and Bill Martineau study a map of the high country above Chuhuichupa, where Martineau had visited an imperial woodpecker nest in the late 1940s. (*Photo by Tim Gallagher*)

him because the horse knew the way home. Bill talks fondly about his father, but I definitely got the impression he was cut from the same cloth as Huck Finn's dad.

Like most cattlemen, Bill's father hated wolves and he would search for their dens every spring. Whenever he found one, he made Bill climb into it and pull out the young cubs. Sometimes he would let him play with them for a while. "They were just like German shepherd pups," said Bill. But his father always killed them before they rode away.

This antipathy toward wolves is common in the Sierra Madre, and most people I spoke with were glad that the Mexican wolf was extinct. (It had been exterminated using the deadly poison bait 1080, supplied by the US government, which didn't want wolves coming north across the border.) One man I interviewed told me a particularly grim story. He said people had sometimes tried raising wolf pups, but they would always put a snug piece of fence wire around their necks. If they ran away—which he said they invariably did—the young wolves would later choke to death as they grew too large for the wire collar. The ranchers did not want them coming back and preying on their livestock.

Bill described the imperial woodpecker perfectly, including its call, and told me that an American had approached his father in 1948, asking him if he could show him some imperial woodpeckers. Bill's father knew where some of these birds lived in the high country above Chuhuichupa and took him and young Bill on a several-hours-long ride into the mountains to a place named, appropriately enough, Pitoreal Pass. Tragically, they found a dead imperial woodpecker lying at the base of its nest tree—a huge pine snag with a nest hole on the trunk, high above them.

Curious what might be inside the cavity, the older Martineau tied two lariats together and attached a small log to one end, which he threw over a limb above the nest hole. He then fashioned a sling for Bill, tied the other end to his saddle horn, and backed up the horse, hoisting his eight-year-old son sixty feet in the air.

"You fall out of the sling and you're dead," he shouted to his young son. His father finally got him right beside the nest hole and Bill reached inside. He pulled two partially feathered young from the nest. They were already dead though still warm to the touch. He thought perhaps both parents had been shot and the young had starved.

When the American saw the dead nestlings, he broke down and wept. "It's just like me to be a day late and dollar short," the man said, sitting on a log covering his face with his hands as tears streamed down his cheeks. "The birds are going to go extinct, and there's nothing I can do about it."

Bill had a number of other encounters with imperial woodpeckers in his life, but the last time was in the mid-1980s when he was guiding a trout researcher in the mountains of Durango. While hiking through some excellent pine forest habitat near El Salto, he heard the distant toot of a *pitoreal*—a sound he hadn't heard for years—but he didn't see the bird.

A couple months after I interviewed Bill Martineau, I was looking through the bird collection at the San Diego Natural History Museum. The tag on an imperial woodpecker specimen (Number 29855) caught my eye. It had been collected by W. M. Fuelscher in the high country not far from Chuhuichupa, which was spelled phonetically as Chewy-Choopa, and added to the collection in 1949—very late for an imperial woodpecker specimen, most of which were collected in the late nineteenth and early twentieth centuries. I thought immediately about Bill Martineau's story and wondered whether this specimen might be the same adult imperial woodpecker that Bill and his father had found in 1948, with the American—and if the man were W. M. Fuelscher. The bird was collected in the same general area at the same general time and, according to the museum's curator of birds, Phil Unitt, this was the only specimen the collection ever obtained from W. M. Fuelscher.

So far, I haven't been able to find out anything else about Fuelscher. There is a historical landmark called the Fuelscher House in San Diego, but I couldn't find any current residents in the area with that name. Going through some death records I did find a William Fuelscher, who died in 1972 at the age of seventy-seven in Southern California. Perhaps he was the man who went with Bill Martineau and his father and this specimen was the very bird they found dead at the base of the tree at Pitoreal Pass, with its young, among the last of their kind.

◆　◆　◆

Reading between the lines in *Unknown Mexico*, I get the sense that people began leaving the Lumholtz Expedition after that first rugged crossing of the Sierra Madre. Just a few months later in May 1892, Lumholtz disbanded the entire party. "Dr. Lumholtz decided that the main object of the expedition, the proof of the existence or non-existence of Cliff Dwellers, could be better accomplished by his traveling alone," wrote Meeds.

It may well be that Lumholtz had actually already given up on the idea that he could find the lost tribe who built the cave dwellings, and the large group he was traveling with made it impossible to do the kind of intimate study of native peoples at which he excelled.

"I determined to study these interesting people . . . and as this was not practical, even with the present reduced size of the expedition, I gradually disbanded the entire company and at last remained alone," he wrote. He sold off most of his animals and equipment in order to keep going, and then rode into the mountains on a single mule.

At first, most of the tribes he encountered were distrustful of him. Many had been persecuted by whites in various ways. But Lumholtz "managed to make my entry and gradually to gain their confidence and friendship, mainly through my ability to sing their native songs, and by always treating them justly." Sometimes he would arrive in a new area and ride along singing their songs at the top of his lungs. And they came to accept him. "I stopped for months with a tribe . . . roughing it with the Indians," he wrote, subsisting entirely on what they ate after he'd used up his own supplies. He created extensive vocabularies of the languages of the Tarahumara and Tepehuán tribes, as well as the now lost Tubares.

Although Lumholtz did not meet any Apaches face-to-face,

they were certainly aware of his presence. He sometimes saw their tracks around his camp or found "small bunches of yucca leaves tied together in a peculiar way known to the Mexicans as signs intelligible only to the Apaches." Perhaps the Apaches were fascinated by this peculiar chap or thought him mad and decided to give him a free pass through their territory.

On his third and most extensive expedition, Lumholtz spent three years, from March 1894 to March 1897, traveling mostly alone or occasionally hiring one or two native people to help him. This helped him to "win the confidence of their tribesmen" and also allowed him to get to know them and their culture.

Lumholtz returned to the United States with huge amounts of data and artifacts as well as in-depth information on the customs, religions, traditions, and myths; vocabularies of their languages; and their melodies and dances, much of which would have been lost if not for his efforts. On his final expedition to Mexico, Lumholtz actually recorded sixty melodies on a graphophone, an early sound-recording device.

Lumholtz pointed out some references to the birds among the legends of the Tarahumara: "The giant woodpecker during the wet season rises high up toward the sun; that is why he gets his tail burned"; and "In winter time they sing of the giant woodpecker." Although Lumholtz doesn't explain the significance of these sayings, the first one must be a myth about how the imperial woodpecker got its black tail (similar to Native American legends in the Pacific Northwest about how the raven became black), and the second may be because of the bird's association with the sun, which is no doubt sorely missed in the cold, bleak Sierra Madre winters. According to Huichol legend, the nocturnal animals of the world—mountain lions, jaguars, wolves, coyotes, and foxes—shot arrows at the sun on its first journey across the sky, and the giant woodpecker and grey squirrel were the only ones to defend him. "They would rather die than allow the Sun to be shot," wrote Lumholtz, "and in the west they placed *tesvino* [beer] for him. The jaguar and the wolf killed the grey squirrel and the gigantic woodpecker, but to this day the Huichols offer sacrifices to these . . . hero-gods and call the squirrel father. From their diurnal habits it is believed that these animals are the Sun's companions and delight in his company. The woodpecker carries the colour of the sun on his magnificent scarlet crest."

◆ ◆ ◆

Another famed Norwegian explorer, Helge Ingstad, journeyed through the Sierra Madre some four decades after Carl Lumholtz and also encountered imperial woodpeckers. He, too, went in search of a lost tribe—in this case, the Sierra Madre Apaches, who by then were only a shattered remnant with perhaps fewer than two dozen surviving members.

Another restless overachiever like Lumholtz, Ingstad had a burning desire to accomplish great things. After completing a law degree, he set up a legal practice and was well on his way to a successful, comfortable, prosperous life but gave it all up after a few years, selling his practice and heading off to the wilds of Canada. When asked the reasoning behind his decision, he replied: "I was afraid of getting rich and getting stuck."

Ingstad spent four years in the wilderness around the Great Slave Lake, hunting and trapping to survive. He stayed for a time with the Chipewyans (an indigenous people who live in the arctic and subarctic regions of Canada around Hudson Bay and parts of the Northwest Territories, Manitoba, Saskatchewan, and Alberta) and became fascinated by their culture. Sometimes sitting around the campfire the men would tell old tales of how some of their people had wandered away to the south countless years (or perhaps centuries) earlier and never returned. Ingstad later found out that the Apaches and Navajos of the American Southwest had originally migrated from the north and spoke an Athabascan language closely related to that of the Chipewyans. Hoping to record their traditional way of life, Ingstad traveled to Arizona in order to talk to the White Mountain Apaches on the reservation. Many there still remembered Geronimo and the wars they had fought against the whites. They told him that the Apaches who had gone south to the Sierra Madre still lived in the traditional way.

Ingstad assembled a team to travel with him through the mountains of Mexico. The first person he chose was Yahnozah, a seventy-six-year-old Apache who had fought side by side with Geronimo and knew all the old haunts in the Sierra. In a famous photograph of Geronimo standing with three other Apaches, all armed with rifles and still on the warpath, Yahnozah is the man on the far left. Although he was old, he assured Ingstad that he could find his way around the Sierra Madre blindfolded and that if they ran across any of the Apaches who had fled there after Geronimo's surrender, they would know him and still be his friends.

He also intended to take Juh, son of the famous Apache war chief of the same name, but Juh backed out at the last minute. And he spoke with the son of Victorio, who also declined. He even briefly considered taking the son of Geronimo, but then decided his name alone might still cause anxiety among the Mexicans. He finally chose a young man called Andrew Little, the son of an Apache mother and a Mexican father, who had been kidnapped by the Sierra Madre Apaches as a boy and adopted into the tribe. Little knew the area well and could speak Apache, Spanish, and English fluently.

Together they headed south from Arizona in November 1937

wegians, who sometimes came to Mexico on pilgrimages, hoping to revisit some of the sites their illustrious countrymen Lumholtz and Ingstad wrote about.

I put the DVD on right away, and it was great: a silent movie with title cards describing the action while a series of lively Mexican ballads played in the background. The explorers went through places I'd seen myself. I was especially excited when the title card read, "The Blue Mountains"—the Sierra Azul, where Elvin Whetten, Jose Perez, and others had seen imperial woodpeckers in the 1940s and '50s and where many specimens of the species were collected. No imperial woodpeckers appeared on the DVD, however.

Helge Ingstad later famously discovered the lost Viking settlement at L'Anse aux Meadows in Newfoundland, Canada. Various archaeologists had pondered for decades where the Norse settlement called Vinland might be. Most of them had searched far to the south, because they were looking for the wild grapes for which they thought it had been named. But Ingstad surmised that "vin" had nothing to do with grapes but was an Old Norse word meaning "meadows." He also closely read the Icelandic sagas to try to determine the distances and directions traveled by the Vikings.

Ingstad and his teenage daughter, Benedicte, set off in 1960 to explore the coasts of northern Newfoundland and southern Labrador. Traveling mostly by boat, they explored every tiny bay and harbor they found and asked the local people if they knew of any old ruins in the area. Miraculously, in a tiny fishing village at the far northern tip of Newfoundland, a fisherman told them, "Yes, come with me." And he took them right to the spot.

"I remember it clearly," wrote Benedicte Ingstad. "My father was very excited when he saw the shape of the ruins and how they were placed in the terrain."

"This must be it," Ingstad told his daughter. "It all fits so well.

This must be where Leif Ericson landed." And it proved to be true. The houses were all of the Nordic type and were dated to the year 1000 AD, when Ericson established the settlement at Vinland.

It was a fitting pinnacle to a lengthy and spectacular career of exploration, but it was far from the end of his life. Ingstad, who was born in 1899, passed away on March 29, 2001, at the age of 101—one of the few people to have lived in three centuries.

5 ♦ There Is Blood in This Soil

John Hatch's four-wheel-drive pickup blasted down the lonely highway, streaking through the darkness like a swift mountain wind. The road to Creel is a good paved highway, rare in the Sierras. Nonetheless, I was concerned; this was only my third journey to Mexico in search of the imperial woodpecker, and I'd already broken that cardinal rule again: never travel at night in the hinterlands of Mexico, because anything can happen. But it was December 2009, the days were short, and Creel was a good seven-hour drive away. If we traveled only in the daylight hours, we wouldn't have time to explore when we finally got there.

An important part of my search, Creel was near where several imperial woodpecker sightings had taken place over the years—most recently in 2005—though none of them was confirmed with a photograph or video, which is necessary for a sighting to be taken seriously by the scientific community. Years earlier, I'd been handed a musty old topographic map by a dying man—David Allen, son of Cornell ornithologist Arthur A. Allen—and it was just like a treasure map, showing a large forested area where imperial woodpeckers had supposedly nested in the early 1970s. David never had a chance to check out the place himself, though it was something he'd always wanted to do. In 2005, as he lay dying of cancer, David gave the map to me, as though passing a torch. I needed to look around the place to see if the habitat was still decent. I also hoped to find Paul Salopek's old friend, Benito Parra, to ask him about the imperial woodpecker.

Creel is an interesting place, one of the main jumping-off points for exploring Barranca del Cobre (or Copper Canyon), which is justifiably billed as the "Grand Canyon of Mexico." A train goes right through Creel and has for many years been one of Mexico's popular tourist activities, taking passengers from sea level at Los Mochis all the way east to Chihuahua City, some four hundred miles away, in the process reaching altitudes of 7,500 feet or more, chugging through one of the most ruggedly beautiful expanses of the Sierra Madre Occidental. It is a spectacular journey.

The train used to get held up periodically by armed banditos, who blocked the tracks and walked through the train, collecting money, jewelry, and other valuables from the passengers. The last time this occurred was in 1999, with devastating results for everyone involved, including the thieves. During the course of the robbery, a middle-aged Swiss tourist kept taking videos of the banditos. Apparently, he didn't understand a word of Spanish or English and thought the robbery was part of the entertainment. After warning him several times to stop videotaping, one of the robbers sprayed him with a burst of bullets from an AK-47, killing him and seriously wounding four other passengers.

From that day, the train has always carried guards, placed strategically through the railcars, well armed with automatic weapons to discourage robbers. But an even greater deterrent are the local *narcotraficantes*, who were outraged by the attention drawn to Copper Canyon, an important drug-growing area. None of them wanted to attract the notice of law enforcement agencies. Some of the drug growers owned shares in various lodges and tourist facilities on the canyon rim—which were great for laundering their drug money—and didn't want tourists to become afraid to go there. The *narcotraficantes*' hit men quickly tracked down all of the bandits, subjecting them to fates that would have made Tony Soprano blanch. One man was tied up, doused with gasoline, and burned alive.

The killings of the bandits sent the message that tourists were off limits and, thanks to that 1999 train robbery, the Barranca del

Cobre corridor became one of the safest tourist areas in all of Mexico—despite its numerous drug crops. An unwritten understanding existed between the drug growers and many tour guides who operated there. The guides knew exactly which areas were okay to take tourists to and which to avoid. Some of them took travelers on foot or muleback down spectacular mountain trails—cleverly skirting the drug-growing fields—en route to picturesque Tarahumara villages. Most tourists didn't have a clue about the area's narcotics cultivation.

The recent government crackdown on the *narcotraficantes* threw everything in the region into turmoil, however, and now no travel in the Sierra Madre is completely safe. Even the sleepy tourist town of Creel had a drug-related massacre in August 2008 when, during a wedding party at a local dance hall, three pickup trucks pulled up and several gunmen, dressed in black and wearing ski masks, leapt out and began firing AK-47s at more than a dozen men who had been standing in front, talking and celebrating. The shooting continued for nearly ten minutes as nearby tourists walking in the street fled into shops and restaurants, cowering behind any shelter they could find. Fourteen people were cut down, including a one-year-old infant who was killed in his father's arms.

◆ ◆ ◆

After a quick presunrise breakfast, John Hatch and I were back on the road. We had stopped in the middle of the night at a small hotel run by Mennonites. Between the Mormons and the Mennonites, who make up a significant percentage of the population in some parts of Chihuahua, I sometimes felt as if I were somewhere in Iowa. I passed many burly, ruddy-faced, white farm boys the first time I strolled down the main street in Nuevo Casas Grandes, all wearing brand-new dark blue denim bib overalls, long-sleeved cotton shirts, and crisp white farmer hats—the typical going-into-town getup of Mennonite farmers. Their wives and daughters strode six feet behind them, clad in long nineteenth-century-style dresses with their hair tied in tight buns and covered with white caps. The Mennonites tend to stand apart from the Mexican culture, and many speak only German, despite the fact that they first began moving to Mexico in significant numbers in the early 1920s. Both the Mormons and Mennonites are traditionally hardworking and ambitious, and they have been remarkably successful—to the consternation of some Hispanic Mexicans who view them as outsiders.

◆ ◆ ◆

As we continued driving toward Creel, I thought about David Allen, who had seen an imperial woodpecker during an expedition to Durango with his father and mother in the 1940s. With a tough, no-nonsense personality, David could be intimidating. He lived down the street from the Cornell Lab of Ornithology on Sapsucker Woods Road and would sometimes come storming from his house in a rage to confront motorists who drove by too fast. He also came to the lab periodically to complain about various activities there and in the surrounding Sapsucker Woods Sanctuary. Of course, he had a perfect right to—he had played a vital role in creating the place, drawing up plans for the sanctuary in the 1950s, laying out the trails, and supervising the construction of the pond and wetlands. When I first arrived at the Cornell Lab of Ornithology in 1990, several lab staff warned me that David might drop in sometime and give me a hard time. As it turned out, when we finally did meet it was nothing like that, because we had something very much in common: we both greatly admired his late father, Arthur A. Allen, the famed Cornell professor who founded the Lab of Ornithology in 1915.

At the age of twelve, when I first got interested in bird photography and falcons, one of the first pictures I saw of a peregrine falcon nest was the portrait Arthur Allen took at Taughannock Falls, near Ithaca, New York, in the 1930s. With the picturesque waterfall as a backdrop, an adult peregrine perches on a branch overlooking the nest ledge and her young. I loved that image the instant I saw it, and when I came to the lab more than two decades ago for my job interview, I asked to be taken to the old peregrine eyrie—still beautiful but sadly lacking the main ingredient, the falcons, which had vanished from the site nearly half a century earlier during the DDT era. A short time later as I was looking through the lab art collection for illustrations and photographs to decorate my office, I found a framed picture of Arthur Allen sitting at his office window, gazing out at birds as he held a camera and long telephoto lens. I immediately hung it on my office wall.

A couple of weeks later, David was visiting the lab, and someone brought him around to meet me. The instant he stepped into my office, he spotted his father's portrait and smiled broadly. From that moment on, we were good friends, and he would often stop by to talk about fly-fishing, with which we were both obsessed, and birds—especially rare ones like ivory-billed and imperial woodpeckers.

When Arthur Allen was leaving on his famed 1935 expedition to film, photograph, and make sound recordings of the vanishing birds of America—including the remnant ivory-billed woodpecker population in northeastern Louisiana—David begged to go along, but at only eight years old, he was far too young. His father promised to take him on future expeditions, and David later became a key participant in everything his father did.

Allen did take his wife Elsa and David (then twenty years old) with him on a six-week expedition in the wilds of Mexico, driving the atrocious back roads of the Sierra Madre in a station wagon and a sedan, both laden to the gunwales with camera and sound-recording equipment. Due to postwar shortages, the cars didn't have any shock absorbers, which made for a horrendous ride. Arthur Allen was then sixty years old but apparently had no complaints.

"From El Salto we made our way to Durango where several of our countrymen were most cooperative in helping us locate our objective—the imperial ivory-billed woodpecker," he wrote in his 1951 book *Stalking Birds with Color Camera*. (At that time, many people called the bird the "imperial ivory-billed" or "Mexican ivory-billed" woodpecker, and some even considered it to be just a southern race of the American ivory-billed woodpecker, despite the bird's much larger size, its preference for high-altitude pine forest rather than bottomland swamps, and other characteristics that separated it from the other species.) "We were hopeful of finding a nesting pair that we could study, record, and compare with the more northern ivorybills, which we had observed in 1935 [in Louisiana's Singer Tract]."

Chester Lamb, a prominent museum collector, had told Allen about seeing the species a few years earlier in the mountains of Durango and had pointed him to the area. Allen really knew he was hot on the trail when logger John Zahala told him he had seen one of the birds just two weeks earlier at his logging camp El Progreso, about thirty miles north of Coyotes in the state of Durango. They wasted no time in racing to the spot.

"The trail led over a rough mountain road, up and down canyons, but ever rising to about 9,000 feet," he wrote. "Here the pines were much larger, and there was evidence of large woodpeckers having worked recently over the dead trees." They found piles of stripped bark under some recently dead trees that looked similar to what Allen had seen in Louisiana, where the ivory-bills use their chisellike bills to pry chunks of bark off trees (though they were usually hardwoods in Louisiana, not pines like in the Sierra Madre) to get at the huge beetle larvae inside. It was mid-May, and birds were just starting to nest in the mountains. They saw colorful trogons, bluebirds, and thick-billed parrots. David watched a pair of the parrots going in and out of an old cavity that imperial woodpeckers had probably excavated. But where were the woodpeckers? Could they be sitting on eggs in a nest cavity somewhere?

It was not until late afternoon on the third day that David sighted a lone female imperial woodpecker flying across a canyon west of camp, heading for a nearby mesa. The next day the search kicked into high gear. The Allens hired two Mexicans to help them, and at dawn they fanned out over the area the bird had been flying toward the previous afternoon. Then Arthur Allen had a breakthrough—he heard a familiar tinny nuthatchlike call that seemed identical to the ivory-billed woodpecker calls he'd heard a decade earlier in Louisiana—and he went racing toward the sound.

"Slipping through the great pines, I soon had an excellent view of the great bird near the top of a dead spire, whacking off large pieces of bark, examining the trunk beneath, and occasionally giving those familiar tin-trumpet calls," wrote Allen. "With my binoculars I could see its yellow eye and easily recognized it as a female imperial with no red on the head."

Allen noted how similar it looked to an American ivory-billed woodpecker and that the difference in size wasn't apparent until it took off. He said the flight was straight, direct, and ducklike, without the bounding undulations of the pileated and many other woodpeckers. He never saw it again after it flew, but his son David spotted an imperial woodpecker later in the day, flying across the same canyon where he'd had the sighting the day before. Arthur Allen put a camera and telephoto lens on a tripod and trained it on a cavity in a nearby pine snag, hoping it was an imperial woodpecker nest hole or roost and that he might still achieve the distinction of becoming the first person to photograph the species in life. But it was a futile effort.

"For several days we haunted this spot, but we never saw it again, nor did we find any fresh cuttings," wrote Allen. "Regretfully we decided it must nest later in the season and gave up our quest."

Besides being the first to spot an imperial woodpecker on their 1946 expedition, David also had the distinction, during a later expedition in the Alaskan wilderness, of being the first person ever to locate a bristle-thighed curlew nest, which brought him international attention.

David went searching for imperial woodpeckers again in the early 1970s, funded by *National Geographic* magazine. He had heard seemingly credible reports of imperial woodpeckers still existing in remote areas and hired a man with a string of mules to take him deeper into the hinterlands of the Sierra. But after a couple of weeks, the man got tired of the quest and ended up abandoning David and taking his mules back with him. David had to walk all the way to a tiny mountain village and wait a week before a logging truck came through and gave him a ride out.

Enormously frustrated, David felt he was just inches away from finding nesting imperial woodpeckers, so when he got to a town with a telegraph office, David wired the editor at *National Geographic*, pleading for more funds to keep going a little bit longer, to follow just one more promising lead. But they turned him down. Whether he was truly that close to a great discovery is impossible to tell.

Shortly after David quit his search and went home to Ithaca, he heard about some imperial woodpeckers sighted by two Mexican university students, who had been working on a study farther north in the Sierra Madre in the Copper Canyon area. Graduate students of Bernardo Villa, a prominent biologist who held an important position in the Mexican government, the students marked up a topographical map with a red felt pen, drawing thin zebra stripes across the area where they had seen imperial woodpeckers. Villa passed the map along to David, and he in turn had given it to me.

The men who saw the woodpeckers were not bird experts but mammalogists, there to study bats. It's possible that they may have seen a different species such as a lineated woodpecker or a pale-billed woodpecker, although the altitude was probably too high for those species but perfectly fit the imperial's preference.

David vigorously pitched *National Geographic* on the idea of a follow-up expedition to check this new lead, but the editors refused. So David never had a chance to return to the Sierra Madre and dreamed of doing so for the rest of his life. Decades later as he presented the map to me, he said, "I sure wish I could go with you."

Both men who had drawn up the map had died young—one of a serious illness, the other in a helicopter crash. Bernardo Villa was still alive at that time, so I asked my friend Eduardo Iñigo-Elias, a Mexican biologist at the Cornell Lab of Ornithology, if he would visit Bernardo Villa the next time he went to Mexico City. When he returned to Ithaca, Eduardo told me that Villa was in his nineties and had recently had a stroke. He did vaguely remember the students and the map he had given to David, but the crucial details we hoped for had vanished from his memory.

A short time after David gave me the map, I delivered a eulogy at his memorial service. That was about three years before I began my own quest, but even then I knew that I had to resume his search for the imperial woodpecker.

◆ ◆ ◆

John pulled off the highway onto an old logging road in the southern part of the area marked on David's map. We had been skirting the edges of the area, stopping to hike in places and examine the habitat, but this dirt road was in remarkably good shape (for the Sierra Madre), and we hoped to use it to drive deep into the forest. The trees were mostly second-growth pines, though they formed a forest that seemed to stretch on forever. But then, just as we were starting to feel as if we had reached a really remote area, we suddenly came out into a long, wide strip of perfectly flat earth. All of the trees, rocks, and debris had been removed to create a landing strip for flying drugs out of the mountains.

John hit the brakes and quickly brought the truck to a halt. The last time he'd been there, huge boulders had been scattered by the military all along the cleared strip to make it impossible to land a plane. Obviously, drug growers had gotten men to clear the boulders out of the way by hand. Labor is a cheap commodity in the Sierra Madre.

We quickly drove back the way we'd come and entered the forest through another access point, eventually stopping at a place along a high cliff where a couple of Tarahumara women sat weaving baskets in a patch of sunlight. The air was fresh at that altitude, with a pungent aroma of pine wafting through on the mountain breeze. The view was spectacular, endless deep gorges and pine-clad ridges: a landscape vast enough to make a human feel small—and perhaps enough to provide refuge for the imperial woodpecker.

After a few hours of hiking through the forest without seeing or hearing any evidence of imperial woodpeckers, we returned to the highway, and John drove me to the mountain village of Pitoreal, where he took a picture of me posing next to the sign. If only finding a living *pitoreal* could be that simple. From there we drove to tiny El Divisadero, one of the stopping points for the Barranca del Cobre train, where hordes of passengers are dumped for fifteen or twenty minutes to get a quick look at one of the most spectacular canyon viewpoints along the route and buy a Tarahumara souvenir or grab a quick meal from a street vendor. Barely a whistle-stop, El Divisadero has a luxury hotel perched on the canyon edge, right in the heart of David Allen's 1970s map.

And here, in 2005, a husband-and-wife birding couple from the United States reported seeing an imperial woodpecker.

At first, the sighting seemed suspicious, coming just a few months after we at Cornell had announced the rediscovery of the ivory-billed woodpecker in Arkansas. Many people wondered whether our discovery might in some way have inspired this sighting. The story hit the internet in a Listserv posting from John Spencer, an American birding tour guide who lives in Baja California. "Possible Imperial Woodpecker sighting!" read the subject line; the post went on to say:

> Ron and Sarojam Makau . . . are avid bird watchers, who live (part-time) near Cabo Pulmo, [Baja California, Mexico]. They are both professors at UC Riverside in the Biology Department.
>
> They just got back from the Copper Canyon trip. They had some fantastic news . . . they are sure, absolutely sure, that they saw an Imperial Woodpecker (!) near Divisadero on the north rim of Copper Canyon.
>
> I questioned them closely, but they were sure, based on the description in [the] Peterson [Field Guide to the Birds of Mexico] . . .
>
> They swear that they saw the female, [which] has a very unusual reverse crest. They both are experienced birders and are biology professors at UC Riverside. They have birded all over the world and are really good birders. I believe their sighting.
>
> They saw the bird about 30 feet up a pine tree, clinging to the trunk. They were about 50 to 60 feet away, with good light. They observed the bird for about 2 minutes; during that time the bird turned her head and the crest was seen at several angles, definitely

matched the drawing in Peterson for the female. The bird flew off with slow heavy wing beats (described as Raven-like flight). No sounds were heard. The sighting was about 0700 on the trail near the big hotel on the canyon rim.

When I first tried to locate Ron and Sarojam, I got nowhere, as did several other birders who had tried and then assumed that the reported sighting must be a hoax. Others had speculated that, even if these birders had seen something they honestly believed to be an imperial woodpecker, they were wrong and must have actually seen a Steller's jay, which also has a crest, and somehow mistaken the smaller size and color of the bird.

I let it go for a while as I traveled through other parts of Mexico but finally decided to look for the birders one more time—and this time I succeeded. Their last name was actually Mankau and had been misspelled in the Listserv posting, and both were professors emeriti at the University of California, Riverside. I found their phone number and email address and tried to contact them. Still, I had no reply to my emails or telephone messages for months.

Then, on perhaps the hundredth time I called, Ron Mankau picked up the phone. Both had retired and now spend most of the year on the southern coast of Baja California. He was at their home in Riverside briefly to pick up a few things. I asked him to tell me in detail about their sighting. He said they saw the bird clinging to the trunk of a pine tree up ahead while they were walking on a trail near Divisadero. Unfortunately, someone was coming back up the trail from the opposite direction and walked right past the bird, flushing it before the Mankaus get there. Otherwise, they would've had a spectacular view of it, so their sighting wasn't quite as good as John Spencer had described it on the Listserv. The bird was backlit, so they only saw it in silhouette and couldn't make out any color. But he told me it definitely had the body shape of a woodpecker and behaved like one, clinging to the trunk of a pine tree. And it was huge. But most important, it had a large crest curving noticeably forward.

After speaking with him, I had no doubt that Ron Mankau was honest and had not made up the story about their sighting. I found the sighting to be credible, but after spending a few days examining the habitat there and in other places depicted in David Allen's map, I came to doubt that it was still suitable for supporting breeding pairs of imperial woodpeckers. Although the woodlands are vast and difficult to survey adequately, most of the places I checked were second-growth forest with few snags available for nesting and foraging. But I couldn't help wondering how this area looked forty years ago when those Mexican grad students claimed they had found imperial woodpeckers. If only I had come here then. Even now, despite the lack of old-growth forest, I could certainly imagine a lone *pitoreal* wandering through this area.

◆　◆　◆

Paul Salopek had come to Creel three months earlier to celebrate Don Benito's ninety-ninth birthday, but it turned out to be a sad time. Just two days earlier, some thugs had abducted his favorite granddaughter, a lively thirty-nine-year-old schoolteacher, and raped her, afterwards killing her with an axe. Everyone told him she had died in a car accident.

Don Benito lives in a casa with a red roof, a short distance off the road to Creel, at the end of the Choguita Valley. That's all the information Paul gave me before I flew to Mexico. After John and I left the main highway, we drove up a riverbed toward a tiny church we saw farther up the valley, looking for someone who might know where Don Benito lived. We spotted some children who told us his home was all the way back in the direction from where we had come, so we turned around and bumped our way back down the stony riverbed.

We finally found the red-roofed house and wondered why we hadn't noticed it right away, before taking this long detour up the valley. A middle-aged man wearing a jean jacket and an old white straw cowboy hat was fixing a barbed-wire fence in front of Don Benito's house and told us the old man wasn't there. He was very sick and staying with his daughter in Creel, he said. He tried to explain how to find the house, but it was complicated, and he finally just squeezed into the truck with us, and we all drove to Creel together.

Benito's daughter, Maricruz, met us at the door, wearing a felt hat and a serape, and ushered us through the house and into Benito's dimly lit room. He looked ghastly, more dead than alive, with a huge abscess on the right side of his face and a colorful bandana wrapping his head. So old and frail—with taut yellow skin as thin as parchment, one eye completely shut and sunken, and the right side of his face drooping—he looked as ancient as an Incan mummy pulled from a centuries-old cave in the Andes. He was completely unable to hear, and to communicate with him, Maricruz had to write questions in big block letters on a legal pad, holding it a few inches in front of his one good eye. At first he misunderstood who we were. Maricruz told him we were friends of Paul, but he thought Paul was actually there with us.

"Pablito, Pablito," he called out several times as he tried to sit up higher in bed. Then he lay sadly back down as he realized Paul was not there. It was nearly impossible to get coherent answers from him at first. But the painting of the imperial woodpecker we held up seemed to release a flood of memories. He told us of the great influenza pandemic of 1918, when so many people, sometimes entire families, had died in Creel. That was also when they had the worst snowfall they'd ever experienced before or since, he said, with snow piled several feet deep—and suddenly *pitore-ales* began showing up right in the village, apparently driven down from the higher country by the severe weather. As he spoke, it was like he was right back in 1918 in his mind.

We were quiet as we left Don Benito and drove away from Creel. It was all so sad. I got in touch with Paul as soon as I could and told him how gravely ill Don Benito was and that I was sure he would not live much longer. Paul was a visiting professor at Princeton then, but he flew immediately to El Paso, rented a car, and made the seven-hour drive to Creel to visit him one last time. Paul wrote a moving tribute to his old friend a few months later in a blog post on the internet journalism site Globalpost:

> Don Beni was born on September 6, 1910, at the headwaters of the Conchos River, a piney mesa that even today could pass for a haunt of the Marlboro man. His father was a traveling seed merchant, his mother a Raramuri Indian. His earliest memories were of blood and hunger. Pancho Villa's rabble and the federal cavalry ranged the mountains, pillaging local farmsteads in turn. By the winter of 1916, he and his seven siblings were reduced to chewing on dry corn-husks. His sisters would sprint for the trees at the sound of distant hoof beats, evading gang rape. His mother rubbed clay into their faces to convince raiders the girls were poxed.
>
> "Those were times of great necessity," he said without visible emotion. "No tortillas, no peace, no hope."
>
> I asked him about Mexico's current woes. "There is blood in this soil," he would mutter, waving away harsh memories with a gnarled hand. "It's rising up again."

On March 15, 2010, less than three months after I visited Benito Parra, another massacre took place in Creel, and the police captured it on video remotely. At the time, I was in a different part of Mexico, in the mountains of Durango. The video was shown on Mexican television and can be viewed at http://tinyurl.com/bv34vd9. It shows a group of gunmen blocking an intersection shortly after dawn, harassing motorists, and pulling some out of their cars. In one scene, the camera zooms in on one of the gunmen snorting huge pinches of cocaine from a plastic bag. Then several men carrying AK-47s approach a residence and begin firing inside, the flare of the muzzle blasts lighting up the inside as they shoot. According to reports, nine members of a Creel family were killed. And yet no one was arrested and no investigations have been launched. The frightening thing is that the command and control center operating the video camera is right in Creel. There, as in many Mexican cities and villages, the police are afraid even to respond to emergency calls, and horrendous crimes are committed with impunity.

Shortly before his surrender in 1886, Geronimo (*at right*) poses with several of his warriors—including Yahnozah (*at left*), who guided Helge Ingstad in the 1930s. (*Courtesy of Arizona Historical Society*)

6 ◆ Twilight of the Sierra Madre Apaches

John Hatch and I left Colonia Juárez early in the morning to drive to Elvin Whetten's ranch, all the way on the eastern side of the state of Chihuahua. Now ninety-five, Elvin spent much of his early life running cattle in the high country of the Sierra Madre and, according to his daughter Nelda Villa and several other people, he knows a lot about the imperial woodpecker.

A widely respected, self-taught expert on the Sierra Madre Apaches, Nelda has been a vital source for many books written about them. She and her husband, Efraín, came with us in John Hatch's big club cab pickup on a crisp December morning. We were headed well out of the range of the imperial woodpecker into the arid high-desert country east of Chihuahua City, where the Apaches suffered one of their most staggering defeats in 1880. In some ways, Apaches have much in common with the imperial woodpecker, grizzly bear, and Mexican wolf—all had been destroyed in the race to exploit the resources of the Sierra Madre.

Nelda and Efraín Villa stand at a viewpoint along the famed Barranca del Cobre, or Copper Canyon. She is an acknowledged expert on the history of the Sierra Madre Apaches. (*Photo by Tim Gallagher*)

Elvin's ranch, called El Rincon (The Corner), stands at an altitude of 4,688 feet and is incredibly remote, a two-hour drive on a rough desert road—this after we'd already driven five hours on paved roads, traveling right through the middle of Chihuahua City and on into the hinterlands to the east. Elvin owns more than ten thousand acres there, consisting mostly of dry open country with high, rocky hills nearby and a massive rock outcropping called El Pulpito (The Pulpit) towering above it. He also owns Rancho El Gavilan, high in the Sierra Madre, but in Mexico a person can be land-rich and cash-poor, and both of Elvin's properties are anything but luxurious.

When he first bought Rancho El Rincon in the mid-1950s, Elvin moved a large herd of cattle down from his remote mountain ranch to a railhead near Casas Grandes in a classic old-time cattle drive. From there, the cattle were loaded aboard railcars and shipped (along with the vaqueros and their horses) closer to the new ranch in eastern Chihuahua, where they were unloaded and the cattle drive continued. We stopped briefly at the old depot where the cattle had come off the train. It had fallen into ruin decades earlier, and the hot desert wind now blew sand over the long-abandoned rails.

Elvin came out to meet us as we pulled up in front of his ranch house. He walked with a cane but in other respects seemed spry and healthy, still cowboy-lean and standing tall in his pointy boots and hat. He wore faded blue jeans and a plaid cowboy shirt with snap buttons. Elvin's striking pale-blue eyes stood out from his leathery, sun-baked face. He shook hands with me warmly and invited us inside.

Elvin's ranch house is simple—an old adobe main building with a log cabin extension built onto it. The inside has a bare concrete floor and a fireplace set into the far wall, with a blazing pine fire spreading warmth throughout the room. On the wall above the mantel hang framed pictures of famous Apaches such as Geronimo and Victorio—and also one of Lupe, an Apache woman captured by Mexicans in 1915 when she was twelve years old. A lookout for

Ninety-five-year-old Elvin Whetten had many memories of the imperial wood-peckers he had seen decades ago in the Sierra Azul. He recalled once seeing several dead imperials piled in front of a sawmill. (*Photo by Tim Gallagher*)

her band of Apaches, led by the infamous Apache Juan, Lupe was captured after warning the others of the Mexicans' approach. (She pulled on a string that led all the way to a bell where the rest of the Apaches were camped.) Some believe her capture may have led to a subsequent killing and kidnapping involving a Mexican family, the Fimbres family, with whom she was living—which ultimately had tragic consequences for all of the Sierra Madre Apaches. Nelda had known Lupe years ago, and she'd had many long talks with her. Although Lupe had at first been reluctant to speak to her, she eventually became close to Nelda and told her all about her life and the ways of the Sierra Madre Apaches.

The vaqueros, including one of Nelda's sons, were just unsaddling their horses after a long morning of riding the range, tending to the cattle. We sat in easy chairs near the fireplace as I spoke with Elvin

about the Apaches and desperados from the old days before interviewing him about the imperial woodpecker. He remembered the
big woodpeckers well, although he said they were never common.

"You could always find them, because their calls carried so far—
about a kilometer," he said, his voice gruff and a little shaky as he
spoke. The birds were usually in pairs when he saw them, but he
could often hear other pairs answering their calls. I asked him to
describe the call for me.

"I couldn't imitate it," he said. "Nothing else around sounds
anything like it. It's kind of like a whistle or the toot of a toy horn,
which is why the Mexicans called it the *pitoreal*. A *pito* is a kind of
toy horn."

The vaqueros sitting in chairs around the living room laughed
as he said this, because *pito* is also slang for penis, but Elvin didn't
seem to notice. *Real*, of course, means "royal," so some people
translate the name as "royal pecker." But this earlier usage of the
word *pito* as a child's toy horn applies much more accurately to
the imperial woodpecker. People had always described the call of
an ivory-billed woodpecker as sounding just like the notes of a
child's toy horn or a penny trumpet—and Arthur Allen had said
that the calls of the ivory-billed woodpecker and imperial woodpecker were identical. So the people of the Sierra Madre named
the bird after the toy horn but added the adjective "royal" for the
power and volume of its call, as well as its immense size.

Elvin said he once rode his horse past a sawmill near the base
of the Sierra Azul in the mid-1950s and saw a pile of dead *pitoreales*, maybe six in all, that someone had shot. But he didn't believe
shooting caused the birds to vanish from the area a couple of
years later. What really wiped out them, he said, was when loggers
removed all of the standing dead trees and took them to a pulp
mill, because after that the birds had no place to nest or forage. He
had not seen any of these birds since about 1960, though he spent

a lot of time in the Sierra Azul well into the 1990s. But he did tell me one very interesting thing during our conversation that I hadn't heard before: his son, Maurice, had seen an imperial woodpecker just five or six years earlier at the southernmost part of the Sierra Azul. I was stunned to hear this and made plans to interview Maurice, who lives in Colonia Juárez, as soon as possible.

That evening, Nelda cooked a dinner of thin flank steaks with frijoles, tortillas, and squash. Afterwards, Elvin, John, and I sat talking for nearly three hours as the vaqueros played poker on the kitchen table. We planned to drive early the next morning to Tres Castillos (Three Castles), a group of three rocky outcroppings where famed Apache war chief Victorio made his last stand against the Mexicans in 1880.

◆　◆　◆

We ate a full breakfast of bacon, potatoes, scrambled eggs, tortillas, and bread with the vaqueros. Ninety-five-year-old Elvin put away an amazing amount of greasy bacon. Maybe that's the secret of his longevity.

It took us three hours to reach Tres Castillos on dirt roads far worse than those we'd traveled the day before. We could plainly see the three huge rock outcroppings looming above the plain, only a mile or two away, but we were having trouble reaching them. We kept hitting muddy areas and sinking in the mire. Each time that happened, we had to back up quickly to avoid getting stuck and try another route. In several places our way was blocked by *arroyitos*, or small gullies, just deep enough to be impassable.

Shortly before the Battle of Tres Rios, Victorio and his band of three hundred Apaches fled Texas to come here, tired and low on food and ammunition, because the site had an expanse of water nearby and shelter in the rocks.

The Apaches suffered a devastating defeat and the death of their leader, Victorio, at Tres Castillos in 1880. (*Photo by Tim Gallagher*)

Joaquín Terrazas—an Indian fighter and brother of Luis Terrazas, the governor of Chihuahua—was determined to destroy Victorio and his band. He knew the direction the Apaches were heading and that they would have to stop at Tres Castillos to rest and water their horses. Terrazas sat for hours at the top of one of the three buttes, scanning the horizon with binoculars. When he finally saw the dust from the groups of Apaches converging on Tres Castillos, he ordered his second in command, Juan Mata Ortiz, to bring a detachment of troops and set up an ambush. Everything was in place by the time Victorio arrived—one of the few times in history that someone had gotten the jump on the Apaches. According to reports, Victorio was riding in the lead on a white horse when the Mexicans opened fire, but he and most of his people made it to the buttes and piled up rocks as fortifications against the attackers.

The Apaches were trapped. A horrendous battle ensued the rest of the day, and that evening the wail of the Apache death songs echoed through the barren stones of Tres Castillos.

The next day, most of the remaining Apache warriors were gunned down. According to some reports, Victorio took his own life, stabbing himself in the chest rather than surrendering to his enemies. The men still living were lined up in an arroyo and shot. The Apache women and children were sold into slavery and sent away, some as far as Mexico City.

◆ ◆ ◆

When John's truck finally made it to the second butte, where the major battle had taken place on the first day, we saw where Terrazas had hidden in the rocks at the top of the escarpment, and we looked out over the plain ourselves with binoculars. Climbing over to the other side of the massive outcroppings, we found the defensive walls the Apaches had erected nearly 130 years earlier: stone walls piled up layer by layer, reaching about four feet tall—one of Victorio's trademarks.

Elvin had found two old rifle shells there years ago, left over from the conflict, one of which had misfired, but all I found were a couple of tail feathers from a juvenile red-tailed hawk and a few shards of Indian pottery. Far below, Elvin poked around with his cane, looking for more bullet casings.

These buttes, looming high above the plain, are now largely forgotten, as are all too many historical sites in Mexico. Yet a horrendous battle had been fought here. A lot of people had died. And the Apaches really never recovered from this devastating blow.

After Tres Castillos, Geronimo became the warrior most renowned among the Apaches, and he would later play a role in avenging this defeat of his people at the buttes. He already had a particular hatred for Mexicans, because years earlier he had promised the authorities in the state of Chihuahua that he would not raid in the area, and in turn was to be left alone. But in 1858, a group of four hundred Mexican soldiers rode across the Sierra from the neighboring state of Sonora and attacked Geronimo's camp while he and all but a handful of warriors were away. More than a hundred women and children, including Geronimo's family, were slaughtered. "When all were counted, I found that my aged mother, my young wife, and my three small children were among the slain," wrote Geronimo in his 1906 autobiography. "We will attack them in their homes," he swore. "I will fight at the front of the battle."

Men who fought against Geronimo said he was an unstoppable force. When he was younger and still bore the name Goyathlay (One Who Yawns), he had a dream that no bullet could harm him. Forever after that, he felt no fear as he attacked his enemies, always charging fiercely at them, often through a hail of gunfire. One time, armed only with a knife, he attacked a force of Mexican soldiers, who, after shooting their rifles at him, fell to their knees, praying to St. Jerome (Geronimo) for mercy. From that day forth, he was called Geronimo.

Geronimo's people called themselves the *Shis-Inday*, or "Men of the Woods," but everyone else knew them as the Apache—from the Zuni word for enemy, *apachu*—and they struck terror in neighboring tribes as well as white settlers. Their culture was based on raiding—making lightning-fast sneak attacks on ranches, settlements, and other tribes' villages to steal horses, cows, corn, and other necessities—sometimes killing people or carrying them off in the process. Then they would disappear into the mountains, many times fleeing all the way to their great stronghold in the Sierra Madre Occidental of Mexico, close to Elvin's ranch on the Rio Gavilan.

By the mid-1880s, most people in the United States were fed up with the Apaches and deeply resented their raids. To them, attacks by hostile indigenous people seemed a grim anachronism and had no place in a modern society. In 1882, Geronimo and his Apaches had returned to Arizona's San Carlos Reservation, but in May 1885, he fled with thirty-five warriors and more than a hundred women and children and returned to the old ways—raiding settlers in the United States and Mexico, then vanishing back into the Sierra Madre.

President Grover Cleveland ordered a detachment of the Fourth Cavalry, led by Lieutenant Henry Lawton, to pursue Geronimo until he was captured or killed—no matter where the pursuit led, in this country or in Mexico. A "hot pursuit" treaty between the two countries had been signed a couple of years earlier, giving the cavalry carte blanche to go after the Apaches, so there was nothing to stop them—except the daunting nature of the Sierra Madre.

Lawton's cavalry troop and several Native American scouts ventured into the Sierra Madre in early May, just as the hottest part of summer was beginning, and spent four months scouring the mountains. The temperature often reached 120 degrees Fahrenheit, the heat sometimes so intense that the men couldn't touch the exposed metal of their rifles or place their hands on a sun-scorched rock without being burned. Many of their horses soon went lame, leaving most of the cavalrymen on foot, and before long, many of them had worn through the soles of their boots. But Lawton was relentless in his drive to capture the small group of renegade Apaches, and he kept on, despite the intense suffering of his men and despite his own suffering.

Thanks to the work of Native American scouts, the cavalrymen stayed on the trail of the Apaches, but invariably, whenever they got in position to attack Geronimo, the Apaches would slip away on foot and blend back into the mountains they knew so well. But their escapes took a toll, because the Apaches usually had to abandon their horses, cattle, and food and live off whatever plants and small animals they could find. It was a difficult life, especially for the women and children (still numbering more than a hundred), who could not survive indefinitely on the run.

Finally, in late summer, Geronimo met with the Americans to discuss a possible surrender. When he learned that all of his friends and family had been relocated to Florida, he was noticeably distressed and seemed to lose heart. On September 4, 1886, he surrendered unconditionally to Brigadier General Nelson A. Miles.

For the United States, this was the last gasp of the Indian wars. Geronimo eventually went from being one of America's worst nightmares to something of a national hero, a quaint reminder of the Old West with its cowboys and Indians and cavalry. He even attended the 1904 St. Louis World's Fair and the following year rode in Theodore Roosevelt's inaugural parade.

But in the Sierra Madre Occidental of Mexico, a number of warriors had refused to surrender with Geronimo and instead returned to their Mexican stronghold, from which they continued to launch raids, although rarely into the United States. The Apaches would come sweeping down from the high country in the dead of night, driving off cattle and horses, which they led back into the mountains, taking them up steep canyons on trails so narrow that one or two Apaches could easily hold off a dozen or more pursuers, picking them off one by one or sometimes just rolling boulders down on them. Sometimes they also carried off children to help bolster their dwindling tribe.

After the Apaches attacked the family of Mexican rancher Francisco Fimbres in 1927, killing his wife and carrying off his three-year-old son, Geraldo (possibly in retaliation for Lupe being abducted from the Apaches years earlier), Fimbres devoted his life to killing Apaches. He would organize posses and take them on what he called "extermination campaigns," leading them deep into the mountains, attacking any Apaches they could find. Sometimes he would return with two or three Apache heads—of both men and women—slung from his saddle horn. One newspaper photograph of Fimbres from the 1930s shows him posing with a fistful of Apache scalps. He even attempted to enlist the aid of various American bounty hunters and gunslingers in his vendetta. While America was in the midst of the Great Depression, Mexico was still fighting Apaches.

After Fimbres had ambushed and killed three Apaches and left their bodies where they lay, someone passing by later found that the Apaches had buried the bodies in three tidy graves. Next to the graves they also left the body of Fimbres's young son Geraldo, dressed like an Apache, with leather clothing, moccasins, and a knife. His throat had been cut.

The Mexican government quietly deputized ranchers to track down the remaining Apache holdouts. These posses did not offer the chance to surrender and live on a reservation but were relentless and brutal in their quest. In one shoot-out in 1933, a posse killed some two dozen Apaches, most of them women. (So few male Apaches were left that many of the remaining warriors were women.) Grenville Goodwin, an American anthropologist, estimated in 1934 that only thirty to forty Sierra Madre Apaches remained, "fighting a losing battle in Mexico, and it seems only a question of time before they are exterminated."

In the late 1930s, Helge Ingstad recorded a story of a young Apache girl who had been captured by a Mexican vaquero and adopted soon after by an American couple. Looking over the edge of a steep canyon, the vaquero had spotted a small wickiup far below. He rolled a boulder down the side of the canyon, and it crashed through the structure, flushing an elderly Apache woman and her four-year-old granddaughter. He shot and killed the woman, perhaps hoping to claim a bounty for the dead Apache.

Carmela, as the girl was renamed, was twelve years old and living in Los Angeles, California, when Ingstad located and interviewed her.

"They named me Bui [Owl Eyes]," she said. "There were only women and children in our camp. First there was Nana (grandmother), then four younger women and three children besides me. . . . We lived in caves and small huts made out of grass. We were always afraid that somebody would come to get us, and we often moved from one place to the other. . . . We ate a lot of mescal and dried meat and also some green grass. We did not have many things, only a few large hides, a knife, an iron needle, and a cup. That was probably all . . . Nana had just sewn a brand-new beautiful dress of buckskin for me, but then I was captured."

Carmela kept the leather dress, her most prized possession, for the rest of her life. She graduated from high school and later became a nurse, though she never married. Carmela passed away suddenly in her forties in the 1970s, still living with her stepmother.

"Every evening we knelt and lifted our hands toward the sky," said Carmela, describing her young life in the Sierra Madre. "Everybody was quiet, not a word was said. But I don't know which God we prayed to."

No one knows exactly what happened to the last Apaches. Barely a handful survived into the late 1930s. Perhaps they dispersed and were assimilated by other indigenous tribes. Perhaps they all died. Or perhaps they fled to the remotest reaches of the Sierra Madre, far beyond the reach of their pursuers.

◆ ◆ ◆

Pedro Fimbres is the son of Francisco Fimbres's brother Cayetano, who had fought side by side with Francisco against the Apaches. Don Pedro is ninety years old now but has a timeless look about him: tall and thin with brown weathered skin and dark eyes, he could easily have been the subject of a medieval painting of a Spanish nobleman in a castle in Andalusia. He was dressed in dark blue jeans and a tidy gray cowboy shirt with pearl snap buttons when I visited him at his saddle shop in Colonia Juárez.

As we spoke about the Sierra Madre Apaches and his family's history, I noticed the limb of a tree, riddled with holes, hanging on the wall outside. It was obviously from an acorn woodpecker granary tree, where the birds stash their acorns. Don Pedro told me the limb came in a cord of firewood he bought several years earlier. He liked the look of it, so he hung it outside his saddle shop.

In the old days, when he traveled frequently on horseback in the mountains, Don Pedro had often seen *carpinteros* like the ones that bored holes in the limb, and he enjoyed their antics. As he talked about his experiences, it quickly became clear he was an excellent observer, so I pulled out my woodpecker illustrations and invited him to look through them, asking if he remembered ever seeing any of them. The first one in the stack was the acorn woodpecker.

"*Sí, sí,*" he said, pointing at the granary log on his wall and talking animatedly. "*El poquito carpintero.*"

He paused for a moment when he flipped to the picture of the lineated woodpecker, then shook his head. But when he looked at the imperial woodpecker, his whole face lit up. "*Ah, sí, sí. El pitoreal . . . carpintero gigante,*" he said in an excited singsong voice. He obviously knew the bird well and was genuinely enthusiastic. *Pitoreal,*" he said again, holding the illustration gleefully. "*Muy bonito carpintero.*" He gushed about the bird, telling us how beautiful and amazing it was. He had often run across them when he was younger, but only in the high country, in the great mesa pine forests.

Don Pedro told us about the birds in remarkable detail and corroborated Elvin Whetten's recollection that they had not been common. He sometimes went weeks without seeing any but would then run across a group of five or six or more. They were difficult to miss because they were so noisy, their trumpetlike calls echoing through the forest. And they were very approachable. One time he was traveling on horseback with another man when they came across a group of them. The man told him he had heard that the birds have a diamond bill, and he wanted to shoot one to see if it was true. Pulling out his saddle gun, the man shot one of the wood-peckers, shattering its shoulder and bringing it tumbling to the ground, shrieking loudly in distress. As the two men went to pick up the bird, the other *pitoreales* flew in, chattering excitedly, just a few feet away. The man wanted to shoot more of them, but Don Pedro wouldn't allow it. He could see no point in it.

Don Pedro was lucid and his observations detailed. He told us these groups of *pitoreales* were usually about twenty kilometers apart, which gave me a better idea than anything else I've read about their population density and how far they ranged in their foraging. He'd also watched some imperial woodpeckers raid the granary of a group of acorn woodpeckers. The huge woodpeck-ers would pry off the bark of the tree with their massive pearl-white bills, he said, sending acorns raining to the ground, then drop down to eat them as the tiny acorn woodpeckers flew around, furiously protesting the theft.

In the 1990s, Martjan and a colleague had interviewed people in the Sierra Madre who mentioned this same behavior. Before that, nothing in the scientific literature of the species suggested that imperial woodpeckers ever stole food from acorn woodpeck-ers. Now my interview with Pedro Fimbres offered independent corroboration of this behavior.

Few people living in the Sierra Madre have read anything about these birds. All they have is their own observations. This made it all the more clear how important it was to continue my interviews. Anything that could be found out now, while a few witnesses to the imperial woodpecker still live, would add to our knowledge of the species. And if by some miracle these interviews led me to a pair of the birds, still nesting in some remote corner of the Sierra

Madre, perhaps the imperial woodpecker could yet be rescued from extinction.

Don Pedro had most of his imperial woodpecker encounters in the Sierra Azul—the same area where Elvin Whetten had seen them. This was no doubt the place where many imperial woodpecker specimens had been collected in the late nineteenth and early twentieth centuries—many of which are tagged simply "Near Colonia Garcia" or "Near Colonia Pacheco," two old Mormon colonies adjacent to the Sierra Azul. Reading the diaries of local Mormon hunters and guides who lived in the mountain colonies at that time, I found that a couple of them were the actual collectors of imperial woodpecker specimens now housed at the Philadelphia Academy of Natural Sciences, the Royal Ontario Museum in Toronto, and the Smithsonian Institution in Washington, DC. The Blue Mountains (Sierra Azul) came up again and again in those early records as an area teeming with deer, wild turkey, grizzly bears, black bears, wolves, and mountain lions. Perhaps enough suitable habitat still remained to support a small number of imperial woodpeckers.

Don Pedro had never heard of people shooting the birds to eat, although many people had reported over the years that the Tarahumaras and others liked to eat *pitoreales*. But again, Don Pedro was speaking from his own personal knowledge, and perhaps he couldn't imagine eating a woodpecker.

At one point, we began talking about the bird's common name in Mexico, *pitoreal*, which Don Pedro thought was a pathetic name for such a beautiful and mighty bird. We told Don Pedro that in the United States the bird was called the imperial woodpecker—or *carpintero imperial*. His eyes lit up. "*Ah, muy bonito,*" he said. That is a beautiful name for the bird.

Once during the 1970s, Don Pedro's father had asked him if he ever saw *pitoreales* anymore. He said some gringos had come to Nácori Chico inquiring about the birds.

I wondered whether this could have been author George Plimpton, who had gone on his own search for the imperial woodpecker with his friend Victor Emanuel in the 1970s and wrote a wonderful article about it for *Audubon* magazine in 1977 titled "Un Gran Pedazo de Carne"—which literally translates "A Great Piece of Meat" and is how a man Plimpton interviewed in the Sierra Madre described an imperial woodpecker he had killed and eaten fourteen years earlier.

In answer to Cayetano's question, Don Pedro told his father, no, he hadn't seen any *pitoreales* since the 1960s. Cayetano nodded. They must have gone the way of *los lobos*, the wolves, he said.

◆　◆　◆

John suggested leaving El Rincon in the afternoon to try to get to the major paved highway before dark. Elvin was surprised we were going so soon and seemed disappointed. He had enjoyed our conversations, and we had become friends. We shook hands, and he invited me to come back and visit anytime.

We had only been driving about a half hour when we went around a bend in the dirt road and suddenly a military vehicle pulled out ahead of us, blocking our way. A team of men clad in dusty desert camouflage fatigues, some wearing balaclavas and goggles to cover their faces, raced out to meet us, automatic weapons gripped in their hands. They were dead serious, ordering us out of the truck at gunpoint. One man stood guard over us—his weapon hanging casually from a leather strap over his shoulder, the barrel pointing at us as his finger rested on the trigger—while most of the men ransacked our belongings in the truck. The man in charge took our identification papers and asked each of us our name as he looked at our driver's licenses.

After a thorough search—which even involved opening the

hood of the truck and removing the cap on the power-steering pump—they finally let us go. By then, it was almost dark. This was part of the Old Outlaw Trail, which smugglers had been taking to and from the United States for more than a century and a half. It is still a busy conduit, with drugs and illegal immigrants moving north and weapons, stolen cars, and other contraband moving south from Texas. Nelda said she had seen cars hidden in the bushes along here before and also that a woman with a couple of kids had recently been arrested along this stretch, her car filled with AK-47s to sell in Mexico.

It was pitch dark as we drove through the center of Chihuahua City. I was very glad John was driving. A couple of young men at a red light were juggling flaming torches, hoping for tips. At another red light, a man raced out to our truck and tried to wash our windows with a spray bottle and squeegee. John waved him off, so he left the wiper stuck in the upright position and the windshield a blur from the spray. We had to stop a short distance down the road and put it back in the down position to clean off the windshield.

Before leaving Chihuahua City, we passed a small park with a monument to Joaquín Terrazas of Tres Castillos fame, the only memorial that exists to celebrate the man and the military action in which he took part. It was surreal. We could barely make out the shape of the monument in the dark—a stone monolith with a plaque, long forgotten like the Apaches, the wolves, the grizzlies, and the *pitoreal*. Like everyone else, we sped past in the dark, not risking stopping to read the plaque.

Although the Apaches never had a chance to get even with Terrazas, they did exact a terrible revenge against his second in command, Capitán Juan Mata Ortiz. The Apache chief Juh swore an oath against him: "For you, Capitán Gordo [Fat Captain], no bullet, no spear, no arrow—fire!" Juh and Geronimo bided their time, waiting patiently for a couple of years before striking when Mata

Ortiz was captain of a regiment of soldiers garrisoned in the town of Galeana on the high plains east of the Sierra Madre, far away from the battle site.

The Apaches had developed an elaborate plan. A small group of them stole some horses in Galeana and rode swiftly out of town, hotly pursued by Mata Ortiz and his troops. The rest of the Apaches were hiding as the Mexicans rode past and opened fire, cutting off the trail back to town. Mata Ortiz understood the situation immediately and broke to the east, leading his men on a frantic retreat up the side of the highest available ground—a rocky pinnacle now called Cerro Mata Ortiz (Mata Ortiz Hill), which rises alone above the surrounding desert. The Mexican soldiers dismounted and started piling up rocks, trying their best to set up a wall to hide behind. The Apaches took their time, advancing slowly, some pushing a rock in front of them as they crawled up the hill, drawing the fire of the Mexicans. When they got close enough, they just sat there, carefully picking off the soldiers one by one, except for Mata Ortiz. The Apaches were under strict orders not to kill the capitán. They had brought a pile of firewood to the barren hill with them just for him. After several hours, only two Mexicans remained alive, Mata Ortiz and one other man, who fled down the rocky hillside. The Apaches let him pass so he could tell the townsfolk what happened. They tied up Capitán Mata Ortiz in a pit at the top of the *cerro* and burned him alive. The frightened villagers in Galeana huddled in the church, watching the smoke rise from his distant pyre.

No tourist signs mark the way to Cerro Mata Ortiz, but the rocks the Mexicans piled and hid behind are still there, like the walls that Victorio's Apaches had erected at Tres Castillos, silent witnesses to two long-forgotten massacres.

Famed ecologist and essayist Aldo Leopold visited the Sierra Madre Occidental in 1936, when wild wolves and grizzlies still roamed there. (*Photo courtesy of Aldo Leopold Foundation/www.aldoleopold.org*)

7 ◆ The Song of Aldo Leopold

The essays in Aldo Leopold's book *A Sand County Almanac* are lyrical—more like prose poems than conventional essays—and deeply moving. One of my favorites, "Song of the Gavilan," is about a special place in Mexico's Sierra Madre where Leopold had an epiphany that profoundly changed his life. The Rio Gavilan country is also one of the places I went searching for the imperial wood-pecker.

"The song of a river ordinarily means the tune that waters play on rock, root, and rapid," wrote Leopold. "The Rio Gavilan has such a song. It is a pleasant music, bespeaking dancing riffles and fat rainbows laired under mossy roots of sycamore, oak, and pine . . . but there is other music in these hills, by no means audible to all. To hear even a few notes of it you must live here for a long time, and you must know the speech of hills and rivers. Then on a still night, when the campfire is low and the Pleiades have climbed over the rimrocks, sit quietly and listen for a wolf to howl, and think hard of everything you have seen and tried to understand."

Leopold had first gone to the Rio Gavilan area in early September 1936 with his old friend and hunting buddy Ray Roark, riding trains all the way from Leopold's home in Madison, Wisconsin, to El Paso, Texas, then on to Casas Grandes, Mexico, and finally to the lumber town of Pearson—now called Mata Ortiz, after the man killed by the Apache leaders Juh and Geronimo—in the foot-hills of the Sierra Madre. From there, Leopold and Roark mounted up and road horseback west into the high country, following the old Mormon wagon road through the pine forest toward Colonia Pacheco, a small mountain settlement established by the Mormons in 1887. They stayed that night with Clarence Lunt (John Hatch's maternal grandfather), who would be their guide as they traveled in the Sierra.

The next morning, Lunt led the men westward, high into the mountains, up and over the Continental Divide, to spend a week camping in the upper gorge of the Rio Gavilan, where wild wolves and mountain lions still ruled, where they would go bow hunting for the abundant deer on the surrounding mesas and ridges. A stag-geringly beautiful place, its magnificent yellow pines and Douglas firs rose majestically skyward.

Lunt took them to the Sierra Azul, which the Mormons had viewed as a hunting paradise since they first arrived and which they treated like a vast cornucopia that could never be used up. Even in 1936, Leopold saw more deer there than he had ever seen in a single area.

One of the Mormon diaries I perused was particularly interesting, because the man who wrote it, Hyrum Albert Cluff, was among those who had collected imperial woodpecker specimens. I found his name on the foot tags of five imperial woodpeckers in two different collections. At some point a museum collector must have come into the area and put out the word that he would pay for the skins of this species.

Cluff and his friend Ernest Steiner were constant hunting companions, sometimes spending days and even weeks scouring the Sierra Azul for game. Cluff's diary entry for October 21, 1901, starts out fairly typically: "I and Mr. Barker and Ernest Steiner started out trapping. We were gone six weeks. We caught and killed five bear, eight lions, eleven turkey, eleven fox, and thirty-two deer." (Incredibly large game lists like this were common in the Mormon diaries.) But then the entry took a startling turn: "The last bear we killed pretty near got Ernest and myself. It was a large silver-tip [grizzly] bear, and he came within ten feet of us with his mouth open, and had it not been for the dogs, he would have gotten both of us."

The story as handed down by his family is that Cluff and Steiner had killed a half-grown bear and then leaned their guns against a nearby tree as they examined the kill. At that instant, an enraged mother grizzly burst out of the trees and chased them. The men took off in different directions, each climbing a separate small tree. The grizzly was right behind Steiner, who couldn't climb high enough to stay out of her reach, and she stood erect right below him, growling and striking fiercely at him with her claws. Steiner had enormous feet, and the bear tore the soles right off his hobnail boots. Luckily for the two hunters, their dogs kept racing wildly around, barking and snapping at the bear. Every so often, the bear would turn from Steiner and run after the dogs for a few seconds, but not long enough for the men to climb down and get their guns. Finally, Cluff told Steiner to wave his foot tauntingly at the bear to hold its attention. As soon as he saw an opening, Cluff dropped from the tree and sprinted for his gun. The grizzly saw him at once and charged, but Cluff fired a single shot and dropped the bear virtually at his feet.

Like Cluff, Steiner also has his name on the foot tag of an imperial woodpecker specimen from the Sierra Azul—a male collected on March 1, 1902, which now resides at the Smithsonian Institution. Cluff has a male and a female at the Academy of Natural Sciences in Philadelphia collected in July 1902. But the most interesting are three specimens at Toronto's Royal Ontario Museum collected by Cluff in 1903. Sadly, they are obviously a family group—a male, a female, and a young bird, probably only recently fledged when it was collected. I pored through everything Cluff wrote that year and came up with an unusual entry on May 25, 1903: "I caught three bear and killed some birds and skinned them." In his entire diary that is the only entry that lists something he killed without saying exactly what it was—like a turkey, bear, or deer. It is also the only time he mentions skinning anything, and I believe the birds he killed that day are probably the Royal Ontario Museum's imperial woodpecker specimens.

◆　◆　◆

Perhaps the Rio Gavilan and the Sierra Azul moved Aldo Leopold because the environment was so altogether different from those he had studied in the United States, many of which had been despoiled and mismanaged to the extent that they no longer functioned as ecologically complete, self-sustaining systems. The fabric of these places had been torn, whereas the Gavilan was then still whole. Trained as a forester, Leopold later became a professor of game management at the University of Wisconsin, Madison, where he developed comprehensive management plans for vast areas, wrote numerous journal articles, and authored the 1933 book *Game Management*. Leopold had spent a lifetime focusing on the individual parts of the puzzle, trying to figure out what steps could be taken to improve certain aspects of a given area, such as boosting the number of deer or other game for the benefit of human recreation. In some ways, he was the ultimate eco-technician, using science and technology to change ecosystems, hopefully for the better. But as he spent time in the perfectly functioning natural environment of the Gavilan, he realized that he had somehow lost sight of the forest for the trees.

"It was here that I first clearly realized that land is an organism," he wrote. Before going there he had "seen only sick land, whereas here was a biota still in perfect aboriginal health."

He also wrote, "There are men charged with the duty of examining the construction of the plants, animals, and soils which are the instruments of the great orchestra. These men are called professors. Each selects one instrument and spends his life taking it apart and describing its sounding boards. The process of dismemberment is called research. The place for dismemberment is called a university. A professor may pluck the strings of his own instrument but never that of another."

This is a devastating self-critique, startling in its directness. When he wrote it, Leopold was himself a university professor engaged in scientific research, dismembering one instrument in the orchestra, fully understanding the functioning of one piece of the puzzle but unable to hear the music: "For all are restrained by the iron-bound taboo which decrees that the construction of instruments is the domain of science, while detection of harmony is the domain of poets."

Leopold saw that the Gavilan country—its pristine old-growth forest, uneroded mountainsides, clean-running streams, the eerie howls of the prowling wolves at night—was a place unto itself, which should be preserved for its own sake, so that its wild music might continue. He was so impressed with the place that he came back the following year with his brother Carl and eldest son Starker, then twenty-five, and stayed from late December through early January, hunting the rimrocks and mesas in the high country above the river gorge. These mountains would become important to Starker, too, who later worked in Mexico for the Conservation Section of the Pan-American Union, wrote a major book on the natural history of the country entitled *Wildlife of Mexico*, and became a professor at Berkeley and prominent conservationist.

Aldo Leopold wrote to the US Forest Service and others, trying to set in motion the process of saving the Gavilan and setting it aside as a reserve. In a remarkable document—a one-page form he filled out for the Ecological Society of America—he clearly spelled out his intentions.

Location: on summit of Sierra Madre, in Chihuahua, Mexico, north and west of Casas Grandes, west of Colonia Pacheco.

Reservation needed: Yes, badly.

Legal protection needed: Complete withdrawal as a Wilderness Park from which new roads are excluded.

Suggested procedure for obtaining it: Some international joint effort. Example: U.S. might offer to finance an international research station, provided Mexico acquired the land and gave it suitable protection. The research station should make comparative analyses of floras, faunas, watersheds, and land-use [on] both sides of the border, using this area as its "control."

Amount disturbed from virgin condition: retains its full flora and fauna (save only the wild Indians) and has only one introduced species (the wild horse). Most of area has been grazed temporarily during lulls in Indian trouble and bandit trouble.

Actually, the last encounter the people in the Colonia Pacheco area had with "wild" Apaches took place after Aldo Leopold's 1936 visit, though the influence of the Apaches had already waned long before. Their presence had deterred the settlement and exploitation of the Gavilan country for at least two and a half centuries.

When the form asked the size of the area in question, Leopold wrote that no maps were available then, but he estimated the area to be about two million acres—a staggering amount of land and an incredibly bold, visionary proposal. What a great national treasure it could have been for Mexico. What a world treasure.

Aldo Leopold filled out the form in July 1941. On December 7 of that year, Pearl Harbor was attacked, pitching the United States headlong into World War II, which ended these and so many other conservation efforts and created a huge demand for lumber. This is what caused the final destruction of Louisiana's Singer Tract—last known stronghold of the ivory-billed woodpecker—which was largely clear cut during the war, with full realization and no care that it would most likely doom that American national treasure. It also took a heavy toll on the pine forests of the Sierra Madre, and the lumber boom became even stronger in the postwar years, when many new houses were built. A steady stream of lumber trucks headed northward across the US border to feed our insatiable hunger for wood.

Several years later, in 1948, Aldo and Starker planned to return to the Gavilan to spend July and August there together. But that spring, while helping a neighbor fight a grass fire, Aldo Leopold had a heart attack and died.

Starker decided to carry on with his plans for the trip and wrote to Floyd Johnson, who had guided them in 1938, inquiring how much logging and cattle grazing was taking place in the area. Apparently Johnson's response was positive, because Starker wrote in a follow-up letter, "I am most gratified to learn that the lumber trucks have not yet reached the 'Breaks of the Blue' [another local name for the Sierra Azul] and that you concur in my tentative selection of that as a study area."

Traveling with Starker were Ward Russell and Alden Miller of the Museum of Vertebrate Zoology at Berkeley and Robert McCabe, who had been a student of Aldo Leopold at the University of Wisconsin at Madison, and they would be in the Sierra Madre from mid-July through early September.

As they made their way into the high country, Starker's heart sank. Several new sawmills had opened in the Colonia Pacheco area, and logging roads were pushing right up to the edge of the Sierra Azul. They passed fourteen logging trucks during their ride up the mountain, and cattle were grazing everywhere. Erosion had degraded the hillsides, and the Gavilan was no longer the river he remembered. He wrote a lament titled "Adios, Gavilan," the following year for *Pacific Discovery* magazine. "The river bluffs were studded with crusty old junipers and oaks just as I had remembered them," wrote Starker. "But the river itself was not the same. What had been a narrow channel winding between grassy banks was now a wide, scoured trough of cobblestones left by summer floods."

The side canyons and much of the Sierra Azul were still pristine and wolves and mountain lions still hunted there. Indeed, in an oral history recorded in 1992, Ward Russell extolled the virtues of the Sierra Azul as he had seen it in 1948. "Best trip I was ever on," he said. "That was the most beautiful country I ever collected in. There were no roads in it yet. It had everything except the grizzly." But the area was being spoiled fast. When Starker returned for a few days in 1952, the Gavilan country was overrun with loggers, but there were still some imperial woodpeckers around. "Chino Whetten [Elvin Whetten's younger brother] states that there are still a few imperial woodpeckers in remote areas SW of here," wrote Starker. "He has seen one or two himself, but everybody still hunts them, for no particular purpose. They are shot because they are scarce—a curiosity."

It's a sad story, made all the worse by thinking that there had been a chance, back in 1941, when we might have saved this vast wilderness. If only more people had listened to Aldo Leopold.

Starker did find some imperial woodpeckers after that, not near the Rio Gavilan but in an area "approximately 100+ miles due west of Chihuahua City," he wrote in a 1961 letter to James Tanner. He had traveled on exceedingly rugged logging roads to the crest of the Sierra Madre, where he could look west to the Pacific Ocean. "This area is being logged right now, and the tall yellow pine timber shrinking before the chain saw," he wrote. "Big woodpeckers were moderately numerous in that region, but undoubtedly will decrease, perhaps disappear, with the loss of the tall timber which is an essential component of habitat." He went on to write: "I may say that in all of Mexico I never saw such tall pine trees as we saw in that area."

◆　◆　◆

When driving the back roads to get to Rancho El Gavilan, just a few miles from where Aldo Leopold camped in 1936, I was riding in front with John Hatch in his four-wheel-drive club cab pickup with Nelda and Efraín Villa in the backseat. Nelda's family had owned the ranch since the late 1940s, and she remembered Starker Leopold well.

We had hit the road early after spending the night at a small hotel in Madera, and we stopped briefly at an archaeological site called Cuarenta Casas (Forty Houses). The *casas* in the place-name refer to a cluster of cliff dwellings in some natural caves in a river gorge. Early Spanish explorers found the site, but it was already long abandoned. Archaeologists believe that the structures were built in the early 1200s and occupied for perhaps 150 years.

Near where we parked our truck, we stood in a pine forest at an elevation of 7,300 feet and gazed down across a gorge at the old cliff dwellings far below. We spoke with Martin Martinez, who works at the site, and asked if he'd ever seen any large woodpeckers in the area. He said that he had, less than two years earlier, in June 2008. He had been sitting in the small headquarters building when he heard a strange call outside, like a toot or whistle—loud, piercing, and unlike anything he'd ever heard. He wasn't even sure it was a bird, so he came racing out of the building. And there it was: a huge black-and-white crested woodpecker on the trunk of a pine tree. It flushed instantly and flew powerfully away through the woods. What struck him about it was that it was so large and thin with a longish tail and a distinctive black-and-white plumage. He told us he had been working there for twenty years and had never seen anything like it before or since. He emphasized how big and elongated it looked in flight. He said he later described the bird to his elderly father, who nodded and replied, "Oh, yes, that is a *pitoreal*."

His description of the bird and its call were near perfect, and the sighting was tantalizingly recent. And yet, he'd seen only one of these birds in twenty years. I couldn't very well stake out a place like this for months hoping to catch another glimpse of this mystery bird. But it did encourage me to believe that there might still be a handful of imperial woodpeckers in these mountains.

A short time later, we made our way through the bleak, scruffy logging town of El Largo and headed upward into the higher mountains. It was all second- or third-growth timber though some trees had already grown to a decent size.

My great hope was that we would be able to drive up into the Sierra Azul to see what it looked like now, though Nelda had warned me several months earlier that it would be too dangerous. But it was winter now, and it seemed unlikely we'd encounter anyone in the high country. And indeed, when we got to the spot where a logging road veered uphill on the left, we turned onto it, seeing no one. It was barely a road at all, just two deep ruts winding upward through the forest. We bucked and ground our way along, almost reaching the top of the ridge. According to my GPS, we had passed the 8,000-foot level, and another ridge that rose in front of us must have been another thousand feet higher.

The view was spectacular, opening into a broad vista of distant ridges and pine forest. John pointed out the locations of Colonia Garcia and Colonia Pacheco in the distance, though my view of the villages was blocked by trees. From these mountain settlements, hunters had come in the old days after deer, bear, turkeys, and mountain lions in the Blue Mountains where we stood. The Sierra Azul were still hauntingly beautiful. Though it was December, the weather was pleasant, windy and brisk but sunny with patches of snow lingering in the shady areas. While John, Nelda, and Efraín sat beside the truck, eating sandwiches and speaking softly in Spanish, I took a long hike higher on the ridge. The place had been logged—perhaps numerous times—but the power of these mountains was still palpable. It was exhilarating to stand there with the pine-scented wind blowing hard against my face, bringing tears to my eyes. Most of the trees were smaller than what would have been there in the 1930s when Aldo Leopold came here, but some had grown to a decent size, and there were some good standing snags, which I photographed. One of them even had some huge and fairly fresh woodpecker excavations gouged out low on its trunk, although I had no way of determining what species had made them.

On his travels through the Sierra Azul (where imperial woodpeckers were seen at least into the 1950s), the author found woodpecker workings on a dead pine. (*Photo by Tim Gallagher*)

Later, as we drove down from the Sierra Azul and continued on our way to Rancho El Gavilan, John pointed to another distant ridge and said it was the Sierra Tabaco—an area with some of the last old-growth pine-oak forest in the area, although not a lot of it.

Ornithologist Martjan Lammertink and naturalist Roger Otto had interviewed a man in the mid-1990s who'd had two seemingly credible imperial woodpecker sightings in the Sierra Tabaco in that decade—one in 1990, the other in 1993.

"This report is considered credible because Mr. Quintana mentioned coming upon the Imperial Woodpecker in recent years rather nonchalantly, when we had not yet shown any special interest in the bird," they wrote in a scientific paper. "His quick selection and description of the Imperial Woodpecker were totally convincing. Besides, the Pale-billed Woodpecker and Lineated Woodpecker do not occur in this part of Mexico." Quintana took them to each of the spots where he had seen a bird, and they were both in snag-rich patches of suitable old-growth forest, in shallow canyons on the eastern slope of the mountains. They went on to write: "Since Mr. Quintana rides daily through the forest and came upon the bird only twice in the past five years, it is understandable that such an occasionally visiting bird would leave no traces."

Both of the birds Quintana reported were females, so Martjan and Roger speculated that both sightings might have been the same bird, wandering alone through the mountains. But Quintana also said that another man he knew named Rafael Romero had told him about seeing a *pitoreal* with a red crest about 23 kilometers southwest of the Sierra Tabaco. If true, this would make a huge difference, showing that there might truly have been a number of these birds hanging on into the 1990s, scratching out a living in these remote places. And it would boost the hope that a few still remained. Martjan and Roger couldn't locate Rafael, so they dismissed his sighting, writing: "Experience shows that such secondary reports are highly inaccurate." I'd spoken to John Hatch about this, and he planned to help me track down Romero and Quintana to find out more about their sightings and see if they'd had any subsequent ones.

The Sierra Tabaco has become very dangerous in recent years, although Martjan and Roger had made it through all of their travels without any close calls. But Roger told me about an incident that took place a couple of years later, when he was traveling alone near the Sinaloa border. He had parked his truck in a remote canyon and spent the night there. The next morning, he got up early, packed up his truck, and was just about to leave when a middle-aged man and his three sons suddenly emerged from the canyon, each carrying an AK-47. One of the sons, about twenty years old, went berserk, striking Roger hard with the butt of his gun and shouting into his face. Roger could barely understand what the man was saying. He seemed to be telling him to go up the trail, and Roger thought, *Oh, no, this is it*. But he was actually asking him why he had gone up the trail. Finally, the father interceded and got his son to cool down. They told Roger to leave right away and never come back, which he was happy to do.

Shortly before we reached the outer boundary of the Whetten property at Rancho El Gavilan, John asked Nelda about the man whose property we were driving across. She said that he and his uncle had been murdered just a month earlier.

◆　◆　◆

We dined on steak, potatoes, gravy, and tortillas that night, using the supplies we'd bought earlier in Madera, then sat before a blazing pine fire that lit up the cabin's main room. Like most ranch houses in the Sierra Madre, this one is rustic—a stark but cozy log cabin with a concrete floor and no plumbing or electricity except for that generated by a tiny solar panel on the roof, which supplies only enough juice to run one or two lightbulbs. There was no refrigerator, and Nelda just left the eggs, milk, meat, and other perishables on the kitchen table. It gets very cold at night away from the fire.

Nelda had moved to Rancho El Gavilan at the age of ten and largely grew up there, eventually marrying Efraín Villa, whose family owned the adjoining property. It was from this ranch that Nelda's father, Elvin, and brother, Maurice, had ridden horses into the high country of the Sierra Azul and seen imperial woodpeckers in the 1940s and '50s.

◆ ◆ ◆

While visiting Rancho El Gavilan, I hiked up the canyon to Guacamaya Falls, which are named for the thick-billed parrots (called *guacamayas* by the Mexicans) that come to bathe in the spray of the waterfall on the hot, dry days of summer. The parrots used to come here by the hundreds, but due to habitat destruction, the pet bird trade, and shooting, people now feel fortunate if they see fifteen or twenty of these raucous, colorful birds.

Aldo Leopold had been here when the parrots still abounded and wrote about them in an essay titled "Guacamaja." The parrots were the "imponderable essence" of the place, a great motive power without which the whole Sierra Madre would seem diminished, a quality he dubbed the *numenon*, "the significance of which is inexpressible in terms of contemporary science . . . It stands in contradistinction to *phenomenon*, which is ponderable and predictable, even to the tossings and turnings of the remotest star."

While visiting the Rio Gavilan area, the author hiked to Guacamaya Falls, named for the thick-billed parrots (called *guacamayas* by the Mexicans) that bathe in the spray of the waterfall during the summer. (*Photo by John Hatch*)

Great beauty still exists in the Gavilan country, but the final words in Aldo Leopold's "Song of the Gavilan" lent a poignant edge to my experience of it:

> Science has not yet arrived on the Gavilan, so the otter plays tag in its pools and riffles and chases the fat rainbows from under its mossy banks, with never a thought for the flood that one day will scour the bank into the Pacific, or for the sportsman who will one day dispute his title to the trout. Like the scientist, he has no doubts about his own design for living. He assumes that for him the Gavilan will sing forever.

PART II

THE FINAL
EXPEDITIONS

Longtime ivory-billed woodpecker searcher Bobby Harrison joined the search for the imperial woodpecker, the ivory-bill's closest relative. (*Photo by Tim Gallagher*)

8 ◆ From Ivory-bills to Imperials

Bobby Ray Harrison is a bearded good old boy from Alabama whom I often went searching for ivory-billed woodpeckers with across the South. We were together on that amazing day when an ivory-bill flew past the front of our canoe in an Arkansas bayou, swinging up to light for an instant on the trunk of a tupelo.

"It's a thirty-two-year dream come true, Tim," he said, sitting on a fallen tree trunk, tears in his eyes. He and I were the first qualified observers in sixty years to positively identify an ivory-billed woodpecker at the same instant—and it changed our lives forever.

So it was natural that I would want Bobby to go with me to search for imperial woodpeckers in the wild Sierra Madre. Bobby and I go way back. He used to call me all the time in the late 1980s when I was editor of *WildBird* magazine. An avid bird photographer, he would get me on the phone and gab for an hour or more. It was often hard to get him to end the call. He has a thick Southern drawl, and he would always say: "Hey, this is Bobby," in a voice remarkably similar to Elvis Presley's. I knew instantly that the afternoon would be shot.

After a few calls, he started to grow on me, and eventually I started looking forward to hearing from him. He was funny, with a self-deprecating humor I appreciated, and he made fun of me, poking holes in my uptight veneer . . . making me laugh at myself. Something about his calm, slow delivery helped me relax after working so hard, slogging away sometimes twelve hours a day to get my monthly magazine out. It was nice being able to kick back and talk to Bobby, like having my own private analyst.

I finally met Bobby in the mid-1990s at an annual conference of the North American Nature Photography Association (NANPA). By then it seemed like I'd known him all my life. Bobby was in his early forties then, big and burly with a beard and short brown hair, thinning on top. Amazingly gregarious, he walked easily up to anyone he saw and drew the person into conversation. We eventually both became members of NANPA's board of directors and would get together a couple of times a year for board meetings, usually building a few extra days into our schedules after the meetings to explore the surrounding area, photographing wildlife in the Rocky Mountains, the Great Plains, the Everglades, and other interesting places.

But despite talking to each other on the phone all the time and going on several trips together, we somehow didn't share the knowledge with each other that we were obsessed with the ivory-billed woodpecker. We both had first become interested in the bird by reading the same issue of *Life* magazine in the early 1970s, which had a feature about researcher and bird book author John Dennis, who said he had found ivory-bills in the Big Thicket area of east Texas. Dennis had been ridiculed for his claim. Maybe that's part of the reason Bobby and I didn't discuss the bird. Being an ivory-bill searcher was generally considered akin to believing in Sasquatch or claiming to have been abducted by a UFO.

I had stacks of books, articles, and notes about the ivory-bill and had been tracking down and interviewing people who had seen the species in the 1930s and '40s. But Bobby had done me one better. He had a place he called "The Ivory-bill Room"—an entire den devoted to the bird, complete with paintings, sculptures, commemorative ivory-bill whiskey bottles, calendars, and other collectibles that only people like us would appreciate.

We might have gone along for many years more without knowing about our mutual obsession except that he dropped out of sight for a couple of weeks and I asked him where he'd been. He said he had gone camping and then tried to move quickly to another topic. Because he seemed evasive, I persisted.

"Where?" I asked.

"Oh, you know, I was in southern Louisiana," he said. "Thought I'd photograph some wading birds down there."

"Hmm," I said. "Why would you go there instead of Florida, where it's so easy to get close to the birds?"

He didn't answer.

"And where exactly did you go?"

"Well, I was along the Pearl River," he said. "There's some nice places there."

This was in 2000, just over a year since a turkey hunter named David Kulivan had seen a pair of unusual woodpeckers at the Pearl River Wildlife Refuge while he was sitting at the base of a tree, clad head to foot in camouflage. His description of the male and female birds fit the ivory-billed woodpecker perfectly. It seemed clear to everyone who interviewed him that either he had seen a pair of ivory-bills or the entire sighting was a hoax. But most people who spoke with him—and this included a couple of extremely skeptical ornithologists—believed he was telling the truth. A lot of birders and other ivory-bill searchers had rushed to the Pearl River.

I was stunned. "Are you an ivory-bill chaser?" I asked.

He was silent for a moment and then said, "Yes, I've been interested in them for years."

"Me, too," I said, and it was obvious a great load suddenly lifted off his shoulders. We started sharing all the ivory-bill knowledge and resources we had individually amassed, making photocopies of articles, book chapters, as well as sighting records we'd collected from people who claimed to have seen the birds. Our obsession increased, and we started going on trips together across the South—Louisiana, Mississippi, Alabama, Arkansas, Florida—interviewing anyone we could find who might have seen one of the birds.

We met some amazing characters along the way. Portly, cigar-smoking Fielding Lewis (the Louisiana State boxing commissioner), who could easily have stepped out of a Tennessee Williams play, had taken some snapshots of an ivory-bill in the early 1970s, though not everyone believed they were real. Ninety-nine-year-old Richard Pough, a giant among twentieth-century conservationists and first president of the Nature Conservancy, was still haunted by the image of a lone female ivory-bill he'd seen in 1943, hanging around in the remnants of the species' last known stronghold in Louisiana's famed Singer Tract even as logging crews felled the last trees. That sad image impelled him to shape the Nature Conservancy into a group absolutely dedicated to saving vital habitats.

Our search for the ivory-bill was awkward at times. Someone would tell me about a person who had seen a bird fitting the description of an ivory-bill in the 1950s or '60s, and I'd start an internet search for the person's phone number. I had my laptop computer set up to get on the internet through my cell phone, so I'd sit in parking lots or along the side of the road in little towns throughout the South, trying to look people up. Sometimes the person had moved out of the area years earlier, so I'd have to do a search of the entire state. This would often yield twenty or thirty people with the same name, and I'd dutifully go down the list like a salesman making cold calls, phoning each person and saying: "Hi, this is Tim Gallagher from Cornell University. I'd like to ask you about the ivory-billed woodpecker you saw in 1956." More often than not the person would reply, "Whut the hay-ell?" And I'd say, "Sorry, wrong number," and go to the next number on the list. Sometimes I would actually find the person—and have a fascinating talk about his or her ivory-bill sighting. Sometimes my interviewees would tell me about other people they knew who had seen ivory-bills, so I'd search for them, casting my net again.

I had just gotten back home in midwinter after an extensive trip through the South with Bobby, checking on sighting reports in the White River area of Arkansas and several places in Louisiana, when I got an email from Mary Scott, a hard-core ivory-bill chaser in Arizona who maintained a website about the bird. She had heard about a kayaker in Arkansas named Gene Sparling who'd had an interesting woodpecker sighting in a place called Bayou de View. Mary sent along a link to an Arkansas canoe club Listserv, where Sparling had posted a long, detailed report about his ten-day paddle down the bayou, which included his description of the mystery bird. It sounded like a great sighting, only six days old. I'd never had such a fresh trail before, so I found Sparling's phone number, and called him. Friendly and talkative, he took me through the finer details of his sighting again and again, and he seemed honest and believable. I decided to ask Bobby to do a separate interview with Sparling and let me know what he thought of him.

Bobby called back less than an hour later.

"I think he saw an ivory-bill," he said excitedly. "And I'm going there on Monday to spend a week floating the bayou with him."

I booked a flight to Memphis, Tennessee. Bobby would pick me up on his way to Bayou de View.

On February 27, 2004, Bobby and I were sharing a canoe—me in the bow, he in the stern. It was the second day of our float down Bayou de View, a little after one in the afternoon. Gene Sparling had gone off ahead in his kayak. He didn't have a GPS when he first saw the bird and couldn't remember the exact location of his sighting but thought we were within a half mile of the spot. He wanted to search for the place as we paddled along exploring the area.

As we moved slowly with the current, transfixed by the movement of the murky brown swamp water, both of us caught sight of a large bird flying up a side slough toward us. We picked it up in our peripheral vision and, without really thinking about it, our minds ran through the possibilities—large, swift flying, black and white . . . *what is this?* And then it burst into full view, flying across the bayou right in front of us, exposing the darkest, deepest black coloration—a color that makes a pileated woodpecker seem almost brown—but most of all, the snow-white trailing edges of its wings caught our eyes, the most diagnostic field mark of an ivory-billed woodpecker. And just as it pulled up to land on the trunk of a tupelo less than a hundred feet away, we both shouted simultaneously, "Ivory-bill!" And the bird veered away into the woods, landing a couple of times on the backs of tupelo trunks and then continuing on as we rammed our canoe into the side of the bayou, jumping out and abandoning it as we struggled to move as fast as we could through the muck and mire, scrambling over huge fallen logs, tearing our clothes on broken branches and shrubbery. Fifteen minutes later, practically in cardiac arrest from the excitement and sheer exertion of the chase, we collapsed against a massive fallen tree as Bobby said, "I saw an ivory-bill . . . I saw an ivory-bill."

More than a year later, in April 2005, the world became aware of our ivory-billed woodpecker sighting. In that time, I had gone back to Cornell and told John Fitzpatrick, director of the Lab of Ornithology, about our sighting, and he had launched a major search of Bayou de View and the surrounding area, some 500,000 acres of swamp forest. Our research team had had several more sightings, and David Luneau had taken a blurry video of a large black-and-white woodpecker, flying away through the bayou. We analyzed the video in a major reseach paper for the journal *Science*, making the case that the bird was an ivory-billed woodpecker.

National Public Radio was the first to break the story on its program *Morning Edition*. Thousands of people across the United States heard about the ivory-bill rediscovery during their morning commute, and many broke down and wept, having to stop their cars at the side of the road until they could pull themselves together.

After a year, Bobby told me he was glad people's interest in the bird was dying down. He was sick of everyone crowding down there, floating through the swamp en masse and making it more difficult for him as he set out hand-carved decoys of the birds, hoping to attract an ivory-bill and film it. One of the times Bobby set up a decoy at Bayou de View he actually did shoot some footage of a large black-and-white bird flying swiftly past his decoy twice. But what good is one more blurry videotape?

Bobby went on to establish the Ivory-billed Woodpecker Foundation, a nonprofit organization dedicated to searching for bird species—such as the ivory-billed woodpecker, Bachman's warbler, eskimo curlew, and imperial woodpecker—that are so rare they have dropped off the radar and may be extinct. I went looking for ivory-bills with him whenever I could get away, but my sights had already moved to Mexico, where I was searching for the imperial woodpecker.

Bobby wanted to join me in these expeditions, but shortly before we planned to go to Mexico together, his wife, Norma, had a horrific car accident that left her a near invalid for months, and then she was diagnosed with breast cancer. Bobby did not want to leave her and go to Mexico, but he continued to be deeply interested in the project. I went to Mexico three times without Bobby in 2009, exploring the mountains and interviewing people about the bird. He was finally able to join me for a week in January. I had just recently returned from the Sierra and was planning a major expedition with Martjan Lammertink that would last from late February through much of March, but I really wanted Bobby to go to the Sierra Madre.

◆　◆　◆

Only a month after my last trip to Mexico, my plane landed again in El Paso. Bobby, John Hatch, his wife Sandra, and I met up, loaded our gear into their van, and headed south to their home in Colonia Juárez, about three hours away.

Instead of taking our usual route west through Columbus, New Mexico, John drove to the nearby international crossing at Santa Teresa. After filling out the paperwork at the Mexican border station, we headed south through the harsh dry lands of the Chihuahuan Desert. Soon the mighty Sierra Madre Occidental came into view on the right—its distant ramparts covered with a fresh layer of snow. Heavy snowfall a few days earlier had closed all the passes.

The author holds up a photo taken by Richard Heintzelman in 1956, showing the same area before the old-growth trees were cut down. (*Photo by Tim Gallagher*)

The difference in size between an imperial woodpecker (*bottom*), an ivory-billed woodpecker (*center*), and a pileated woodpecker is striking. (*Photo by Bobby Harrison*)

(Illustration by John Schmitt)

Richard Heintzelman told the author that if he could locate this unusual rock outcropping, he would be very close to where William Rhein filmed an imperial woodpecker in 1956. (*Photo by Richard Heintzelman*)

When shown Richard Heintzelman's 1956 photograph, Tepehuán villagers in the high country near Taxicaringa' instantly recognized the distinctive outcropping called Los Pilares (The Pillars). (*Photo by Tim Gallagher*)

A side view of Los Pilares, taken in 2010. The forest is much more dense and the trees shorter than in 1956. (*Photo by Tim Gallagher*)

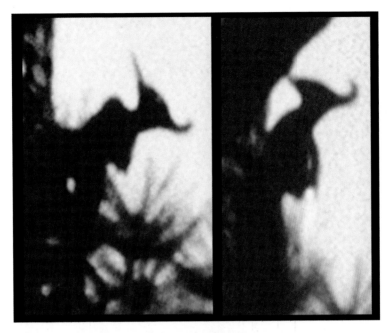

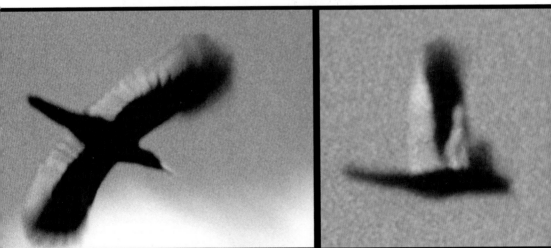

William Rhein's 1956 film of a female imperial woodpecker is the only photographic documentation in existence of a living imperial woodpecker. (*Photos by William L. Rhein, courtesy of the Cornell Lab of Ornithology*)

John L. Ridgway's illustration of an imperial woodpecker pair appeared in an 1898 issue of *The Auk*, along with an article about the species by E. W. Nelson. (*Courtesy Wikimedia Commons*)

Excellent habitat still exists on some of the remote mesas the author explored in the mountains of Durango. (*Photo by Tim Gallagher*)

Large trees still remain in high-mountain areas surrounded by cliffs, which made it too difficult to harvest the timber. (*Photo by Tim Gallagher*)

The infamous drug cartel Los Zetas, made up of trained paramilitaries who left the Mexican armed forces, controls the area on the other side of the Rio Taxicaringa, making it too dangerous to explore. (*Photo by Tim Gallagher*)

Mexico only has road graders to use for snow removal in the Sierra Madre, which are completely inadequate, so all the mountain roads usually just close whenever a decent amount of snow falls. I might have been pushing my luck going there a second time in winter, but at least it wasn't prime drug-growing season.

When we got to John and Sandra's house, John gave us each copies of a book his father, E. LeRoy Hatch, had written years earlier entitled *Medico: My Life as a Country Doctor in Mexico*, which provided a fascinating look at this area in the 1940s through '60s and also gave us insights into John. Bobby was especially taken with the story of Lofty Loftus, an old-time desperado who supposedly robbed a bank in the United States in the 1930s and fled south on the "Old Outlaw Trail" into Mexico, where he holed up in a cave in the Sierra Madre for the rest of his life. Lofty paid for everything with old gold coins he kept stashed somewhere in the backcountry. John's father was the local doctor and always cared for Lofty when he was ill. One time when he thought he was on his deathbed, Lofty confessed to Dr. Hatch that he had murdered his bank-robbery partner years earlier in a scene straight out of *Treasure of the Sierra Madre*—both men were afraid to fall asleep all night for fear that the other would kill him. When his partner reached for a tin cup, Lofty thought he was going for his gun and blasted him to eternity. He then pushed the dead man into a nearby gully and covered him with rocks. Lofty carried several heavy bags of gold coins—which they had hauled south on mules—and stashed them in a pit the ancient Indians had dug there, high on a rocky hillside, and covered it with dirt and rocks.

Well, apparently Lofty wasn't quite ready to die yet and rallied from his illness, but he was still in bad shape. He denied the story he had told about the robbery and murder. But Dr. Hatch kept pestering him about it, and eventually Lofty said he would take him to the spot. By this time, Lofty was bedridden, so Dr. Hatch and a friend took him on a stretcher in the back of a truck on the incredibly rough back roads of the Sierra. Though they carried Lofty piggyback all over the mountainside, digging here and there, they never found his hidden treasure cache.

◆ ◆ ◆

After breakfast the next morning, we left to visit Elvin Whetten's son Maurice, whom I had interviewed on the phone a month earlier but was eager to meet in person. As we pulled up in front of his house, Maurice was standing at a table in the yard with a blazing cutting torch, working on some pieces of iron, which he set down when he saw us. Maurice resembled his father—the same tanned, leathery face and striking pale-blue eyes. He was in his sixties, wearing a white straw cowboy hat, plaid cowboy shirt, blue jeans, and pointed leather boots. He had the hands of a worker, soiled and thickly calloused with a couple of broken nails, one blackened and painful looking. He greeted us warmly, shaking hands with each of us, and invited us inside as his little Chihuahua danced around our feet, yapping incessantly. His house was cozy, with a warm fire in the hearth.

"I don't remember the exact year," said Maurice. "But it was within the last ten years, I'd say. We were having an Easter campout, and I got up early and went outside. Everyone else was sleeping in. I heard the bird calling from some trees on a bluff behind me. After a little while, I saw him fly over, and then he was calling on the other hillside."

It took him a minute to figure out how best to describe the call of an imperial woodpecker. "It was very distinctive," he said. "You can't mistake it. Nothing else around here sounds like it. Just *anh*, and then a little while later, *anh*. And it was loud as a peacock."

"How far away could you hear it?" I asked.

Maurice Whetten poses with an illustration of an imperial woodpecker. He saw many of these birds in the high country of the Sierra Azul in the 1950s. (*Photo by Tim Gallagher*)

"More than a kilometer," he said. "The sound really carried on a still day. I used to see these birds a lot when I was a teenager in the 1950s. They'd nest in these old dead pine trees or sometimes in a live pine with a dead top. I'd see one or two of the birds at a time.

"I think when loggers started cutting all these dead trees for pulpwood is when the big woodpeckers disappeared," he told us. "They started logging heavily in the '50s, but when they opened that pulp mill, they really got all those big dead trees out of there. They were using winch trucks to pull the trees out, hooking a steel cable to them and winching them right up out of the canyons. So the birds didn't have any trees to nest in. I think that's what happened to the [thick-billed] parrots, too. There used to be thousands of parrots. Now, there's still a few left, but you don't see them like you used to."

When I asked if he had been excited to see an imperial woodpecker for the first time in more than thirty years, he said, "Oh, I don't know. I just thought: there's one of those woodpeckers." It didn't occur to him to rush right over and wake his family to see this amazing sight.

"When did you stop seeing imperial woodpeckers regularly?" I asked.

"It was in the 1960s," he said. "I don't remember seeing any in the '70s."

He'd never seen a dead imperial woodpecker, but he had often heard about people shooting them. "Almost everyone carried a rifle or a pistol in those days," he said. "The big woodpeckers were pretty tame. You could walk right under them. And people would shoot parrots, too. I don't know why they did it—maybe just for the fun of shooting them or to get a few feathers. Some people are just destructive. It's a shame."

"How often do you go to that place where you saw that last imperial woodpecker?" I asked.

"We used to go camping there every year, but now, with all this violence going on, it's too dangerous," he said. Opium poppies and marijuana now grow right alongside the creek where he used to camp with his family.

"There are still some huge pines in the Sierra Tabaco—some that three people couldn't even reach around," he said. "They're down in the canyon. And I do know Genero Quintana. I think he might live in Casas Grandes now. You should ask about him at the restaurant in town.

"If you do go to the Sierra Tabaco, you might want to look at some of the dry washes. Someone who knows how to do it can find gold there."

"Another treasure to look for if we don't find the birds," I said.

"The gold collects in basins," he said. "It's heavier than the sand. You pan for it, and what you get has a lot more sand in it than gold. But you put it in a chamois and pour mercury on it. The dirt and mercury go right through the chamois, and what you have left is pure gold."

"Oh, yeah," said Bobby, snorting. "That's all we need. Mercury poisoning is bad."

"Gold fever's bad, too," I said, and we all laughed.

Before we left, we asked Maurice who might be able to help us explore the area. His wife, Alma, had grown up on a rancho just west of Santa Rita, not far from where he'd had his sighting, and still had a lot of family there. That tiny village would be the jumping-off point on our trek to the spot where Maurice had his last imperial woodpecker sighting. We planned to rent some horses or mules in Santa Rita, ride for several days through the high country, the entire length of the Sierra Azul—about twenty-five miles— and descend into Geronimo's old stronghold. Having explored this general area in December, I was eager to get back.

"You should look up Ramiro Dominguez," said Maurice. "He's married to my wife's sister and has a house in Santa Rita." Ramiro also owns three large ranchos in the mountains, one of which is actually called Rancho Pitoreal. We would pass it en route from Santa Rita to the place where Maurice had his sighting.

Maurice also told us about another man, Nino Villar, who lived in the area. "Nino spends a lot of time in the mountains," he said. "If any of those birds are left there, he probably would have seen them."

Santa Rita was a five-hour drive away, so we were eager to get on the road. For the moment, the weather report seemed promising, but weather reports for the Sierra Madre are notoriously unreliable. The winter storm the week before had really hammered the area, so I was grateful we hadn't arrived a few days earlier, as Bobby and I had originally planned.

When we finally left town and headed southward, the Sierra loomed large on the horizon to the right of us, covered with snow. We passed the rocky knoll of Cerro Mata Ortiz, out on the desert to our left.

After several hours we drove through the logging town of Mesa del Huracán—which should really be called Mesa del Tornado, because it was given the name after a devastating tornado (not a hurricane) swept through the area decades ago, causing massive destruction. It is still a major logging town, with industrial-scale sawmills.

It was foggy and raining constantly as we made our way higher into the mountains to El Largo, the last major town before Santa Rita. It was just a big mud hole after all the rain that day and the earlier snowstorm, though John said it never looks good, even at the best of times.

People trudged grimly down the muddy streets; or drove, slipping and sliding in their pickup trucks, or rode sullenly on mules, head down, hooded sweatshirts cinched tightly around their faces. We were trying to get to the local general store to talk to the man who owned it, who would be able to lead us the rest of the way to Santa Rita, but the bridge in the middle of town had fallen into the creek in the downpour, and we couldn't get to the other side.

John finally left Bobby and me in the truck and walked off into the gray twilight, found a place where he could get across the creek on foot, and disappeared on the other side. Grim-faced men kept walking past, glaring into the truck. We nodded quickly at each of them as they passed then looked forward again, toward where John had disappeared.

After a while, John returned, having found the man from the shop, who said he would drive ahead of us and lead us to the village of Santa Rita. It took some time to find another way over the creek, but eventually we found the man and his old red pickup truck. He waved at us to follow him and then took us up a treacherous mud road higher and higher into the Sierra, our tires spinning wildly here and there as we struggled to keep up.

Our guide stopped at a shallow creek that cut across the road and pointed up the other side toward the village of Santa Rita, which lay in a high valley surrounded by pine-clad mountains. After we shook hands, he turned around and headed back to El Largo.

A scattering of huge pines grew in the village, one even protruding through the roof of an empty cabin. The ground was still covered by several inches of snow. At the first house we came to, a bright-pink stucco casa, we knocked on the front door to ask where to find Ramiro and Nino. A man in his sixties came outside to speak with us, staggering drunk but willing and eager to help. We showed him the illustrations of four species of Mexican woodpeckers, and he instantly picked out the imperial and then launched into a story about riding horses up on a mesa not far from here with his son three years earlier and running across one of the birds. He said neither of them had ever seen one before, and his son had even wondered if it might be some kind of strange mountain grouse. The man drew his pistol and shot the bird, injuring it, and quickly threw a blanket over it as it squawked loudly. The two had brought lunch with them, and they decided to rest awhile and eat there. A short time later, his son stood up and went to check on the bird. The instant he lifted the edge of the blanket, the huge black-and-white bird burst out and flew away. Apparently, it had only been stunned.

Although he was intoxicated, his tale had some interesting

details, which would have been difficult to fake, drunk or sober, and seemed to have a ring of truth. It was nearly dark, so we had to leave to see Ramiro and find out where we could stay—either by using whatever shelter was available or setting up a tent: not something we were eager to do in the steady rainfall.

Following the man's directions, we had no problem finding Ramiro's house, a sturdy, white one-story surrounded by an oddly out of place wrought-iron fence. In front of the house, a totem-pole-like object rose twenty feet above the ground, built of stacked steer skulls, perhaps thirty in all, and topped with deer antlers. Ramiro, who was thin with gray hair and looked to be in his late sixties, greeted us warmly with a strong handshake and invited us inside, where he introduced us to his wife and son, and we sat together at the kitchen table.

None of them had seen an imperial woodpecker or knew much about them, but a short time later Nino Villar came in and introduced himself. Younger than Ramiro, he wore a cowboy hat and had dark hair hanging over the collar of his coat and a bushy black moustache. He instantly picked out the imperial woodpecker illustration and described an encounter he'd had with one many years earlier, in 1960, when he was ten years old. He and his father had ridden horses into the high country above Chuhuichupa, near Pitoreal Pass—the same place where Bill Martineau's father had hauled him up to an imperial woodpecker nest to get the dead young in the late 1940s. Nino's father had spotted the woodpecker foraging on the side of a tree and made a point of showing it to his son. His father had seen them often when he was younger, but by 1960, the birds had become scarce, so he wanted Nino to get a good look at it. That was the only one Nino ever saw.

Nino arranged for us to stay the night in a rustic cabin in Santa Rita owned by one of his relatives, which was great, because the temperature was plummeting.

No one had stayed for a very long time at the cabin, which was cluttered and dusty inside. Although it was nice to get out of the damp, foggy weather, the cabin was freezing. It had a metal fireplace in the center of the room, but the only wood available was some old, damp oak, which would not stay lit, even when we split it into thin chunks of kindling with an axe and stuffed newspaper under it. The fire would burn brightly for several minutes, as if the wood were starting to ignite, but as soon as the newspaper was gone, it quickly sputtered out. When the owner of the cabin stopped by for a visit, we explained our predicament. The man smiled and said he'd be back in a few minutes. He returned carrying a one-gallon plastic milk jug, half full of gasoline, which he doused liberally over the wood. He then struck a match and tossed it into the fireplace, and with an explosive *whoosh*, the wood burst into flames with an intensity that pushed us back. He laughed and walked out the door with his jug. The fire kept us warm, but the place reeked of gasoline all night.

We got up before dawn, and John cooked a big breakfast of scrambled eggs with onions and jalapeños, which we put into flour tortillas and eagerly wolfed down. A short time later, we picked up Ramiro, who put his chain saw in the back of our truck, and the four of us headed into the high country to reach the place where Maurice had seen the imperial woodpecker. We had originally planned to take a quicker route, going down and around and ending up right where he had camped, but it would involve having to make four crossings of rivers that had been turned into raging torrents by melting snow and rain. Instead, we decided to drive up higher in the mountains and make our way along the ridges to get above the place where the bird was seen. This would take us through the three ranchos Ramiro owned, including Rancho Pitoreal, worth visiting for the name alone.

It was a tough slog. We were obviously the first people to drive on the old logging road for quite some time. At first the road was muddy and had places with long, deep puddles where ice had frozen as thick as plate glass on top. We would break through the ice immediately and push along in four-wheel drive, with water splashing up to the wheel wells. As we went higher, the dirt track we were on was covered with nearly two feet of unbroken snow, a week after the last storm. Worse, we kept coming to places where pines had fallen across the road, blocking our path. If they weren't too big, we would jump out and horse the broken trunks and branches out of the way. Several times Ramiro got out his chain saw and buzzed through a sizable log.

Eventually, we reached Rancho Pitoreal—a disappointment, all small second-growth pine forest. Yet the imperial woodpeckers that had once been there had left such an impression that someone named a rancho after them. We continued through Ramiro's other two ranchos, which total about twelve thousand acres in size. Some large pines grew in several areas along the way, although they were all second growth.

After three more hours of slow, tough driving—including sloshing a mile or so down a shallow creek—we finally stood on the ridgetop right above where Maurice had seen and heard the imperial woodpecker. The bird may well have been calling from one of the trees where we now stood, a humbling thought. The wind whipped loudly and powerfully as Bobby and I strained our ears, hoping to hear birdcalls or drumming, and scanned the areas with our binoculars, searching for any sign that the great woodpeckers might still be there. The weather conditions were terrible, making it difficult to see the birds even if they were present. We spent a couple of hours hiking and examining the habitat. The trees along the ridgetop and hillside were small and scattered sparsely, though a few huge pines stood below along the river.

We stopped at two more places and hiked around, but worse

Maurice Whetten said he heard an imperial woodpecker calling, then saw it fly across this canyon as he stood at a campfire beside the creek one morning less than a decade ago. (*Photo by Tim Gallagher*)

weather was quickly descending upon us. The wind had picked up to a howling crescendo, whipping the treetops, and then the rains came hard—near torrential. We started racing back to Santa Rita, bouncing along the terrible old logging track and through the long stretch of creek again.

Bobby had been joking earlier in the day about the roughness of the drive into the mountains in a perfect Elvis Presley imitation, "I'm all shook up!" But the trip back really got to him, and by the time we finally reached Santa Rita, he was uncharacteristically quiet and didn't even eat before going to bed. That night, the rains continued to pour, lashing down for hours, sometimes punctuated by thunder and lightning. Later in the night, I woke up briefly, and it was oddly silent. I was just glad it wasn't raining anymore—and went back to sleep—but the temperature had plummeted, and the rain had turned to snow. We awakened to several inches of snow on the ground and the snow was still falling heavily.

John saw the ramifications of this instantly. "We need to get out of here right away," he said. "If they close the passes, we could be stuck here for a week or more."

This crushed our plans to explore the Sierra Azul and get above the old Apache stronghold. But maybe if the weather conditions were better down south, we could drive to the barranca country near Copper Canyon and search more of the area in David Allen's old treasure map. We decided to race to Madera and assess the situation when we got there. John knew a man who owned a hotel there, and he would ask him to call another hotel in Creel to inquire about the weather. If it looked good, we would head that way. If not, we would take the other route and return to Colonia Juárez—if we could get across the final pass.

El Largo looked even more depressing in the dusky morning light as we passed through again: bleak muddy roads filling with snow, stray horses stumbling aimlessly with no owners in sight. Driving through the high country en route to Madera was terrible, the snow almost knee-deep. We passed several stuck cars—people racing, like us, to make it over the pass before it closed. Some had already dug out their cars and were turning back.

Eventually, only one set of tire tracks was visible in front of us, and then we saw the truck, its bed piled high with firewood, tires spinning uselessly in the snow. We drove around it and forged ahead, cutting our own trail through the fresh-fallen, knee-deep snow like some great river barge. The world was muffled and silent, but when we finally reached the highest pass at 8,125 feet our worries were still not over, because the road downward was slippery. In some places, the road overlooked lofty precipices with no guardrails. Even Bobby, who laughs and jokes his way through most situations in life, looked grim.

We safely got through the high passes, and by the time we reached Madera, the snow had eased somewhat but was still falling steadily. John stopped at the hotel where he usually stays, and the man at the desk reported that Creel was being hammered by snow, so we gave up on going farther south. Instead, we visited William Randolph Hearst's crumbling hacienda, Babicora, not far down the road. This once-glorious estate—Hearst's south-of-the-border San Simeon where famous movie stars and other celebrities dropped in to go hunting or just to spend time in an exotic locale—had covered a million acres of land, much of it old-growth mesa pine forest, rich with game, surrounding the village of San Jose Babicora. Visitors would ride the train from El Paso to Madera, where they would be met at the station and taken to the hacienda in a horse-drawn wagon. Sandra Hatch's grandfather had once seen Ernest Hemingway on the train, en route to Hearst's hacienda, in the 1930s.

Hearst's brand—the letter *H* with splayed lower legs and a downward-curving arc on top—was etched into the concrete floor of the entryway along with the date: 9-21-36. The place was a mess, rubbish strewn on the floor, crumbling plaster here and there, a fountain in the courtyard choked with weeds—but it had once been beautiful. Even more beautiful had been the primeval mesa pine forest that had once covered much of the surrounding

William Randolph Hearst's brand is etched into the concrete floor of the entryway at Hacienda Babicora, his once-grand Mexican estate, now a crumbling ruin. (*Photo by Tim Gallagher*)

land. If only Hearst had seen the value of saving this amazing place when it was in near-pristine condition, the imperial woodpeckers would still be there. It made me sick to think of it.

In March 1941, just a few months before the United States entered World War II, E. M. Barnum, a lieutenant colonel in the US Cavalry, had written a letter to James Tanner about Babicora. An article he read about Tanner's work with ivory-billed woodpeckers in Louisiana had inspired Barnum to contact him. He had visited Hacienda Babicora in November 1938 and '39 as a guest of the manager, Kelly Simmons, and spent most of his time hunting, but Simmons had urged Barnum to go with him on a horseback-riding trip to an area where they could see imperial woodpeckers. "Had I not been transferred to Boston, I certainly would have made the trip," he wrote. Barnum raved about the amount of game and other wildlife in the area. "[T]he destruction of wild life is 75 years behind [the United States] . . . I saw several wolves (lobos not coyotes) and we shot one from the car. Unfortunately I saw a bald eagle shot from a fence post at a distance of 100 yards. They are considered varmints at the ranch."

Clearly, the people running Babicora were not environmentalists. But Tanner was intrigued by Barnum's letter and quickly wrote to Kelly Simmons, bombarding him with questions about the imperial woodpecker: How common is it? What kind of country does it live in? How does it feed? Simmons basically replied that he was a cowman and not a student of bird life but was glad to tell him what he knew about the species. "All the imperial woodpeckers I have seen in Mexico are located in a general region comprising the Sonora-Chihuahua line, which runs along the top of the Continental Divide, these birds being found in the highest of the high country, or, down here, around from seventy-five hundred to nine thousand feet altitude," he wrote. "I don't think I would call it common at all, but it is easily found if you know where to look. I never saw it except in the high pine timber . . . I have noticed that these birds (and they seem always to be found in pairs) return each evening to a certain tree or group of dead trees, either to feed, roost, or nest. I know that it is almost impossible to kill one with a shotgun unless at very close range, they seeming to have the capacity of carrying off more small bird shot even than a turkey."

Simmons wrote that imperial woodpeckers could be found with some certainty within a two-day horseback ride of the hacienda and ended the letter, "If I could in the future help you in any way toward your end of obtaining more information, photographs, etc., you may feel free to call upon me.—Kelly Simmons, Babicora Development Co., Hacienda Babicora, Madera, Chih., Mex."

There is no record that Tanner took him up on his offer. Pearl Harbor was attacked a few months later, and Tanner enlisted in the United States Navy.

◆　◆　◆

When we got to Nuevo Casas Grandes, we started looking for Rafael Romero, the man who had supposedly seen a male imperial woodpecker in 1994. Martjan Lammertink and Roger Otto had heard about him from Genero Quintana. John had recently found out where Romero lived, but when we stopped at his house and spoke to his wife, she told us he had left to work on a remote rancho on the other side of the Continental Divide. Unreachable by telephone, he was often away for months at a time.

At that point, we decided to try to track down Genero Quintana, who lived with his daughter in a tan-colored house up a side street in Casas Grandes. Don Genero greeted us at the door. In his late seventies, he had a kind face, dark and creased from the sun, and a thick shock of gray hair combed back. He wore blue jeans and a white cowboy shirt with light-blue stripes. His wife and daughter as well as some teenagers all sat with us at the kitchen table as I asked him about his imperial woodpecker sightings.

Fifteen years earlier, Martjan and Roger had met Genero when he lived on a ranch in the high country and passed through the Sierra Tabaco almost every day, caring for his cattle. His sightings had been in shallow canyons where patches of big trees and numerous snags remained, but he said he had not seen any other imperial woodpeckers after the lone female in 1993.

◆　◆　◆

Genero Quintana holds an illustration of four Mexican wood-pecker species, including the imperial. He had told Martjan Lammertink and Roger Otto of some credible imperial wood-pecker sightings he'd had in the Sierra Tabaco in the early 1990s. (*Photo by Tim Gallagher*)

On our last full day together in the Casas Grandes area, John took us to a graveyard containing his family plot. Bobby had wanted to see the gravesite of the old outlaw Lofty Loftus, whom John's father had buried beside his family graves. It was marked with a simple piece of granite, perhaps four inches wide by a foot long, inset into the grass, with his name chiseled into it. John also showed me the graves of his mother and younger brother who had been killed years earlier when a trailer broke loose from a truck just as they were passing in the other direction. "If they had gone by just a second earlier or later they would have been okay," he said.

After leaving the cemetery, we passed another group of Mexican law enforcement officials, headed in the opposite direction on the highway. They did not wear camouflage like the *militarios* who had stopped us in the desert but were even more frightening, driving in a convoy of several black pickup trucks with machine guns mounted on top of the cabs, each manned by a soldier clad head-to-foot in black with his face completely covered by a black balaclava and goggles under a black helmet with flared rims resembling a World War II German helmet, which gave them a disconcerting Darth Vader look. John explained that they had been attacking *narcotraficantes* and kept their faces covered so no one could identify them and retaliate against them or their families.

That same day, John's friend Roberto called to say that he had been held up in broad daylight in a Sam's Club parking lot in Chihuahua City. The people pulled guns on him and drove away in his pickup truck. A wave of carjackings, robberies, and other serious crimes had been sweeping through the state of Chihuahua.

◆ ◆ ◆

That afternoon, we drove to Arroyo de los Monos, a fascinating little canyon with ancient petroglyphs on its walls, including the earliest known illustration of an imperial woodpecker, perhaps eight centuries old. The petroglyph lies about twenty feet up a cliff, and we scrambled up the side of it to a grassy ledge so we could take pictures. It had been chilly and overcast, occasionally drizzling, all morning, so the first pictures we took were gloomy. But then the

This petroglyph, near Casas Grandes in the state of Chihuahua, is the earliest known depiction of an imperial woodpecker, and may have been drawn eight hundred years ago. (*Photo by Tim Gallagher*)

sun came out, bathing the petroglyphs in rich, warm afternoon light, so we took all the photographs again. Bobby was completely in his element, setting his camera on a tripod on the cliff and taking pictures of the petroglyphs from every possible angle.

The author visits a petroglyph site near Casas Grandes in the state of Chihuahua. (*Photo by John Hatch*)

It was a good end for Bobby's journey through Mexico. He would not return again—not out of fear or because it was so grueling to get around in the Sierra Madre, but because he felt depressed by the hardships and deprivation people face every day in Mexico.

It was nearly dark as we left the arroyo. The next morning we would drive to El Paso and then fly back to our homes. Less than a month later, Martjan and I would be traveling to the mountains of Durango to explore the place where a dentist from Pennsylvania had taken the only known footage—in fact, the only known photographic documentation of any kind—of a living imperial woodpecker in 1956. The idea filled me with a mix of excitement and dread. Still, I was eager to start preparing.

9 ◆ The Last Explorers

One of the most committed imperial woodpecker searchers in the twentieth century was William Rhein, a dentist in Harrisburg, Pennsylvania, who launched three self-funded expeditions to the Sierra Madre Occidental in search of the bird in the 1950s. It's hard to say what motivated him to embark on such grueling and dangerous journeys. He had an excellent income from his dental practice, a nice home, and no children, so he and his wife could afford to indulge themselves. Instead, he chose to drive south with a few buddies and spend up to two months at a time roughing it in the outback of Durango, living on beans, booze, and tortillas.

When Rhein first traveled to the Sierra Madre of Durango in 1953, it was a place where lean hombres rode tall in the saddle, sporting the same large, broad-brimmed sombreros that Pancho Villa and his men had worn during the Mexican Revolution. Many still packed aging nineteenth-century six-shooters in leather holsters and knew how to use them. One day Rhein and his friends had to drop and take cover when an Old West–style shootout broke out as they were walking to their hotel in the town of Tepehuanes.

Yet Rhein went to the Sierra Madre Occidental not once but three times—in 1953, 1954, and 1956—mounting major expeditions he personally funded into the rugged backcountry of the state of Durango, one of the least-populated parts of Mexico. But by the time he had finished, he had done what no one else had ever accomplished: he had photographically documented a living imperial woodpecker.

These guys were mostly World War II veterans, and perhaps they missed the thrills, danger, and sense of camaraderie they'd experienced in combat. Rhein had served in the Pacific as a dentist,

William Rhein (*at right*) with brothers George and Walter Kohler during his 1953 expedition in the Sierra Madre Occidental. (*Photo by Frederick Hilton*)

but he'd had some close calls. One night, he and four other men were playing cards in a shack when he suddenly heard the telltale pop a Japanese grenade makes when its pin is pulled. Rhein dived out the window just as the grenade came flying into the shack. Two of the men with him died in the ensuing explosion, but he came out unscathed.

Rhein loved a challenge and tended to excel at anything he put his mind to. At one point he took up golf and was coached by legendary pro Ben Hogan, eventually becoming the state golf champion of Pennsylvania in his age group, after which he moved on to other pursuits. He and his wife Wilma took up figure skating and mastered it, after which Rhein moved on to hybridizing rhododendrons.

Bird study was a lifelong obsession with Rhein and, as with his other passions, he developed his skills to a professional level.

Although he did not have a degree in ornithology, he was an ornithologist to the core, as well as a gifted bird photographer and cinematographer. Rhein's lucrative dental practice provided all the funds and time he needed to do anything he wanted, and the imperial woodpecker was the ideal species for an obsessive quest—a bird that had barely been studied and never photographed alive.

To prepare for his 1953 expedition, Rhein visited famed Cornell ornithology professor Arthur Allen, who had searched for imperial woodpeckers during a joint National Geographic Society–Cornell University expedition in 1946. Allen provided Rhein with maps, advice on where to go, and the names of people to contact in Mexico. He even loaned Rhein a huge parabolic microphone and a wire recorder (an early sound-recording device that recorded sound onto thin steel wire) in case he got a chance to document the bird's voice, which had also never been done.

Rhein and his three friends—Frederick "Fritz" Hilton, Walter Kohler, and George "Flip" Kohler—loaded up his Chevy panel truck with all their gear and headed south in the late spring of 1953, driving all the way from Harrisburg, Pennsylvania, to the city of Durango, Mexico, some 2,500 miles away.

I had a chance to speak with Fritz Hilton a couple of times recently. He is in his mid-eighties, retired in Louisville, Kentucky, after a long career as a professor and medical researcher at Johns Hopkins. At twenty-seven years old, Hilton was the youngest member of the expedition. He had first become acquainted with Walt Kohler and Bill Rhein in the late 1930s when he was thirteen years old. Hilton was interested in birds and nature, and a friend of his family introduced him to Kohler, who ran a small zoo. Kohler in turn introduced Hilton to Rhein, who became a mentor to him in his study of birds and wildlife illustration. Like Rhein and Kohler, Hilton had also served in the Pacific during World War II. He was just beginning the second semester of his freshman year at Cornell

During William Rhein's first expedition to Mexico in 1953, Walter Kohler poses in front of a fallen tree trunk where two imperial woodpeckers had been foraging just minutes earlier. (*Photo by Frederick Hilton*)

University when he took a leave from his studies and joined the US Navy. Kohler's brother Flip was the only person on the expedition who was not a veteran of the war. A case of childhood polio had left him with a pronounced limp, which prevented him from enlisting in the military.

Rhein and his friends took the long route to Mexico, stopping in Florida to look for ivory-billed woodpeckers before heading for Durango, capital city of the state of Durango. (Rhein had seen an ivory-billed woodpecker on an earlier trip to Florida and was one of the very few people who, like Arthur Allen, had seen both the ivory-billed and imperial woodpeckers.)

When they got to Durango, they left their vehicle in the city and rode an old steam locomotive northward to the town of Tepehuanes. The engineer let Walt Kohler drive the train a good part of the way, and when they reached Tepehuanes, they and the other passengers had to jump out and help turn the locomotive around on a huge turntable so it could make the return trip. From there the trio hitched a ride west on a logging truck that took them higher into the mountains near where the Allens had seen the imperial woodpecker seven years earlier. But the trail had gone cold. Although they found snags with huge cavities obviously excavated by large woodpeckers, the workings were not fresh. They estimated that the imperial woodpeckers had vanished from the area about five years earlier.

Disappointed, they hitched a ride back to Tepehuanes on the next available logging truck and then returned to Durango on the train, pondering what to do next. Ultimately, they decided to head in a different direction, this time driving southward through the mountains to Los Laureles, a logging camp and village about a day's Jeep drive from Durango on a rough dirt road. The road was used to haul lumber from the mountains as well as silver, gold, and zinc ore from various mines.

They stayed in a rustic cabin in Los Laureles, and there they found their first imperial woodpeckers, including a pair with two young. Fritz spent a great deal of his time in the cabin, sketching the local birds while Bill, Walt, and Flip went out exploring. Some of the local people were suspicious of them because of the strange equipment they carried, such as the odd-looking metal parabola, which was bigger around than a sledding disk, and the wire recorder. This was in the early days of the nuclear age, and many of them suspected the Americans were searching for uranium. Unfortunately, the bulky sound-recording equipment proved to be impractical for the job at hand. They had to use six truck batteries to power the setup, which did not allow them the mobility they needed to follow an imperial woodpecker closely and record its calls—which is too bad; no recording of the bird's voice exists,

William Rhein (*at right*) watches as a parabola is loaded on a pack mule during his 1956 expedition. He had hoped to be the first to record the call of an imperial woodpecker. (*Photo by Richard Heintzelman*)

and no one to date had a better chance to record it than Rhein and his friends.

They would have had a far better chance of fully documenting the species if they had come just a year earlier. Some of the men around the camp, all of whom carried pistols and other firearms, told them they had killed twelve imperial woodpeckers during the previous few months. And sadly, Hilton found the story credible because there were so many imperial woodpecker cavities and other workings nearby but few of the birds.

Walt Kohler did something that might have helped slow the killing of these birds. An avid collector of antique guns, he started buying up old pistols. Many of the sidearms people carried in the Sierra Madre were old six-guns from the 1880s or earlier, and he bought every one he could find—often for only two or three dollars apiece. He carefully packed all of them in a suitcase, wrapping each one individually in a shirt or other article of clothing, latching it tightly before putting it in the back of the panel truck. Somewhere on the way back to Durango, the back doors on the panel truck opened and the suitcase fell out.

As soon as they noticed what had happened, several miles farther down the road, they turned back to retrieve the suitcase. They soon ran into a mining truck heading toward them and flagged it down. The men in the truck said they didn't know anything about a lost suitcase and couldn't help them. There was little Kohler could say in response, but he was suspicious—especially when they didn't find any trace of his suitcase along the road. The next day in Durango, Kohler decided to go to the police and file a report. But he quickly changed his mind when he entered the station and saw the chief of police wearing one of his shirts from the lost suitcase.

As far as I can tell from reading Rhein's letters and interviewing Fritz Hilton, only Rhein and Walt Kohler went back to Mexico in 1954. This time they hired a team of mules and a guide and made an overland trek, crossing the deep canyon of the Rio Taxicaringa and making their way up the other side, toward the village of Guacamayita. They located a pair of imperial woodpeckers with young but were unable to photograph the birds or record their calls.

Bill Rhein's third and final expedition in 1956 was the best documented. That spring, he traveled to Mexico with Dick Rauch and Dick Heintzelman and repeated the long, rough drive to Los Laureles and the journey by mule across Taxicaringa Canyon and up the other side, where they camped. Heintzelman was the youngest member of this expedition and today is retired and lives with his wife in Camp Hill, Pennsylvania, not far from Harrisburg. I was fortunate enough to hear about Dick from his nephew not long after the 2005 announcement of the rediscovery of the ivory-billed woodpecker. I subsequently spoke with Dick several times on the

Richard Heintzelman poses next to the picture he took in 1956 of the distinctive rock formation called Los Pilares. William Rhein was less than a mile from there when he filmed a female imperial woodpecker. (*Photo by Tim Gallagher*)

telephone, and Martjan Lammertink, the woodpecker expert, and I later drove to his home to interview him in person.

Twenty-two years old at the time of the expedition, Heintzelman was not a bird-watcher at all but one of Bill Rhein's patients. During a dental appointment, Rhein had mentioned the expeditions he'd taken to Mexico, and Heintzelman basically said, "Gee, I'd love to do something like that." And Rhein replied, "Well, we're going there next week . . ." Less than two weeks later, young Heintzelman found himself bouncing along a rough logging road in the hinterlands of the Sierra Madre.

On his third and final expedition to Mexico, Rhein finally documented the imperial woodpecker in eighty-five seconds of 16mm Kodachrome motion picture film. But because the film didn't meet Rhein's professional standards, he kept it to himself for decades.

In 1956, the forest around Guacamayita was still classic old-growth mesa forest, with large pine trees in an open, almost parklike setting. (*Photo by Richard Heintzelman*)

The world might very well never have learned about the imperial woodpecker film if not for the efforts of Martjan Lammertink, who tracked down Rhein and interviewed him in 1997. A couple of years earlier, Martjan had completed his fieldwork in Mexico, searching the Sierra Madre Occidental for imperial woodpeckers. He learned of the film's existence by chance only later, as he was going through some of James Tanner's personal correspondence and notes, which were archived at Cornell. Before Tanner had launched his 1962 imperial woodpecker expedition, he wrote to Rhein for advice on where to go. Rhein casually mentioned the film in one of the letters he wrote to Tanner. "At present I have two reels of movie film pertaining to our three trips," he wrote. "One reel includes some very poor footage of a female ivory-billed with several short flight shots taken hand held from the back of a mule."

Martjan was stunned to learn about the motion-picture footage and tried for weeks to locate Rhein, who was then in his late eighties, so he could view his film. Martjan tracked him to Mechanicsburg and, since he had already been planning to fly from the Netherlands to America to visit a friend in Arizona, he arranged a stopover in Newark, New Jersey, so he could rent a car to drive to visit Rhein.

When Martjan finally arrived in Mechanicsburg, he booked a room at an inexpensive motel and called the local Audubon director, whom he had contacted while searching for Rhein. The man was furious with Martjan, because he had told him in a phone call that Rhein had become reclusive, and he had not given him Rhein's address or phone number. He said it was a very aggressive move to come all the way from Europe and just show up on his doorstep when nothing had been arranged. Martjan pleaded with the man, telling him he was a serious researcher who had spent many months in the field searching for the imperial woodpecker. Rhein was one of the last people to have seen one, Martjan told him, and the only person who ever photographed a living one. He finally agreed to meet Martjan for breakfast the next morning. He was surprised how young Martjan was and ended up liking him. He said he would take him to meet Rhein the following morning.

Martjan could barely sleep that night. He couldn't stop thinking about the film. How good would it be? Would it show any interesting behaviors? Would the bird be identifiable? And was it definitely an imperial woodpecker? Martjan had come so far to see this film but had no way of knowing whether it would be worth the effort.

Rhein and his wife greeted Martjan warmly when he came to their house, but the whole meeting almost broke down a short time later, through no fault of his. Apparently, the Audubon director and Rhein were at opposite ends of the political spectrum, and the two suddenly got into a heated argument about a remark Rhein had made. Martjan quickly stepped in and tried his best to smooth things over between the two men, and everyone finally sat down in the living room and watched Rhein set up his old 16mm projector and screen and begin running the film. Although it was only eighty-five seconds long, the film was far better than Martjan could ever have imagined. The bird was easily identifiable and was engaged in a variety of behaviors: flying, foraging, hitching up a tree. The film was a small record but rich with information.

Rhein seemed embarrassed by the quality of the film and made disparaging comments as they viewed it. Yet this was the only photographic documentation ever made of the imperial woodpecker; its importance cannot be overstated.

Rhein at first told Martjan he could borrow the film and have it copied, but later backed out on his offer. But a couple of years later, after Rhein passed away, Rhein's nephew, Ronald Thorpe, sent a DVD of the film to Martjan. Later, Thorpe donated the original film to the Cornell Lab of Ornithology, and it has since been enhanced and analyzed.*

Years later, it was Rhein's film that inspired Martjan and me to launch an expedition to the mountains of Durango to see if this imperial woodpecker may yet still fly in the area Rhein and his friends had explored.

◆　◆　◆

Martjan should have been born a hundred and fifty years ago, he so perfectly fits the mold of Victorian explorers like Lumholtz and Nelson and Goldman—for better or worse. He lives to be a field researcher, studying birds in faraway and often inhospitable locations, and it's always been like that for him. He's one of the most intense and focused people I've ever met.

Martjan began his scientific career long before he earned his PhD—in fact, before he even enrolled in a university. He's been fascinated by large woodpeckers—such as the ivory-billed and imperial woodpeckers—since childhood and, while still in his teens, launched an expedition to Cuba at his own expense (using money he'd saved from working at a dairy factory in the Netherlands) to search for ivory-billed woodpeckers. He learned how to speak Spanish and then flew to Cuba alone, hiring local people to help him search the mountains of Oriente Province, where ivorybills had been seen in the mid-1980s. He spent weeks scouring the area and later wrote a scientific article in which he declared that the ivory-bill was almost certainly extinct in Cuba. A few years

---

*Martjan's analysis of William Rhein's film is featured in a scientific article he and I wrote for the October 2011 issue of *The Auk*, the journal of the American Ornithologists' Union. Read the article and view Rhein's footage and other online extras about the imperial woodpecker at www.birds.cornell.edu/imperial.

later, in the mid-1990s, he headed to the mountains of Mexico and spent months searching for the imperial woodpecker. He later became lead scientist of the Cornell Lab of Ornithology's Ivory-billed Woodpecker Project after our 2004 sighting in Arkansas. But in between his Cuba and Mexico expeditions and several times since, he has worked in Borneo, Myanmar, and other remote and potentially hazardous places. In an Indonesian city during a period of ethnic unrest, he saw human heads hanging from street lamps. It didn't seem a stretch for him to want to join me in the Sierra Madre.

◆　◆　◆

For months Durango had loomed in front of me. It would be my best chance yet to seek answers to vital questions about the imperial woodpecker and its catastrophic population collapse. I would travel through a part of Mexico that was new to me—a notorious drug-growing region for both marijuana and opium—and have to depend on people whom, with the exception of Martjan, I had never met before. But following in the footsteps of Bill Rhein, visiting the very spot where he shot his film of a living imperial woodpecker, was irresistible.

Martjan was similarly driven. When I first told him of my plans to search for imperial woodpeckers, he said, "People said I was crazy in the 1990s to travel through the Sierra Madre looking for this bird. But now . . ." He smiled and shook his head. The level of violence and danger had risen astronomically since his travels more than a decade earlier. But Martjan had come back to my office half an hour later to say: "I may want to look for this bird one more time." Imperial woodpecker fever is hard to shake.

After I returned from my exploratory journeys through the Sierra Madre with John Hatch, Martjan began working on identifying the spot where Rhein had made his film. Since he had been the one who rediscovered the film and tracked down Rhein, this was a special project for him.

In a letter Rhein had written to Jim Tanner in 1961, Martjan found some sketchy clues to where the imperial woodpecker was filmed. Rhein had mentioned driving to the logging town of Los Laureles and taking a mule trip across a canyon toward the Guacamaya Mountains. As far as Martjan could tell, no such mountains existed, but there was a village called Guacamayita across the canyon of the Rio Taxicaringa. Dick Heintzelman, the last surviving member of Rhein's 1956 expedition, had sent me some Kodachrome slides he had taken there, but he hadn't paid attention to which way they were traveling when they left Durango City and wasn't even sure what direction they had driven. But a couple of his photographs showed a large, distinctive rock outcropping. He said that if we could locate that outcropping on a satellite map, it would be very close to where they camped and where the imperial woodpecker had been.

Martjan spent months poring over Google Earth maps on his computer until he felt certain he knew, within a mile or two, where the movie was taken. Even better than that, he located several areas not far from there that still appeared to have excellent forest without any roads or houses nearby. As far as he could tell, they had never been logged. (Decades-old logging roads are usually still perfectly visible in satellite images.) Perhaps these were the kind of remote "lost worlds" that might yet hold imperial woodpeckers. Some of them looked extremely difficult to reach—sheer-sided mesas with forests on top that probably had not been worth the trouble of logging or even climbing to. And these satellite images had been taken only five years earlier in 2005.

Although Martjan was pessimistic about the chances that imperial woodpeckers might still exist, he was excited about exploring the old-growth areas he had located on the Google Earth satellite maps. He started contacting people he knew in Mexico, including Julián Bautista, a forester in the state of Durango, who confirmed that some areas still had excellent forest. He also thought the area was still reasonably safe.

Martjan arranged some funding through Birdlife International and logistical support and a truck through Pronatura Noroeste (the northeastern Mexico chapter of the conservation group Pronatura). The Cornell Lab of Ornithology's Neotropical Bird Conservation Program, headed by Mexican ornithologist Eduardo Iñigo-Elias, also pitched in.

Rosa Vidal, of Pronatura, offered to write us a letter that we could carry with us to show to any military police or *narcotraficantes* we might encounter, stating our business and the fact that Pronatura vouched for what we were doing. Miguel Cruz, of Pronatura Noroeste, who had completed his PhD studying thick-billed parrots in the Sierra Madre Occidental, said his brother Javier, who had a great deal of experience working on wildlife projects in the Sierra Madre and had been his brother's main assistant in all of his thick-billed parrot fieldwork, would accompany us on the expedition.

We planned to leave in late February 2010 and stay until March 20, traveling on a shoestring, camping out most nights and living on beans and tortillas, but that was just the way we liked it. We would be in the mountains of Durango, in the heart of the historical range of the imperial woodpecker.

Originally, the Cornell Lab's multimedia program had considered sending a videographer or even a team to document the expedition, shooting high-definition videos of the habitats and birds as well as mountain residents we would interview. But these plans fell through a few months before we left, after Larry Arbanas—a videographer who works on many projects with the multimedia group—was robbed at gunpoint while on assignment in Mexico. He had stopped briefly at a rest area on the main toll road between Veracruz and Mexico City, when a man suddenly came up behind him and held a gun to his head while another took his car keys and wallet. Then they fled in his rental car, leaving Larry stranded, with only the cutoff shorts and flip-flops he was wearing—no money, no passport, no driver's license, no credit cards. Worse, unknown to the robbers, the trunk of the car contained a quarter-million dollars' worth of high-definition video equipment—a staggering loss.

Yet it could have been even worse. The police told Larry that these same thieves had hijacked a commercial truck and killed the driver.

◆ ◆ ◆

Gazing out the airplane window, over the endless parched lands of Old Mexico, I finally saw the distant escarpments of the mighty Sierra Madre—the mother of all mountain ranges—rising blue through the pale mist along the horizon. From this vantage point, I felt like I could see forever. The entire landscape had a hallucinogenic quality, as if it was covered with water and as if various ponds, streams, and lakes were floating above it.

We took a taxi into the center of Durango to our hotel, which was near the spectacular Spanish cathedral built in the late seventeenth and eighteenth centuries and rightly viewed as one of the most beautiful buildings in all of northern Mexico. The hotel has quite a history, too. Originally a private hacienda owned by a wealthy family in the colonial era, it was converted into a hotel more than a century ago, but its glory days are long past.

Even so, as I stepped inside the old hotel, I was pleasantly surprised. Just past the check-in desk is an elaborate inner courtyard with huge stone pillars, Romanesque arches, a flagstone floor, and painted stucco walls rising on all sides. The halls of the two upper stories overlook the courtyard and sport black iron railings. Potted plants are everywhere, and a suit of armor stands against the far wall. The sitting area has lush leather couches, and framed blowups of historical photographs hang along the lime-green walls. The paint is peeling and the furniture worn, but the place has undeniable charm. Our room was nice, with a small balcony overlooking the cathedral.

We met the field crew from Pronatura in the lobby later in the evening: Rene, a tall, thin, good-natured man from Monterrey who studies maroon-fronted and thick-billed parrots; Marco, a biology instructor from Mazatlán; Oscar, a field technician from Monterrey who seemed to be cultivating a Rasta look; and Manuel, the youngest at sixteen years old, who was from a small mountain community near Madera and worked as a field technician for Pronatura. Manuel would be doing all of our driving on some potentially dangerous roads even though one of his hands was hugely swollen where he'd been stung by bees a couple of days earlier while working on a trout project.

We were disappointed to learn that Javier Cruz would not be going with us after all. At the last minute, he had changed his mind about coming. They told us he hadn't been feeling well and was having dizzy spells. Rene also told us he would not be joining us on the expedition. I felt sure he would have been a good person to have in the field with us, but he would be returning to Monterrey the next day on a bus. We had not even begun our expedition and had already lost two of the Mexican biologists we thought would be accompanying us.

We still had Marco, who works with Pronatura Mazatlán and teaches biology at a university in Sinaloa. Thirtyish, with a four-day beard and wearing a black wool cap pulled low on his head, he seemed terrified at the prospect of traveling in the Sierra Madre and never wasted an opportunity to let us know what a bad idea our expedition was or to tell us another horror story of people who went there and never returned or of recent massacres in the area. According to him, more than a dozen people, including women and children, had been mowed down by automatic weapons just a couple of weeks earlier, in the southern part of the state of Durango, near the border with Sinaloa. When Martjan told him we had come here in late winter because we thought there would be less drug-growing activity and it would be safer, Marco said, no—this is the worst time to go, because they're harvesting the opium crops.

Now it would just be the five of us—Martjan, Marco, Oscar, Manuel, and me—so our expedition would not have any prominent Mexican biologists. Oscar, a field assistant with Pronatura Chihuahua, was younger than Rene and Marco (about twenty-two years old) and had long, unkempt hair and several rings through his eyebrows; he wore a bandana on his head. Clean-shaven Manuel had come from a tiny village in the Madera area said to be the coldest place in Mexico. He works for Pronatura Mazatlán on community outreach with Miguel and Javier Cruz.

Martjan had also had a hard time getting in touch with Julián Bautista, his friend in the state forestry unit, but Martjan finally reached him by phone. We were to meet him at his office the next morning at eight thirty.

When we got back to the hotel, I had a strong impression that my gear had been ransacked. Nothing seemed to be missing—both of my still cameras and camcorder were there, as were my binoculars and several other key items—but my bags had obviously been searched and several zippers left open. Martjan seemed dubious about it at first, but then also became concerned as he thought about all the expensive gear he had. But at this point, nothing was missing, so we just let it go and finally turned out the lights.

The next morning at breakfast, Martjan told me he had some concerns about our journey. For one thing, the truck Marco had driven up from Mazatlán had Sinaloa license plates and no official insignia on the sides. Marco was very worried about this. We could get into serious trouble taking an unknown truck from Sinaloa into these mountains. The people of the Sierra Madre are very insular, and in their view nothing good has ever come from the state of Sinaloa—only drug lords, crime, and exploitation. Our other truck had logos on the sides indicating that it was from a university in Monterrey, which was good, but it was sixteen years old with a lot of mileage, and might not hold up on the rough roads of the Mexican outback. We had really been counting on driving two trucks, in case we had any breakdowns, and also because we would have safety in numbers.

After breakfast, we joined the others in our group and began our trek to Julián Bautista's office. At only eight in the morning, Durango was already heating up, and it would soon be blazing hot outside. The six of us trudged along the narrow streets like a ragtag band of gypsies—past solitary men and women who stood waiting for a bus or car or just enjoying a morning smoke in a doorway.

We ended up walking too far and had to turn back, but finally found the right address, in a barred and locked storefront. It was just past our appointed time of eight thirty, but no one was there yet.

"It's Mexico," said Rene, with a laugh. "They open at nine."

We leaned against the dusty wall together in the clear morning air. High above us, several turkey vultures circled, which made me laugh.

Just a minute or two before nine, a young woman arrived, unlocked the office, and let us inside. Julián Bautista arrived a short time later, wearing blue jeans, a denim jacket, and dark brown leather boots. Short, muscular, with jet-black hair and deeply tanned skin, he looked to be in his late fifties. He welcomed us warmly, and we all shook hands. Martjan wasted no time. He pulled out his Google Earth maps, which he had meticulously marked with the areas of interest, and then set up his computer to play the Rhein film. Julián closed his blinds and dimmed the lights, and we stood around together gazing at the computer screen.

Rhein's imperial woodpecker film always amazes people, and Martjan put on a great show, playing some sections over again in slow motion, stopping and starting to give everyone a better look at the most interesting details. Then we looked at the topo maps again and pulled out several of Dick Heintzelman's pictures that I had printed. Julián's face lit up when we showed him the picture of the rock outcropping near where Heintzelman and the others had camped when the 1956 movie was filmed. He knew the place well.

A conservationist, Julián wants to help maintain the forest so that it is more natural and better for wildlife, but some of his practices are not good from a modern ecological perspective. For one thing, he maintains fire-control units in the forests he oversees even though fire would help the pine forest there, burning out the undergrowth and promoting regeneration.

As we sat talking about the Sierra Madre, we mentioned Marco's concerns about driving a truck with Sinaloa plates. Julián smiled. "I can see why you would be concerned," he said. "You might be all right if you introduce yourself to the village elders and explain what you're doing." He said he would go with us in his forestry truck if we left tomorrow and would spend the day introducing us to some of the key villagers in the area we wanted to explore.

Things at last were falling into place. Then a curious thing happened. More people started coming into the office—first two, then another three. Martjan would go through the entire presentation again—playing the video, showing the photographs, poring over the topo maps—as the people gazed with rapt attention and nodded enthusiastically. Then they would basically wish us well and walk out of the room. (One man laughed when he saw a picture of Rhein's truck on a decent-looking dirt road. "The roads were much better here in the 1950s," he said.) As far as we knew, all of the men were associated with the forestry unit in Durango.

Just when it seemed we were finally finished and could leave, five more men filed inside—but these were different, all native Tepehuanes who lived in the village of Guacamayita, in the heart of the area we wanted to explore. Julián had heard they were in town and invited them over. They had come from the Sierra Madre and were clad in their best city clothes. One man, Carlos, who seemed to be the leader, wore a silk cowboy shirt, a crisp new cowboy hat with a silver buckle in front, and brand-new snakeskin cowboy boots. Another man wore a rodeo belt with a silver buckle as big as a Volkswagen bug hubcap, with "Durango" in huge gold letters and a steer head inlaid in it.

Carlos's younger brother, Miguel, told us he used to drive mules right through the same valley where Rhein traveled in the 1950s. All of them immediately recognized the rock outcropping in Dick Heintzelman's picture as very close to Guacamayita and identified it as Los Pilares (The Pillars). Martjan and I glanced at each other and smiled. Then I looked at Marco. His face was grim. Julián noticed this, too, and asked the men from Guacamayita how safe it would be for us to drive the Sinaloa truck into the mountains.

Carlos looked surprised. "Does it have any insignia?" he asked.

"No, nothing," said Julián, shaking his head.

Carlos and his friends glanced at each other for a second and then told us that it would be far too dangerous to bring that truck up the mountain. There was no telling how people in some of the small villages or on the outlying roads and trails would react to it. Maybe we would be able to explain our way out of trouble, but it would be far better not to attract unwelcome attention in the first place. We would have to leave it somewhere in Durango while we were away.

Martjan began his presentation one more time, handing out the photographs and Google Earth maps and showing the men Rhein's movie on his laptop computer. They gathered closely behind him—some on their knees, some standing—all of them peering intently at the motion picture images unfolding on the tiny screen. Though none of them had ever seen one of these birds, they were genuinely interested and seemed to get more and more excited as we talked about the *pitoreales*. Carlos told us there were still uncut woodlands and big trees in the area, especially in the places we had viewed on Google Earth.

He also warned us that we would be traveling through some dangerous areas to get there and could not safely visit all of the areas Martjan had marked on the maps. Crossing to the other side of the Rio Taxicaringa was completely out of the question, he said. It was controlled by Los Zetas—the most feared drug cartel, made up of paramilitary types who were formerly elite troops in the Mexican military, trained by US Special Forces to be used in drug interdiction, but they had crossed to the dark side, where big money was to be made. As outsiders—and gringos at that—running into a group of Zetas would be the best way to fall off the edge of the Earth and never be heard from again. We decided we would stay on Carlos's side of the river. It was disappointing not to be able to check all of the potential imperial woodpecker sites we had marked on the map, but we could visit the best ones, including the area where Rhein had filmed his movie. And because our search would be limited to a smaller area, we would be able to spend more time there and search the woods more thoroughly.

Julián made an impassioned speech to the men from Guaca-mayita, saying what a wonderful thing it was that we were doing, coming all this way, facing untold dangers to find out more about this bird and this area. It was a historic endeavor, he said, and they should all be proud of the attention being bestowed on their remote little community and eager to help. Carlos and his associates were completely on board, offering us their assistance going in and out of the mountains and finding local people to help guide us through the areas we wanted to check. He and a couple of his friends would drive with us the next day and introduce us to people in the tiny mountain villages, which could help us avoid potential problems. We agreed to meet at four the next morning in front of a convenience store at the edge of the city and drive together into the Sierra Madre with a caravan of three vehicles: Carlos's fancy club cab pickup, our old beater truck from Monterrey, and Julián's official forestry truck.

Martjan and I were beaming as we walked outside into the dazzling Mexican sunshine. We believed we now had Julián's full backing and had made several new acquaintances who lived right where we wanted to search, and they were willing to help smooth things out for us. But Marco still looked grim. He paused beside Carlos's truck, parked right outside, a brand-new club cab truck with gleaming copper-brown metallic paint and darkly tinted windows.

"You don't own a truck like that or wear clothes like theirs on the kind of money you can earn honestly in the Sierra," he said. "They're obviously up to their eyeballs in drug money."

I felt sick to my stomach. I knew he must be right, but what else could we do? *Carlos might be a drug lord, but at least he's our drug lord*, I thought, and I welcomed any help he could provide us getting into and out of the mountains.

We shifted into full expedition preparation mode and made plans to buy our supplies, which would include most of the food we would eat on the expedition as well as two huge plastic drums to fill with gasoline. There would be no place to buy gas once we left Durango, so we had to carry it in with us.

At the parking lot where Marco, Oscar, and the others had their vehicles stored—the next block over from the hotel and guarded twenty-four hours a day—we took the truck Oscar had driven from Monterrey and drove Rene to the bus station. I was sorry to see him go and hoped no one else would drop out of the expedition. I decided to go back to the hotel instead of joining the supply run.

I hadn't been in the room long, when I heard a tapping at the door. I got up and quietly walked to the door and opened it. A man was standing there, just about to put the key in the door. He blanched when he saw me, no doubt thinking no one was in the room. I asked him what he wanted, and he said he just wanted to find out if everything was okay. I said it was and he hurried away. But I didn't feel good about it. Had he decided to come back now to get some of the things he'd seen but hadn't taken when he'd gone through my bags the day before?

I sat back down on my bed and began writing in my notebook when suddenly—*BOOM!*—a huge blast rang out, rattling my windows, followed by sirens and emergency vehicles screaming past. It sounded like the explosion came from just down the street. I jotted down the time: 5:35 p.m.

I told Martjan about the explosion as soon as he came back. He had been inside a big store a good distance away and had not heard the blast, so we went downstairs to ask the concierge about it. Someone had fired a rocket-propelled grenade (the new weapon of choice of the *narcotraficantes*) at the hotel down the street, where several federales were staying. Even downtown Durango had become a war zone.

The next morning we would be dropping out of all contact with the outside world—the part of the Sierra Madre we would be traveling through has no telephones or electricity—so I was eager to get online and send a few emails to my family and friends. Our hotel had a sketchy wireless internet connection that didn't work at all in our room, but I found that if I walked the hallways with Martjan's laptop in my hands, I could often locate hot spots that were good enough to send and receive emails.

About ten o'clock that evening, after I'd found a spot down the hall from our room that had a decent wireless signal and an old couch to sit on, I was typing away madly, when Martjan came out of the room, ashen-faced and shaken.

"We will probably have to cancel our expedition," he said.

"What happened?" I said.

"Julián got an anonymous call," said Martjan. "The man knew about our expedition and was angry. He demanded to know who we are, why we are going there, where we'll be staying, and all the details of the timing and route of our travel."

My heart sank. I saw my dreams of revisiting Rhein's film location fading quickly. "You know if we go home now, we'll never come back," I said.

"Not necessarily," said Martjan. "We might be able to return when it's safer."

"That's not the way things are going now," I said. "Every time I come to Mexico it seems ten times more dangerous than the time before."

Julián had spoken about the situation with Carlos, who apparently was unfazed by the call. He said that since the caller knew we were leaving at 4:00 a.m., we should just leave at 2:30 instead so they wouldn't be ready for us.

"I can just picture that," said Martjan. "Carlos racing up there at ninety miles an hour in his fancy truck as we drag along behind."

I nodded. "What do you want to do?" I asked.

"I don't know," he said. "Julián wants us to meet him in the

Plaza de Armas in twenty minutes. Carlos and Miguel will be there, too."

This was not a happy thought. The town plaza seemed like the classic place for a hit, and we were both nervous about going there. Still, we really had no choice. We talked briefly with Marco, Oscar, and Manuel and asked them to come with us. They were not ready to go right then but said they'd be there shortly.

Just before we left, I turned on my digital tape recorder and slipped it into my shirt pocket to record our conversation with Carlos. But when we stepped out into the darkened streets, Martjan noticed a bright red light glowing in my pocket. It would not have been good to get caught wearing a bug while talking to these guys, so I turned it off.

◆　◆　◆

As we walked down the flagstone streets of the pedestrian mall, the perimeter of the plaza was filled with police, no doubt intending to present a strong police presence after the earlier grenade attack. Their white squad cars lined the edge of the street, red lights flashing on top, but they didn't make us feel any safer. We strolled into the Plaza de Armas in the semidarkness. People kept emerging from the shadows, filling us with a momentary dread. On the far side of the plaza, half a dozen men pounded an intense African rhythm on conga drums, which only added to our tensions. We suddenly felt almost like fictional characters walking through a movie, and the thought made us laugh nervously.

Julián was fifteen minutes late, but we were getting used to that now. We finally spotted him walking not far from the police lines, without Carlos. We all shook hands and walked away together into the shadows. Marco and Oscar joined us shortly after, followed by Carlos and Miguel about fifteen minutes later.

Marco seemed panicked at the thought of driving into the mountains. Although he would not be taking the truck with the Sinaloa license plates, he still felt insecure because of his Sinaloa accent, which he thought might also turn the local people against him. Carlos seemed bored by his paranoia and didn't think there would be any problem driving to Guacamayita. He again suggested just changing the times when we left and returned.

Carlos's confidence made me feel better about our prospects in the mountains, but Julián thought it was a bad idea to go there now and asked us to reconsider. He apologized for his earlier encouragements and said the situation had changed; the area had become far more dangerous in recent days.

"Of course, if you want to go, I'll still go with you as we planned," said Julián. "It's up to you."

Martjan and I glanced at each other.

"Do you want to go ahead with this?" Martjan asked.

I paused for a few seconds, imagining Los Pilares, just a single day's rough drive away. I wanted to go there so badly, I could almost feel the place. I knew in my heart that this would be my only chance to go there, and perhaps the only chance anyone would go there for decades to come. There could be imperial woodpeckers there, but no one would ever know if we didn't go.

I drew in my breath and said, "Yes, yes, I do want to do this."

Julián's face sank, but he nodded and said he would help us. Carlos wanted to leave at four o'clock in the morning, but Julián was dead-set against it.

"The devil walks at that time of night," he said. "Far better to leave at six thirty when it's just getting light so we'll be in full daylight all the way to Guacamayita."

Carlos said that was fine, and we made plans to rendezvous at a convenience store at the edge of Durango. Julián said he would meet us at our hotel about twenty minutes before that so we could load up everything and go to meet Carlos. We left Julián, Carlos, and Miguel and started walking back to the hotel.

Marco had been very quiet but then said, "I'm sorry. I can't do this. It's just too dangerous." He said he would drive the other truck back to Mazatlán in the morning.

I felt sick. There was no way of knowing if we could get in and out of the mountains safely.

10 ◆ No Turning Back

 I got up well before dawn and, as I started repacking my gear, I noticed my camcorder was missing. It had been there the day before when I inventoried my equipment after my bags were ransacked. Someone must have come to our room and taken it when we were meeting Carlos in the plaza. Martjan and I went through everything closely, but the camcorder was the only thing missing. It was a great blow. If we saw an imperial woodpecker flying through the woods, we would have no way of videotaping it in motion or recording its call.

Furious, I stormed down to the night desk with Martjan and complained to the man in charge—the same man who had told us about the grenade attack the day before. He nodded sympathetically as I groused about the stolen camcorder and told him about the man who had tried to get into our room when he thought we weren't there.

"Yes, we've had complaints about him before," he said, adding that they should be able to do something about it this time. "The owner has tiny video cameras hidden in the hallways and can watch who goes in and out of the rooms." He said they would rewind all the tapes and play them back to see if they could see the man coming out of the room with my camcorder. "Check with us later if you come back to Durango," he said.

We both nodded and started walking back to our room to get the rest of our gear. When we got to our door, I looked up at the ceilings and walls for the length of our hallway and saw nothing. I finally shook my head and burst out laughing.

"There aren't any video cameras here," I said. "We'd be able to see them. I think the desk clerk may be in on it with the other guy."

"You think so?" said Martjan.

"Yes," I said. "At least it wasn't an expensive camcorder, and we still have all of our cameras and other gear."

◆ ◆ ◆

We got to the rendezvous point at the convenience store half an hour past our appointed time. Carlos was nowhere to be seen, and Julián had forgotten to bring his cell phone, so we had no way of contacting him. Oscar had given our big plastic gas drums and enough money to fill them up to Carlos. If we didn't connect with him, we wouldn't have enough gas to drive to and from the mountains.

Fortunately, Carlos showed up an hour past our scheduled rendezvous time, with the two containers of gasoline—as large as oil drums—in the back of his truck. Both of them had already leaked around their screw tops, one of which had been screwed down over a piece of sheet plastic to improve the seal. They would be messy and smelly once we started bouncing along on the dirt road.

As we sat in our trucks about to leave, Carlos called out to me and asked if I wanted to ride in his vehicle, which had room for another passenger in the club cab. I thanked him but said I wanted to talk to my friends on the way up the mountain. Actually, I was terrified by the idea of riding into the mountains with a drug grower. If we got stopped at a military roadblock, how could I ever explain what I was doing with him? (In Mexico, if you get arrested, you're basically considered guilty until you can prove your innocence.) And I didn't want to risk getting caught in a crossfire if we encountered a rival drug grower.

Before we hit the mountains, Carlos stopped at a small, trash-strewn pond and filled some water jugs. We had barely driven half an hour before we left the paved road; we would not see another one for a long time.

We'd been driving on the rough dirt road for about an hour in our three-vehicle convoy—Carlos's truck in front; our truck second, with young Manuel driving, me on the passenger side, and Oscar in the middle; followed by Julián's forestry truck, with Martjan on the passenger side—when a pickup truck appeared, following a hundred yards behind Julián's truck, at first carefully maintaining its distance and not getting closer even when Julián slowed down. After twenty minutes of this, the truck abruptly sped up, racing past Julián's vehicle and ours. As they passed our truck, I noticed that the man in the passenger seat had an AK-47 cradled in his lap. They pulled up beside Carlos's truck and drove alongside him for several minutes. The men in the strange truck seemed to be taunting or menacing Carlos and his friends. They finally broke off and drove quickly away, leaving us all in their dust.

We continued on until we reached Las Espinas, a small village in an area Carlos considered safe, then stopped and got out of our trucks. Carlos looked pale and shaken, which was disconcerting, because he had always seemed so calm before. He told us the truck and the men inside fit the description of some people who had murdered someone in a nearby village just a week earlier.

By midafternoon, we had reached Guacamayita, a pretty little village in the high country, surrounded by pine forest and inhabited by the indigenous Tepehuanes. Carlos invited us inside his cabin, where his mother was cooking. She was in her early fifties and pretty, with black hair and dark eyes, and she made tacos for us on a stove made from half an oil drum laid on its side with a flat piece of sheet metal on top. A hot pinewood fire blazed inside it, and we huddled near it to keep warm.

Inside the cabin, an Uzi submachine gun lay in plain sight on a table near the front window. Later as we were preparing to leave and drive deeper into the mountains, Carlos loaded bullets into a clip, which he slipped into the bottom of the gun. He smiled and said the gun was "*por coyotes*," but to me this represented a significant escalation in the level of danger. Because of the scare we'd had driving up the mountain that morning, Carlos was probably no longer willing to go anywhere without an automatic weapon stashed under his seat. Despite the risk of being stopped at a military roadblock and arrested for possessing a firearm, he felt it was far more dangerous to travel unarmed.

After we'd eaten our tacos, we went back outside and stood together talking. Close by was a tiny village store made of rough-hewn wood, where people could buy flour, fruit, soda, hardware, and other general store items. Several men hung around, leaning against the split-rail wooden fence surrounding Carlos's property or squatting on the ground, relaxing in the sunlight near the little store. Although it was only midafternoon on a weekday, most of the working-age men didn't seem to have anything to do. They were all Tepehuanes, but they dressed about the same as other rural Mexicans in jeans and cowboy shirts. Only the women dressed in more traditional long, straight skirts. Some of them spoke in their native language. Most of the men were drunk, which annoyed Carlos's mother, who told us someone had been coming around selling cheap mezcal to the villagers.

"Now many of the men are getting drunk all the time and beating their wives," she said, frowning.

Carlos introduced us to Felix, an elderly villager who'd spent his entire life in the area. Although he said he was in his late seventies, Felix looked far older, with crow's feet deeply etched in his leathery face, baked mahogany brown by years of searing sunlight in the thin mountain air. He wore a thick, weather-beaten plaid shirt with metal buttons and a hole so large that most of his left shoulder poked through, sunburned crimson red. He also wore a white straw cowboy hat, ubiquitous headwear in the backcoun-

Felix, an elderly villager in Guacamayita, remembered the imperial woodpecker well and took the author to the area William Rhein traveled through in the 1950s. (*Photo by Tim Gallagher*)

try of northern Mexico. He was born in Taxicaringa, a larger village in a river canyon about a dozen kilometers from Guacamayita. Taxicaringa means "burnt village" in the Tepehuán language. The name predates the arrival of the Spaniards and refers to an incident between two warring Tepehuán tribes that took place centuries ago.

Don Felix laughed when he saw the flying ivory-billed woodpecker emblazoned on the front of my cap, but said the bird was wrong. Lifting the hat off my head, he pointed at the bird's neck and correctly said that the *pitoreal* had an all-black neck with no white lines on it, unlike the bird on my hat. The birds had been numerous when he was growing up, and he would often see two or three of them at a time and hear their calls, which he mimicked for us: *anh, anh, anh*—a near-perfect rendition of the loud nasal toots of an ivory-billed woodpecker, the closest relative of the *pitoreal*. He didn't remember people shooting them and thought they were fairly spooky if you approached them on foot, but that you could get very close when riding a horse or mule. Loggers started cutting timber heavily in this area around 1954, and he hadn't seen any *pitoreales* since about 1957 or '58.

Carlos wanted to take us to some of the areas in Dick Heintzelman's photographs, so we all climbed aboard the trucks. We pulled out of Guacamayita in a little convoy—Carlos's truck in the lead, followed by our Monterrey truck, and then Julián's forestry truck, all overflowing with people, most of them drunk. A couple of villagers rode in the bed of Carlos's truck, clinging precariously with their fingertips to the rim of a gas drum to keep from falling out.

En route, we ran into an older man and woman standing beside a pickup truck, which appeared to be broken down. One of the men with us talked with them for a couple of minutes, after which they handed him an empty gallon milk bottle made of plastic and a short piece of garden hose. He brought it over, unscrewed the cap of one our gas drums, and stuck the hose into it. Then he started sucking on the hose to get the siphoning action started. A few seconds later, he turned his head quickly to the side and spit out a big stream of gasoline and then filled the milk bottle with gas and handed it back to the other people to put in their truck.

Don Felix had come along to help pinpoint the exact places in Dick Heintzelman's photographs. But before we went to Los Pilares, we stopped at the mesa forest shown in some of Dick's photographs. It had changed drastically. The general terrain was the same, but the massive old-growth trees were gone. A hodgepodge of second-growth pines had emerged among the old stumps, and the thick native grasses had been browsed down to the dirt.

Next we stopped at Los Pilares, which was unmistakable from the 1956 picture. Carlos, Miguel, Oscar, Manuel, and I scrambled up the back of the rock formation and made our way to the top. As I walked along a grassy ledge, I just missed stepping on a big rattlesnake and jumped back. Sluggish in the cool mountain air, it obligingly slithered away after Miguel poked at it with a stick and disappeared into a crack in the rock. An altitude reading I took of Los Pilares with my GPS showed that it stood at 9,244 feet above sea level—well into the heart of the imperial woodpecker's altitudinal range.

We drove higher into the mountains, stopping at the edge of a spectacular canyon. A couple of red-tailed hawks and a Cooper's hawk flew past as we sat on rocks overlooking the canyon. Martjan took a double-knock contraption, consisting of a birdhouselike wooden box and a striker, out of his backpack. Using a rope, he lashed the box tightly to the trunk of a big pine with the open side against the bark so it would act as a resonator. Then he took out the double-knock striker—which resembles two lengths of thick broomstick, about a yard long each, connected with a pivot bolt in the middle. In the typical double-knock drumming of most *Campephilus* woodpeckers—*BAM-bam, BAM-bam*—the second impact sounds almost like an echo of the first. Martjan swung the striker in an arc, hitting it hard with the first stick while the other swung over on the pivot, hitting the box a fraction of a second later, producing a perfect rendition of the natural sound. He had designed the device a few years earlier to use in the search for ivory-billed woodpeckers.

Martjan played some ivory-billed woodpecker *kent* calls, the

Martjan Lammertink uses a device he developed to mimic the distinctive double-knock drum of a *Campephilus* woodpecker. (*Photo by Tim Gallagher*)

sounds closest to imperial woodpecker calls. He then played a recording of a Sierra Madre sparrow—an endemic of these mountains, now extremely rare—which Rhein had also seen and filmed in the area during his expeditions in the 1950s. There was no response. But when Martjan played a barred owl recording, it drew a loud call from a Mexican spotted owl perched in the trees in the canyon below.

We drove to a tiny village called Las Coloradas, which translates "the reds" and is named for the color of the soil. The village consists of only three or four log cabins and a couple of crude adobe dwellings, and is inhabited by one Tepehuán extended family. Julián said the people wanted us to stay in an adobe hovel, but Martjan objected.

"I want to set up a base camp near our study site, so we can start searching first thing in the morning," he said.

Julián frowned. "It is not safe to sleep outside in the mountains," he said. "There are dangerous animals . . . *leones*."

It seemed doubtful that the local mountain lions would be a danger to us, but he probably wanted us to stay there because arrangements had already been made with the elderly couple who owned the adobe. The woman had obviously just swept the dirt floor of the adobe and lit a fire in the crude metal stove. She stood silently holding a corn broom just inside the yard, with her husband beside her, grim-faced and perplexed as Martjan bickered with Julián about where we would sleep.

"It would be very difficult setting up a camp out there, especially at night," said Julián, "and this is very close to where you want to explore anyway."

There may have been other reasons that Julián did not raise. Perhaps word had got out that we were in the area and local people didn't want us snooping around by ourselves and possibly running across their drug crops.

Martjan compromised and pitched his tent on the hard bare ground just outside the adobe. He may have had the right idea, because our little hovel smelled like chickens and goats, which had obviously been living in it until the old couple drove them out to accommodate us. It had a hard-packed dirt floor, with several puddles and muddy spots where snowmelt or rain from the last storm had dripped down through the numerous small holes in the tin roof. The whole thing measured about 11 yards by 6 yards and was divided into two rooms with a wall and a single doorway between them. One room served as a kitchen and bedroom, with a small woodstove made from the top third of an old oil drum that we could use to cook our food and keep the place warm. Across from it stood a crude wooden table and a set of shelves, and in the other corner a bed made of rough-hewn planks nailed atop four pine logs, which stood vertically as legs. The room also had a simple plank bench on two pine logs. Oscar slept in this room, and Manuel slept outside in the back of the truck. I stayed in the other room, which was slightly larger and had a sleeping platform made of planks and a couple of simple tables. Both rooms had a door to the outside, plus the pass-through door between them, each held closed with a piece of string.

The wooden doorframes were only four and a half feet tall, with a six-inch step-over. Even though I bent over completely to go through the doorway between the rooms the first time, at just over six feet tall I bashed my head on the two-by-four at the top. My scalp bled profusely for a few minutes, and after I swabbed it a little, I still looked like I'd been struck by a billy club. I had no way to wash up, so thereafter I had to wear a cap all the time to hide the encrusted blood on my head.

◆ ◆ ◆

Carlos and his friends had left us at Los Pilares before we drove to the edge of the canyon to look around. But he and Miguel came to Las Coloradas shortly before dark to warn us about the dangers of traveling out of the mountains. Julián had planned to drive here and back in the same day, but Carlos urged him to stay put, because it was far too dangerous to make the trip back to Durango unescorted. He advised Julián to wait until the following afternoon, when he would have the benefit of driving in a two-vehicle convoy—and Carlos had some firearms for protection. Julián agreed to stay the night with us before driving back.

With Martjan and me, Carlos was even more emphatic. "Do not under any circumstances try to drive to Durango unescorted," he said, adding that we should also take the precaution of departing a day early, since the person who had made the threatening phone call seemed to know the general itinerary of our expedition. He would meet us at ten o'clock on Friday morning, two weeks hence, and drive out of the mountains with us. Julián would be there, too, in a forestry truck.

We all shook hands, and Carlos climbed back into his truck. Before they left, Miguel walked stealthily over to the herd of goats, perhaps thirty in all, grazing in the short grass near our adobe hut. A couple of them wore neck bells that clanged whenever they moved. He suddenly grabbed a young white billy goat, which sent the rest of the herd racing away. The young goat bleated in terror until Miguel stuck his thumb in its mouth to keep it quiet.

"That's probably tonight's dinner for them," said Martjan.

Miguel held the goat for several minutes, and I wondered if he was going to cut its throat right there. But he finally cinched a white cord around the goat's neck, and carried it to the truck. He tied the goat's makeshift leash to a spare tire lying alongside a big gas drum in the bed of the truck. The goat was still bleating pitifully as Carlos and Miguel raced away in cloud of red dust.

We all crammed into the kitchen area of our little adobe hut— Julián, Martjan, Oscar, Manuel, and me—to cook and eat dinner. By then it was pitch-black outside. A blazing pine fire glowed, popping and hissing in the cookstove, providing the only illumination in the room, except for the headlamps we all wore and turned on for a few minutes from time to time so we could see what we were doing. I chopped up some green peppers, onions, and jalapeños, which Martjan tossed into a big black skillet with the scrambled eggs he was preparing. We didn't have any tortillas, so we scooped the tasty mix up with slices of wheat bread and hungrily gobbled it down. When we finally went to our various sleeping areas, we all quickly fell into a deep slumber.

◆ ◆ ◆

We rose well before dawn and were off on our first long forced march. Our guide was a tall, thin Tepehuán named Antonio, the son of the couple who owned our adobe hovel. He sported a droopy moustache, a jacket too thin for the chill morning air, and some old black dress shoes he wore without socks. They didn't seem the best kind of shoes for scrambling down the jagged talus slopes and along tiny goat trails on the edge of a precipice, but he was far more sure-footed in his smooth-soled shoes than any of us were in our hiking boots.

Since Julián wasn't leaving for Durango until midmorning, he came along with us for the first few hours, whacking the side of a tree here and there with a machete, leaving a small fresh nick so he could find his way back more easily through the woods.

On the first full day of their expedition in the mountains of Durango—from left to right: Tepehuán guide Antonio, Tim Gallagher, Martjan Lammertink, and Manuel Escarcega. (*Photo by Oscar Paz*)

At the edge of a vast canyon, Martjan pulled out his double-knock box, attaching it firmly to the trunk of a pine tree.

"This must be the seven hundredth time I've done this," he said, smiling as he ran through his research protocol: doing several double knocks, waiting twenty minutes, and repeating the sounds. He'd used the box for months in Central and South America, eliciting *BAM-bam* responses from pale-billed, Magellanic, and other *Campephilus* woodpeckers.

"I guess it's like playing the slot machines in Las Vegas," I said. "You have to put in hundreds of quarters before you hit the jackpot."

Martjan grinned. "My parents have been playing the state lottery in Holland for years and haven't won yet," he said. "And they're nearly in their eighties."

"Yeah, but you'll be the one who benefits if they ever win," I said.

We heard some drumming on the mesa below, which Martjan identified as an Arizona woodpecker. In spite of its name, this medium-sized woodpecker is a Mexican species of the pine-oak mountain woodlands with a range that barely extends into Arizona and a tiny piece of New Mexico. Brown and white, with a solid brown back, the male has a red patch on the back of its head. We also heard the loud *waka waka* calls of acorn woodpeckers, which live in extended family groups, gathering acorns to store in their shared granary trees. We heard Steller's jays, a hepatic tanager, treecreepers, and several other birds, but no *pitoreales*.

The hike was tough. We descended a long way down a steep talus slope, and then hiked along a rocky ridge that got narrower and narrower until we reached a bottleneck with sheer drops on both sides. We scrambled across it to get to the mesa, which rose up high on the other side. Its name was Sierra del Huesa (Mountain of Bones)—a spectacular place, with numerous tall pines. The narrow rocky bottleneck had obviously prevented anyone from harvesting the trees; it was simply too difficult to get the timber out.

This was as far as Julián went, because he had to make his way back to Guacamayita and find Carlos before driving back to Durango. He seemed reluctant to go, as though he were worried about us, but finally said, "See you in two weeks." He hugged Martjan and me and then trotted back in the direction from where we'd come. I was sorry to see him go. Of all the people I'd met so far on the expedition, he was the one I trusted most.

When we got the rest of the way across, we hiked quickly up to the higher ground. As we climbed, we heard the raucous calls of large parrots, and I scrambled to try to catch a glimpse of them. But Oscar was the only one who saw them—two spectacular military macaws, flying appropriately enough up the Arroyo del Guacamayas. Nearby, white-collared swifts raced madly around like tiny jet fighters above the canyon.

We made our final push upward to reach the place Martjan had marked on his Google Earth map as the area where Rhein filmed the imperial woodpecker. Based on the most recent information we obtained from Dick Heintzelman and the conversations we'd had with residents of Guacamayita in the previous twenty-four hours, however, we were now convinced that this was the wrong spot. Dick had told us that they camped near Los Pilares and made all of their forays from there. There would have been no reason to come all the way over here. In 1956 there were plenty of huge old-growth pines close to Los Pilares. Martjan had originally thought that Rhein and the others might have come close to this mesa en route from Los Laureles (where his expedition originated) to Los Pilares. But Carlos's brother Miguel, who had led pack mules along that same trail for several years, said that the trail ran miles to the north of where we stood. This spot was rarely visited by anyone, then or now, and the habitat was still nearly pristine. But just because it wasn't the place where Rhein made his film didn't make it any less likely to have *pitoreales*. This area was actually far better than the devastated habitat we had visited the previous afternoon at Los Pilares, which was within a mile of Rhein's film location. Don Felix had told us there had been *pitoreales* all over this area in the 1950s, not just at Los Pilares.

There was also something special about coming to this spot. We had viewed a satellite image of this place, put a red arrow on it in our computer, and now were standing at the exact GPS coordinates. It was eerie being here in this quiet, tranquil place with only the soft, steady *whoosh* of the mountain breeze and some bird sounds— including the artificial drumbeat of a *pitoreal* from Martjan's knocker. Sadly, there was no reply. I wondered, *Are they really all gone?*

We rested for a time, watching a mixed flock of birds moving through an oak tree: a Grace's warbler; a plumbeous vireo. A magnificent hummingbird hovered for an instant nearby then sped away. As we lay there, several turkey vultures soared above.

"This reminds me of something I did with a friend when I was a teenager," I told Martjan. "We were sitting on a ridge like this in California, watching a bunch of turkey vultures soaring overhead, and we suddenly thought how funny it would be to play dead and see if any vultures came down to try to eat us." We both laughed. "I think we lay there for three or four hours, and some of the birds did fly really close, staring at us with their beady little eyes, but none of them landed. By the time we gave up, we both had one side of our face badly sunburned and the other white."

"I did something similar when I was sixteen," said Martjan. "I was on vacation with my father in northern Spain and wanted to get close-up views of lammergeiers and griffon vultures. I tried to buy a dead sheep to attract them, but I couldn't find one."

The areas of uncut forest the author saw in the mountains of Durango were only on steep-sided mesas, too difficult to cut. (*Photo by Tim Gallagher*)

So, always innovative, Martjan went to a toyshop and bough a little baby doll, which he covered with red sauce to look like blood and put it out on a hillside, hoping to attract the massive Old World vultures. They completely ignored it.

◆　◆　◆

In the late afternoon, we climbed back down the steep slope, across the narrow rocky spine, and up the other side to get back to Las Coloradas. The air was so thin and the rocky slope so steep on our last climb, I had to stop three or four times to catch my breath. I hoped I'd be more used to it by the next morning, because we'd be carrying packs loaded with food and water and equipment up a ridge far higher than this one.

When I got back to our adobe hut, I found a full-grown nanny goat standing on my bed platform chewing up a plastic hairbrush she'd taken from my open bag. A short time later, a scruffy, coyote-like dog stopped by and pissed on the doorframe right in front of me. Then a huge black rooster with patches of reddish brown in his plumage strode right inside, as if he were reclaiming his home.

Martjan and I took a walk through Las Coloradas with Antonio. The village has four or five households, all related, who have lived there for at least four generations. We talked to Antonio's parents near their wooden stake fence as their children and grandchildren looked on.

Salvador, Antonio's father, was in his seventies, a tall, dark, reserved man with grayish-black hair and intense eyes. Nicolesa, Antonio's mother, was four or five years younger, lively and full of laughter, with a happy round face and long gray-and-black hair tied back in a ponytail. She wore a long traditional skirt and a light blue cotton shirt. We snapped several digital pictures of them together

Tepehuán guide Antonio and his family live in a log cabin in the tiny village of Las Coloradas, high in the Sierra Madre of Durango. (*Photo by Tim Gallagher*)

as they leaned against the fence and showed them to Nicolesa, who laughed when she saw them on our camera viewing screens and called her kids and grandkids over to see them.

Salvador remembered seeing the *pitoreales* when he was younger and started telling us about them, but Nicolesa quickly took over the conversation.

"They were beautiful," she told us. "I would see them one, two, three at a time, mostly in the high country." But she had not seen one since about the time she first learned how to make tortillas, around the age of ten, which would have been in the early 1950s.

We stumbled back to our adobe in the pitch-black night, our headlamps providing the only illumination. Several feral-looking dogs followed behind, yipping loudly, and a herd of goats scattered ahead of us, with bells jangling. We did our best to prepare

a decent meal, cutting up red and green bell peppers and adding them to a sauce with peanut butter and pouring it over multicolored spiral pasta. Loaded with carbs, we slept like the dead.

◆　◆　◆

Up before dawn again, we drove down an old logging road, trying to get as close as possible to the next area we wanted to explore, but we soon reached a spot where a huge fallen log blocked the road. John Hatch would have buzzed through this with a chain saw in ten minutes, but Antonio didn't seem interested in trying to clear the road. He claimed there were places farther along where the road was washed out anyway, but I didn't see any other bad spots later on the way down. Taking time to clear all of the obstacles on the old logging road would have been well worth the effort, but maybe the local people preferred having some of these roads blocked—to keep strangers from snooping around. An elaborate network of foot trails runs all through this forest, and only the Tepehuanes know the routes.

After walking past the fallen log, Antonio led us scrambling down a deep arroyo, following a barely existent path, with loose rocks and slippery gravel that would have been tough for a goat to traverse. At one point, Martjan slipped and started to fall, his big backpack throwing him off balance. I raced toward him, but luckily, he was able to halt his slide before tumbling over the edge. There was no way I could have reached him in time.

A stream ran through the bottom of the chasm, and we had to walk several hundred yards to find a place where we could get across without wading. But our descent into the arroyo turned out to be nothing compared with the steep climb we had to make to get up the much higher ridge on the other side. I was less than a quarter of the way up and breathing heavily, my heart pounding loudly in my ears. I had to stop several times to catch my breath before I finally crested the ridge. I thought, *The worst is over,* and surged with pride. When I looked back down the arroyo from where we had come and up the other side, the return trip seemed doable.

We walked along the ridge for a while and, on the opposite side of the mesa, Martjan lashed his double-knock box to a pine at the rim of the canyon and went through his usual routine: banging the box a few times; waiting twenty minutes; then repeating the process. I was coming to cherish these moments, because I could relax for a while and catch my breath.

After Martjan had made a few double knocks without getting a response, we scanned the canyon below with binoculars and noticed a disturbing sight—a patch of opium poppies growing in a cleared area near the stream. Martjan and I spoke with each other about it and snapped some pictures. Then we noticed Antonio watching us, so I quickly pointed my binoculars in another direction and started looking for birds, but I was sure he had noticed our interest in the crop.

We continued hiking for a couple more hours, then took a break at the end of the mesa where it overlooked a huge canyon. I took off my backpack and dug around for some food and a bottle of water. As I sat on the edge of the cliff with my legs dangling down, Manuel suddenly called out, *"Incendios!"* and pointed excitedly at the clouds of dark smoke rising from three different places on a forested ridge. This was in one of the areas Martjan and I had seen on Google Earth, where the habitat looked excellent, but Julián had warned us away from it. The Zetas were obviously clearing old-growth forest to make way for more drug plantations, and there was nothing we could do about it. I felt sick about the wanton destruction of such vital habitat. We carefully scanned the other side of the canyon and along the river with binoculars and spotted another drug patch, which stood out boldly, a distinct cultivated square in a shade of green unlike anything surrounding it.

All of us had assumed we would spend all day on this mesa and hike back the way we'd come. But Antonio pointed to a forested area across another steep canyon, and wanted to take us there. My heart sank as I gazed across yet another chasm, deeper than the one we'd crossed that morning. It was an area we had planned to explore on another day. I couldn't help thinking that Antonio wanted to lead us as far away as possible from that opium patch. There wasn't even a real trail going down the canyon from this side. This was the damp, shaded side of the canyon, and we had to push our way through thick vegetation, almost shoulder high in places. Water seeped from the ground on the slope, and we walked along wet, moss-slick rocks and narrow ledges, where the gravel fell away as we stepped. We also had to double back several times because we couldn't get through on the route Antonio had chosen.

By the time we got across the river, it was midafternoon and the sun was scorching hot. We only stopped for a couple of minutes before shouldering our packs and starting to push our way up the dry side of the canyon, with its hot, steep, barren slope of broken scree, hiking back and forth on a tiny switchback trail. For several miles, I had been completely exhausted and light-headed, perhaps falling into a state of heat prostration. My heart alternated between fluttering wildly and hammering like a great pile driver in my chest—*BOOM! BOOM! BOOM!* It took all of my concentration and agility to negotiate the trail, but my strength was quickly fading; somehow, even then, I couldn't admit to myself what was happening. I just kept pushing myself harder, placing one foot in front of the other and ignoring the severe pain spreading through my body. Occasionally, I'd dash several feet up to a bend in the switchback, where I would pause for a couple minutes trying to catch my breath. But it was hopeless. I felt worse and worse with every second and started feeling detached from my body. The sounds around me began to seem muffled and distant, as though I were submerged deep underwater. All I could hear was the incessant pounding, pounding, pounding of my heart hammering in my ears.

When I reached another place where the path vanished for several feet in the broken scree of the steep slope, I paused and drew a deep breath, trying to prepare myself to sprint across it, then burst forward. I only took three steps before a wave of intense nausea swept over me. I retched and instantly my knees buckled and I was falling headfirst . . . and everything went black.

11 ◆ That Was Long Ago, and Now They Are Gone

I came to almost instantly and found myself hugging the trunk of a small tree. Martjan was kneeling above me, holding his broad-brimmed hat over my face to give me shade and asking if I was okay. It took a few minutes to get my bearings and remember where I was and how I got there. By some miracle, I had fallen off the trail headfirst and slid less than ten feet down the steep, rocky slope before the small tree brought me to a halt. If not for the tree, I would have fallen all the way into the arroyo. When I looked back and then forward on the trail, I saw that this tiny tree was the only thing within a hundred feet in either direction that could have kept me from falling to my death. Did my subconscious know I was at the end of my rope and that this was the only place I could fall and survive? Or was it just dumb luck?

Martjan sat down beside me and handed me a small can of papaya juice, which I sipped slowly. He looked worried.

"What happened?" he asked. "Did you slip?"

"No. It was weird . . . like my body just switched off," I said. "I suddenly felt like I was going to throw up, and then I guess I blacked out. I was falling and then I just found myself hugging this tree."

Martjan frowned.

"My heart was beating in a strange way," I said. "It was pounding so hard, it felt like someone was punching me from the inside. And then a few times it just fluttered."

Martjan nodded. "I had something like that happen years ago in Borneo," he said. "It was very hot and humid, and I was pushing myself hard. I didn't drink enough water. I had the same kind of frightening pounding in my chest. I rested and made myself drink a lot of water. But I had that pounding in my chest on and off for six months."

He held out a water container, which I took and drank from greedily. I had been carefully rationing my water—too carefully, as it turned out. I rested for about fifteen more minutes and then got to my feet. I still felt light-headed and held tightly to the tree trunk for a few more minutes, but I wanted to try to get up to the top of the ridge, where I hoped the hiking would be easier. Still concerned, Martjan had gone over to speak with Antonio while I was resting, and they kept looking at me as they talked. When he came back, he gave me his wide-brimmed hat to wear, so I would have some shade on the back of my neck, and he took my cap. He also insisted on carrying my backpack for a while and handed his own pack to Antonio.

I couldn't stop dwelling on what had happened. I felt like I had become a burden to the expedition. What was wrong with me? For my whole life my body had always done what I'd asked of it. Now it was letting me down, and the thought of it cut deeply. But perhaps it was actually I who had let my body down by not knowing or accepting my limitations. At that moment, I realized more fully than at any other time in my life that I could easily die here. The thought was sobering.

I had to rest several more times before reaching the crest of the ridge, but our trek was far from over. We had come back a different way, and it was now closer to walk overland to Las Coloradas than to return to the truck.

Although the last half mile of the hike to the village was on fairly level ground, I must have looked like a zombie, staggering along with a pained, half-dead expression on my face. We had been gone for more than ten hours on our trek, hiking almost

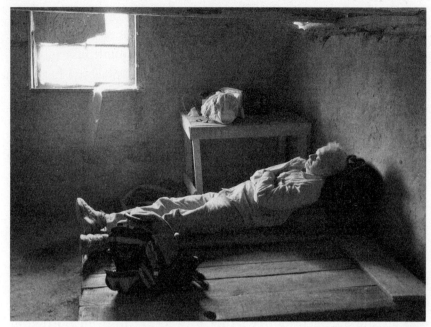

The author in an adobe hut after his dangerous fall. (*Photo by Martjan Lammertink*)

constantly except for that one long rest at the top of the ridge and the brief ones as we were coming up the canyon to help me catch my breath.

As soon as I got back to the adobe hut, I lay down on the wooden planks of my bed platform and fell into the deepest sleep of my life. Martjan snapped a picture of me in the dim natural light of the room as I lay there—like a corpse on a slab at the morgue. I laughed when I saw the image later on his computer.

"The funny part is, that bed's exactly where they would have put me if I'd died out there," I said, and we both laughed.

◆　◆　◆

Martjan had had his own close calls in his work in wild areas. While my blackout had been life-threatening, I'd come close to death a few other times: a fall from a prairie falcon nest cliff had split my climbing helmet and gashed my back in several places; a head-on automobile collision had left me with fractures and deep gashes in my scalp. But Martjan's story of how he had met his Bornean wife, Utami Setiorini, easily outdid my tales with their near-catastrophic experience in the steamy depths of a Borneo jungle.

Martjan had hired Utami, a recent college graduate with a degree in biology, as a field assistant to help him gather data for his project. Martjan is northern European—tall, pale-skinned, light-haired, blue-eyed—and Utami indigenous Bornean—short and dark-skinned with long black hair and deep brown eyes. He was raised Christian, she Muslim. At the time Martjan and Utami met, Martjan was in a relationship with an American woman and Utami was already pledged by her father to wed a man from Borneo in a traditional marriage arrangement. One humid, oppressively hot afternoon, they were walking along a crude dirt trail, recording all of the wildlife they encountered on their study transect.

The sky was quickly darkening, and a torrential thunderstorm threatened to roar through the area any second. As they rounded a corner, they saw a local man cutting up a tree he had just felled with a chainsaw, which was illegal in this protected area. Martjan frowned for an instant but then nodded at the man as he and Utami walked past.

A few minutes later, they spotted an oriental honey buzzard, the first they'd seen. Martjan was pleased, and they paused to watch it with binoculars as it perched in a nearby tree. These unique raptors, which are closely related to kites, feed on the larvae and nests of various wasps, hornets, and bees. Researchers believe their feathers may contain a chemical deterrent that protects them from being attacked by these enraged insects when they feed on their nests—which is fortunate for the honey buzzards but not so good for anyone or anything else who might come along.

This honey buzzard had just finished feasting on a bee nest, and swarms of the angry insects were flying around nearby. A couple of them landed on the back of Martjan's neck, and he reflexively slapped at them, killing them both, which released some of their pheromones—which attract other bees and cause changes in their behavior. Already worked up over the honey buzzard, the bees instantly homed in on Martjan, swarming over him by the hundreds and stinging him repeatedly. And each time another bee stung, the site of the sting would be drenched with additional pheromones, drawing more bees to the attack.

Within seconds Martjan knew that his life was at stake. There was no convenient lake or river into which he could plunge. No escape route. He took off sprinting up the trail, slapping at the bees, trying to brush them off, but more and more of them attacked him—a ghastly nightmare swarm of stinging buzzing bees, trying their best to kill him. He glanced back at Utami—she too was swatting bees—then plunged headlong into the dense jungle vegetation, desperately hoping to find some sanctuary to burrow down into and escape the bees' fury.

But even through the panic of his desperate situation, the logical part of Martjan's mind kicked in and evaluated the situation. In a sudden flash of clarity, he saw he was doing the worst thing possible. It was suicide to run blindly through the jungle. The bee stings would soon overcome him; by then thousands of bees covered him and hundreds had already stung him. He was reeling from the effects. If he collapsed there, no one would find him until it was too late. On the other hand, if he went running back down the trail, someone might be able to help. And then there was Utami. What was to become of her? She might be just as bad off as he was by now. He should be running in the opposite direction, trying to get as close to camp as possible before he passed out.

Martjan raced back to Utami as fast as he could run. By then, she had collapsed to the ground and thousands of bees were stinging her. He grasped her by the arm and urged her to get up and run back to camp, several miles away. She got to her feet and they staggered away down the trail together.

As they spotted the man they'd seen earlier cutting wood, they screamed to him for help. He looked up, squinting his eyes to see them better. They looked like monsters with huge brown heads covered from head to foot with angry stinging bees.

When he realized what was happening, the man dived into the shelter of the rain forest, hiding in dense foliage to avoid becoming a target of the bees himself, but called out as Martjan and Utami ran past, telling them to take the metal fuel can next to his chain saw and douse themselves with gasoline. Martjan quickly unscrewed the cap and poured the pungent liquid over Utami and himself. Then they fell to their knees, gasping for air and shuddering. Just then a deafening clap of thunder broke overhead, unleashing a short but torrential downpour as they sat in the mud, sodden to the skin with gasoline and rainwater.

As the rain began to ease, Martjan looked at Utami and saw that her lips were turning blue. A moment later, her eyes rolled and she collapsed backward into the mud. Martjan picked up her hand and held it tightly.

As she lay in the mud, her body poisoned by the toxic stings of thousands of bees, Utami felt her life slipping away. She had a classic near-death experience, seeing a powerful light beaming ahead of her through the darkness, offering warmth and an end to her suffering. She felt herself moving quickly toward it and made no effort to resist its inexorable pull. But something outside of her was holding her back, preventing her from completing the passage to the light. It was Martjan's hand, the only sensation she felt. And it kept her alive. She opened her eyes and saw his blue eyes gazing down at her. And the two of them bonded in that instant. They knew they would be together forever, come what may.

It was not immediately certain that Martjan and Utami would survive the bee stings. The man finally came out of hiding and helped them walk back to his simple shack, where he cared for them for days, washing the gasoline and mud from their hair and skin; plucking the stingers from them, which were as thick as body hair, using the edge of a machete to shave away as many as he could. The first evening was a sleepless nightmare of vomiting and diarrhea as their bodies reacted to the toxic stings. But as the sun rose the next morning, they were still alive, though the glands on their necks bulged, and they felt like they never wanted to eat another meal.

After they fully recovered, Martjan went to visit Utami's father and threw himself on the man's mercy, explaining the deep bond he had with his daughter. Her father was sympathetic and liked Martjan. But in the strict Muslim culture of Borneo, there is no such thing as casual dating or other ways to get to know a prospective spouse. It's marriage or nothing, and to even be considered, Martjan had to become a Muslim, which he gladly did for her.

Marriage ceremonies are huge in Borneo. People traditionally invite virtually everyone they've ever had any connection with, so Utami's guests came from far and wide in the surrounding area and numbered about fifteen hundred. The Dutch contingent was only Martjan's mother and father, who flew there from the Netherlands to attend the ceremony.

People in Borneo generally dress in the traditional attire of their tribes for the marriage ceremony, which Utami did. So Martjan donned the attire of the Netherlands tribe—the classic floppy hat, baggy blue pants, and wooden shoes of a Dutch boy.

I asked Martjan what he'd thought of Utami's story of the white light at the end of the dark passage.

"Well . . . of course, I think these things have a physiological basis," said Martjan, "but . . ." and his voice trailed off.

◆　◆　◆

When I awoke the evening after my blackout, I had an overpowering thirst. I guzzled a quart of water, started on a second, and felt myself quickly bouncing back. It was such a relief not to be hiking. Martjan cooked another odd pasta dish for dinner—sort of a Dutch-Italian spaghetti dish. I chopped up a couple of onions and some cloves of garlic, and also cut some slices of American cheese into thin strips to put on top of it. Martjan opened a can of sardines with tomato paste and mixed them with the onions and garlic to make the sauce, and we poured the entire strange concoction over the spaghetti noodles—bizarre but tasty to a starving man who had just survived a killer trek through the Sierra. I ate seconds.

After dinner we walked in the dark back to the casa of Antonio's parents, Nicolesa and Salvador, to show them Rhein's *pitoreal* film. Another two-room adobe with a hard-packed dirt floor, their hut was in far better shape than ours, with more homey features: pots and pans hanging on the walls and an old calendar with a pretty picture of a scenic mountain vista. Nicolesa's worktable was draped in a blue tablecloth and held a stack of thick, just-made tortillas and a bowl of large corn kernels. Their children and grandchildren crammed into the main room, sitting in darkness except for the light of the fire in the wood-burning stove. Our headlamps lit up the place as we stepped inside. Nicolesa cleared a spot on her table for Martjan's computer, and Salvador brought some short, round, hand-woven stools for us to sit on.

We started by showing them Dick Heintzelman's pictures as

the computer booted up. They all recognized Los Pilares and were amused at how old the pictures were. And they were completely delighted by the film of the *pitoreal*, especially the part where the bird's crest bounced jauntily as it moved up the trunk, foraging. (I wondered if this was the first time any of them had seen something like a film or television.) They thanked us profusely as we left, and Nicolesa generously gave us all the tortillas she had made, wrapped in a white linen cloth with flowers hand-embroidered on it. I took some ibuprofen to ease my pain-wracked body and drank a quart of water before conking out for the night in another deep slumber.

◆ ◆ ◆

Most days we got under way well before dawn and arrived back in camp after dark. But one day Antonio couldn't guide us because he and every adult in Las Coloradas, Guacamayita, and the other nearby communities were going to a meeting in Taxicaringa to parley with a rival group. His eleven-year-old son, Rubén, would guide us instead. This didn't give us much confidence, but Martjan thought it would be a good idea to take an easier trek and recover our strength. We would return to the place where we'd heard (and Oscar had seen) a pair of military macaws a few days earlier. Perhaps we would have another flyby, and anyway, the more we hung around in this remote area watching and listening, the more likely we were to encounter any rare wildlife that might be there. Martjan went through his double-knock protocol as soon as we reached the edge of the canyon, and we all sat in silence, listening for a response that never came.

Rubén was a nice kid. He wore a thin yellow nylon jacket and dark pants with only huaraches on his bare feet, even though it was probably in the low thirties Fahrenheit when we began our hike. He followed me closely, and whenever I stopped to write in my notebook, sat close beside me, seemingly fascinated by what I was doing. I gave him some chocolate, which he savored, eating it a little at a time and closing his eyes as it melted in his mouth.

After nearly two weeks in Mexico, I was really missing my own wife and children. I felt as if they were on the other side of a vast chasm, impossible to bridge. At times I wondered if I would ever see them again. I wanted to know they were safe. Time and a long, scary drive out of the mountains stood between us.

Martjan was gone for a couple of hours, and when he returned, he went on another long hike, this time with Rubén. They walked all over the high mesa we had explored two days earlier. I walked through most of it again, too, but I stopped for an hour, sitting at the edge of a cliff with my legs dangling. We finally returned to Las Coloradas toward evening. The kids in the village were running wild with no parents to control them. Some clambered around on top of a new log cabin being built in the center of the village. They ranged in age from infants to a few in their early teens, but all of them were playing with each other. Some young children carried toddlers and even babies around with them, with no parents around to cramp their enjoyment. Others chased each other excitedly or played ball in an open dirt field. As it got dark, the children lit a huge, smoky bonfire and took turns jumping over the flames and through the thick smoke, laughing and shrieking with delight.

Rubén came over as we cooked dinner and ended up eating with us. I think he felt like one of us. His little brother (who looked just like him) kept climbing up and peering through the little window at us and laughing.

◆　◆　◆

We woke before dawn the next morning, but no one was stirring at Antonio's casa. Normally, the villagers got up before us and had a fire going and breakfast cooking in their homes while we were eating bowls of cereal. We tried honking the truck's horn, to no avail. The adults had gotten home sometime after midnight, and everyone—men, women, and children—had worn themselves out. It didn't matter. We had already decided to try something different today, exploring the area near Guacamayita where Rhein had actually taken his film, doing double knocks and examining the area thoroughly.

Some of the sites where we ran through the double-knock protocol were nice, with good-looking habitat and huge pines, among which were also numerous large stumps. The big pines may have been spared to act as seed trees.

We had to scramble up steep, rocky slopes at most of the places where we did double knocks. The second one, near Los Pilares, was at an altitude of 9,310 feet. After he did the double knocks there, Martjan played the ivory-billed woodpecker *kent* calls and drew an angry response from three northern flickers, a smaller woodpecker species. They called loudly, and one of them drummed on a big snag.

Although it was sunny, a cold wind blew, chilling us through our winter coats. After going through the double knocks in a few other areas, we decided to drive to Guacamayita to get some more supplies. Manuel and Oscar were desperate to get some more tortillas, and I wanted some, too. But the little store was closed, and there was no one around to open it. We saw one man we hadn't met before. He seemed nervous at first, but when we asked him to give our *saludos* to Carlos, he calmed down and became much friendlier.

We decided to drive to Las Espinas, the tiny village where we had stopped with Carlos on the way up from Durango—where he had gotten out of his truck, white as a sheet, terrified by the armed men in the other vehicle. We were a little nervous about driving alone outside our usual area, but we figured at least the village was inside Carlos's safe zone. But as we left Guacamayita, we saw a lone man walking up the dirt road. He was middle-aged with a bushy moustache and a cowboy hat. Manuel suddenly said, "Ai," and let out a quiet whistle as he saw the AK-47 slung casually over the man's shoulder. There he was, out for a midday Saturday stroll in the sleepy village of Guacamayita, armed to the teeth.

Las Espinas turned out to be much farther away than we thought and the store didn't have any tortillas, so Manuel and Oscar bought a bag of corn flour to make their own. We were nervous as we made our way back to Las Coloradas, sneaking quietly through Guacamayita and then driving as fast as we could go on the terrible roads.

◆ ◆ ◆

We spent a final night in the adobe casa, about which I had mixed feelings. The first time I had walked inside, it seemed like a smelly goat shed—which it was—but now that we were leaving I would miss it.

Sometime after midnight, we were awakened by a loud ruckus and clattering. A couple of burros had come snorting and scrambling through the yard, walking over boards and various metal cans and other junk. I chased them away once, but they soon came back. Shortly after they finally left for good, raindrops started falling hard, clattering loudly on the tin roof and dripping down on me, so the night was mostly shot for sleeping.

In the morning, we took a long, bouncy ride in the truck to the new area, one of the most promising places Martjan had mapped out on Google Earth. Antonio went with us to introduce us to our new guide, a Tepehuán named Rafael, whom we planned to meet at his cabin. We had piled all of our gear—except for the two drums of gasoline, which Antonio said we could store beside the adobe hut—into the camper shell on the back of our pickup truck. I crammed myself back there, too, with Oscar and one of Antonio's younger sons, who was only eight. It was impossible to get comfortable. We had to lie flat on our backs on top of our piled-up gear, which kept shifting as the truck went bouncing down the badly eroded, rocky road. After a short time, we stopped for a minute. Antonio had left his axe leaning against a tree somewhere in the woods near there, and he wanted his son to find it and carry it all the way back home. He had amazing faith in his children's ability to find their way home safely. No doubt it had been the same with him when he was growing up. The innate navigational abilities of the Tepehuanes and their endurance are amazing.

We finally reached Rafael's rancho, a rustic log cabin with no amenities. Short and thin with a sparse beard, Rafael seemed like a good man, quiet and unsmiling but thoroughly dependable, in his thirties with six children. He wore blue jeans, a drab nylon coat, a dirty gray felt cowboy hat, and the ubiquitous huarache sandals of Mexico, even in the winter. My own feet were freezing most of the time, despite wearing thick socks and hiking boots.

After introducing us to Rafael, Antonio set off on foot, traveling overland back to his home—about a two-hour walk away on the network of mountain trails.

We had intended to drive closer to the site where we planned to search for the next three or four days, but Rafael told us we could go only a short distance farther in the truck, so we pitched our camp in a nice area near a spring, with pine trees and plenty of branches lying around for firewood. There were also a lot of rocks we could use to encircle the fire and make a cooking stand for the big round piece of flat iron Rafael had loaned us for cooking.

We pitched our tents, got settled in at camp, and then headed to an overlook to take a peek at some of the places we would soon be exploring. We drove on a rough old logging road but could go only

Martjan Lammertink (*at right*) and Tepehuán guide Rafael search a remote mesa forest for signs of imperial woodpeckers. (*Photo by Tim Gallagher*)

so far before we had to get out and hike—and it was never easy to hike around there. I had come to dread going downhill, because I knew I'd have to walk back up again, always tough at this altitude.

When we got back to camp, we built a makeshift fireplace to brew some coffee. Because we didn't have a coffeepot or filter cone, we just put a couple of spoons of coffee in each cup and poured boiling water over it. When we added milk, the grounds floated on top, and we could skim most of them off with a spoon. But we still had to do some filtering with our teeth and a lot of spitting to get the grounds out of our mouths. Still, it was better than instant coffee.

Manuel and Oscar started playing Mexican music with the truck's CD player, cranking it up loud and leaving the windows open so they could hear it in camp. This bothered Martjan, because he preferred hearing the sounds of nature, but in some ways I enjoyed it. The songs perfectly captured the spirit and atmosphere of Mexico.

◆ ◆ ◆

The next morning, three young goats with reddish-brown fur strode into camp and started nosing around, looking for things to eat. They were curious, and we had to watch them closely so they wouldn't steal anything. A small, shy dog also came by, as light on her feet as a cat as she stepped noiselessly over the leaves, pine needles, and sticks. She had long fur, black along her back and reddish tan everywhere else, with ears like a bear. I wished I could have taken her home with me.

Later we drove to Taxicaringa on one of those terrifying roads for which the Sierra Madre is so famous. At first, it was just a bad road—or really no road at all—as we bounced along through the woods and down a rocky arroyo. But then it turned into a horrendous dirt track running along the edge of a cliff. Our truck made the downhill drive especially terrifying, as the brakes groaned constantly, sometimes making a disturbing grinding sound.

When we were partway down the side of the canyon, Rafael asked Manuel to stop the truck briefly, then pointed over the edge to some wreckage far below. Manuel whistled, then pounded on the back window to alert those of us sitting in the bed of the truck.

"*Camioneta*," he yelled, pointing down at a small pickup truck, lying on its top halfway down the sheer slope. Rafael told us the brakes had gone out when the people were driving down to the village of Taxicaringa, and the truck went off the edge. Everyone was killed.

As we drove on, the spectacular canyon of the Rio Taxicaringa opened up before us. If this were the United States, the area would have become like Sedona, Arizona—a playground for artists, latte sippers, and the wealthy. But here the canyon is impossibly remote, almost entirely detached from the modern world, like a remnant of another century. Here the Tepehuanes live pretty much as they did when Christopher Columbus landed in the New World more than half a millennium ago: huddled beside pinewood fires in crude huts made of adobe bricks they formed from the local clay and dried in the sun or in cabins built of pine logs hewn from the surrounding forest. A scattering of homes with tin roofs and a handful of beater pickup trucks were among their few bows to modernity.

The pretty village of Taxicaringa with its church and adobe casas lay a short distance below us, but we skirted it and headed instead to some outlying ranchos in the canyon to look for some elderly Tepehuanes who we'd heard might know about the *pitoreal*.

We found Virginia (pronounced *veer-heen-ya*) living at a rancho, just up the steep hill from Taxicaringa. She looked to be in her late seventies, with long, straight gray hair tied in a ponytail that hung down the center of her back. She had lived for years with her husband in an isolated rancho called El Hornito, right at the gateway of one of the places we would be exploring, but she had moved closer to Taxicaringa a few years earlier after her husband passed away.

Several adobe huts stood clustered together, some with large tin cans filled with pink flowers on the windowsills. As we stood at the edge of the property, talking to Virginia across a rustic wooden fence, several other women peered shyly at us through glassless windows and open doorways. They all looked remarkably similar to her, with long expressionless faces, straight hair, and traditional Tepehuán dresses reaching almost to their feet, even though they were decades younger than Virginia, with coal-black hair and eyes so dark you could not distinguish their irises from their pupils.

No men were around, just a wide-eyed group of curious children and one small boy, perhaps only three or four years old, who rode wildly about on a horse, jumping over piles of debris and squealing with delight.

Virginia nodded as we asked her about the birds and described them accurately as "*pinto*" (black and white) and said that the black on their plumage had a bluish sheen at times if the light struck it a certain way. But she answered most of our questions with the same refrain: "That was long ago, and now they are gone."

When asked why she thought they had vanished, she answered, "*¿Quién sabe?*" ("Who knows?").

We stood for a time at the fence with her, trying to ask the questions in a different way, to get her to fill in more of the details about this bird, but it was hopeless. We finally thanked her and walked slowly back to our truck, feeling the dark eyes of Virginia and her relatives still locked on us until we drove away out of sight along the canyon edge.

The next person we visited was an elderly man named Gregorio, who lived a couple of miles away, up a steep drive. It was drizzling steadily as we stopped our truck beside a small dirt footpath that led up to his casa. A man sat outside in the rain on a small hand-woven stool, tending a pot of water over an open fire, and greeted the five of us happily, shaking hands with each of us before fetching us some stools and inviting us to sit down. Just as at Virginia's home, several generations of his family were present—the women lean, with straight black hair tied back, wearing long skirts. We sat beside the fire with him in front of a piled rock wall, where several children played.

A jovial, talkative man, Gregorio laughed constantly. It turned out he was Nicolesa's brother, and they were amazingly similar in temperament and outlook. Obviously several years older than Nicolesa, he was a little unsure exactly when he was born.

"I have a paper that says I am fifty," he said, grinning.

We all laughed. He looked much closer to eighty than fifty, with short-cropped gray hair and teeth nearly worn away.

As we spoke with Gregorio, I suddenly noticed three men walking through an orchard behind the casa. All were dressed in black, and one of them carried a rifle. When they saw us, they quickly turned back and ducked out of view. I alerted Martjan in English—which no one but the two of us spoke—and his eyes widened for an instant. But we continued interviewing Gregorio, hoping for the best. The rain drizzled constantly as we spoke with him, and we got wetter and wetter.

A few minutes later, a loud gunshot rang out from behind the house. Then one of the women emerged from behind the casa, carrying a big red rooster by the feet. It had just been killed, and it fluttered wildly in its death throes, spattering droplets of blood all around as she held it upside down by its feet. The rifle had obviously been used to kill the chicken and had never been a threat to us. The men were probably frightened for a minute when they saw us, because they didn't know who we were and thought they might get in trouble over the rifle.

Like Nicolesa, Gregorio knew the *pitoreal* well and said the birds were once quite common in this part of the Sierra Madre. He would encounter a group of a dozen or so of them, and then several kilometers away, another group that size. E. W. Nelson's 1898 article in *The Auk* had also mentioned sometimes seeing groups of eight or nine imperial woodpeckers together like that and then finding more as he traveled farther.

Gregorio added a disturbing detail: a forester in the 1950s had told the local people that the *pitoreales* were destroying valuable timber and should be killed. And he provided them with poison to smear on the birds' foraging trees.

Martjan and I were stunned to hear this. Carl Lumholtz had

written in the 1890s that imperial woodpeckers would often feed on the same huge pine tree for two weeks at a time, until it finally fell over. So smearing poison on one of these trees would certainly be a ruthlessly effective way to wipe out an entire group of the birds. Other roving groups of imperial woodpeckers might move in and feed on the same tree. The thought was chilling. In addition to the destruction of the *pitoreal*'s habitat and random shooting by people who were curious or thoughtless or wanted to eat the birds, logging interests may have engaged in a wholesale systematic destruction of the species, which they claimed was damaging or destroying timber, even though the trees the birds peeled and hacked into were already infested with huge beetle larvae.

Gregorio's story reminded me of Elvin Whetten's sighting of six dead imperial woodpeckers piled in front of a sawmill as he rode past on his horse in the 1950s, far to the north of here in the Sierra Azul of Chihuahua. It all suddenly made sense to me: logging companies had paid people to kill imperial woodpeckers, take them back to the sawmill, and collect a bounty. The logging interests—perhaps including the state forestry department—had killed off the bulk of the imperial woodpeckers. Logging companies had cut down most of the ivory-billed woodpecker's habitat in the United States and killed them off indirectly; here, they had poisoned and killed the birds directly.

My evidence was circumstantial, of course, but these events took place at roughly the same time in two widely separated parts of the Sierra Madre in two different Mexican states. When added to other accounts of killed imperial woodpeckers—such as the twelve birds Fritz Hilton reported killed in this very area the year before Rhein's first expedition—the conclusion was convincing. It's conceivable that the poisoning and shooting had also happened in the other areas between the Sierra Azul and Guacamayita.

Jim Tanner had written about the birds' pattern of disappearance in his 1964 article in *The Auk*. A logging camp would be established in a remote area of old-growth forest and, within a year or so, the imperial woodpeckers would vanish, even though there were then still plenty of big pines around. He surmised that the logging roads opened up these areas to subsistence hunters, who were killing off the big woodpeckers for food.

I'd always had trouble completely accepting this theory. To a subsistence hunter, one animal is probably as good as another: a jay, a turkey, a rabbit, a woodpecker—they were only a food source, one no better than another. So it's doubtful subsistence hunting could have eliminated the birds. A far more likely scenario is that logging interests deliberately killed off the imperial woodpeckers, directing and supporting a large-scale extermination campaign, the same way other people had finished off the Mexican wolves and grizzlies—and the Apaches.

Poison could have been *the* major factor in the crash of the imperial woodpecker and why, now, even though we had to physically claw our way up to these isolated, uncut ridges, we still didn't find any *pitoreales*. The birds had been already long gone from this area, and perhaps from most of the Sierra Madre. Although I don't personally believe that the imperial woodpecker is extinct yet—I find some of the recent sightings to be credible—at that moment the tragic thought dawned on me that it may well be too late to save them.

◆ ◆ ◆

When we finally got back to camp, we started a fire, and all of us stood around trying to warm up in the endless light drizzle. Luckily, pinewood burns well even when wet.

As we stood by the fire, I watched Manuel fill an empty plastic bottle with water and put it right into the burning hot coals at the center of the fire, pushing it in quickly with the toe of his boot. At first the water kept the bottle cool enough to keep it from melting, but eventually it started to elongate and finally become completely misshapen. I guess that meant it was ready, because Manuel dragged it out of the flames with a stick. The bottle was half melted and leaking in a couple of places, but Manuel carefully unscrewed the cap and poured the scalding hot liquid into a Cup-a-Soup container. He let it stand for a few minutes, then mixed up the contents and ate them. I cringed to think about all of the terrible chemicals released into the water by the melting plastic, but perhaps they were no worse than the chemicals the hot soup leached from its Styrofoam container.

Just before dark we drove up a rough track to a spot where we could look down over the high, forested fingers of pine forest we still hoped to explore. We could see Virginia's abandoned adobe casa, El Hornito, far below, on a road no longer passable, so we would have to hike all the way down to it and back up again on an adjacent finger. Virginia had told us she would see one or two *pitoreales* around here—not the big groups Gregorio had seen. But the pines in the high mesa forest where Gregorio grew up had been much larger in the old days than the ones in the area near Virginia's old rancho. The soil is much rockier and more arid in these unlogged fingers, so the trees have never grown as large there.

That evening as we sat around the campfire, a Tepehuán couple walked past on the trail that runs beside our camp, leading four fully loaded pack mules, followed by a young dog that looked like a floppy-eared German shepherd. The woman wore a long, dark-blue skirt. These were not the first—or last—people we would encounter there. The trail outside our camp was a major thoroughfare for foot travelers and people with mules en route to and from Taxicaringa and Guacamayita.

12 ◆ You Will Get There at Best

It rained hard most of the night, and all of our tents leaked, leaving our sleeping bags sodden by morning. Instead of our usual predawn departure, we lingered around camp till well past daybreak, waiting to see if the weather would change. The rain eased to a drizzle, but every so often a sudden cloudburst would drench everything again. Rafael chopped some wood and started a fire about a hundred feet outside camp. (I'm not sure why he didn't build it in our usual fire spot near our tents.) He piled up some wood behind a large eight-foot-long pine log to keep the fire out of the wind and rain, but part of this log was burning, too.

We finally decided to start exploring the new area in spite of the cold, rainy weather. We put on our backpacks and walked a short distance west before plunging into a deep arroyo with thick vegetation. It was a tough slog—a long, winding trek downward before we finally stopped at midmorning for a double-knock session. It was nice to take a breather. We'd had to scramble up higher after first going down. The conditions quickly worsened as we started hiking again, following faithfully behind Rafael. We didn't seem to be on a trail at all as we pushed through soaking wet, waist-high vegetation along the side of an extremely steep mountainside. And then we had to fight our way upward again, before finally stopping for another double-knock session. We were all physically drained, and then the rain, which had eased somewhat, began pouring down again, great cascading sheets of water soaking us to the skin once more.

◆   ◆   ◆

The next morning, the weather turned frigid: clear and windy. As the sky began to lighten, the horizon glowed crimson and menacing.

"Red skies at morning, sailors take warning," I said to Martjan as we stood shivering beside the campfire. He didn't give the old saying much credence.

"Perhaps we're just seeing the last of the old weather front passing," he said. It did look clear and bright outside.

After some coffee and a quick bowl of cereal, we were off, scrambling down once more to explore another isolated ridge projecting away from the main part of the mountain range. A short time later, we hiked past Virginia's old rancho, some of which lay in ruin, about as far off the beaten path as you could go. An old adobe still stood, as well as a cabin and some outbuildings. A profusion of flowers bloomed beside the adobe, despite the cold weather, and I imagined Virginia as a young woman planting them there. But that was long ago . . .

We finally rested at the top of a spectacular mesa, amid a stand of tall pines, though there were also a few stumps where some had been cut years earlier. It was not yet eight o'clock, and we had already hiked a long way from camp, mostly downhill. I was starting to feel a bone-deep fatigue, a cumulative exhaustion. I could also see it in the eyes of Oscar and Manuel—the pained expressions, the grim set of their jaws. It was impossible to be happy, carefree kids under these conditions. They rarely smiled. Martjan was the only one I couldn't read. He always wore the same stoic expression, no matter how difficult and tiring the situation we faced.

Always methodical, Martjan kept going through the double-knock protocol again and again, followed each time by playing ivory-bill *kent* calls at prescribed intervals. He never seemed to get discouraged, at least outwardly. For me, this ritual held a great sadness, playing sounds that may not have been heard in those woods for decades. It seemed so empty there without the *pitoreal*. I thought of Aldo Leopold's description of the native thick-billed parrot as a *numenon*—the "imponderable essence" of a place, without which the landscape would seem empty, like the north woods without the loon . . . or the Sierra Madre without the *pitoreal*.

It was eleven o'clock, and the sun blazed overhead. A strong wind was rising, whistling louder and louder through the canyon. As he put his double knocker and other equipment back into his pack, Martjan glanced up at Rafael. *"Uno mas kilómetro,"* he said. We shouldered our backpacks and headed for the next double-knock point.

We reached the farthest ridge just past noon and stood staring down at the spectacular chasm before us. Across the great barranca we could see the other area we had viewed on Google Earth and had wanted so much to explore—the land of the Zetas, almost certain death for us if we ventured there.

As we gazed across the canyon with our binoculars, scanning carefully, we noticed a disturbing sight: two crude dirt roads bulldozed through the previously virgin forest high up the canyon wall on the Zetas' side. Five years earlier, when the Google Earth satellite photographs had been taken, the area was completely without roads. We compared the Google maps we'd printed out with the scene in front of us, and there was no mistake. Rafael confirmed that the roads were new. Virtually as we watched, more of the Sierra Madre wilderness was vanishing.

There was still a lot of great country. We had hiked past big trees earlier in the day, including one pine we measured at eight feet in circumference. Even so, these trees were nowhere near as large as those that used to grow on the broad, flat mesas of the Sierra Madre with their rich soil. Yet this natural, uncut forest had

From left to right, Martjan Lammertink, Manuel Escarcega, and Tepehuán guide Rafael look across the vast chasm of Taxicaringa Canyon. The paramilitary drug cartel Los Zetas controls the area on the other side. (*Photo by Tim Gallagher*)

plenty of standing dead pines and giants that had already toppled over—plenty of forage for woodpeckers; the way that it should be. We saw one standing dead pine that held an acorn woodpecker granary, where something had sheared off the bark, bringing the acorns tumbling down—just as old Don Pedro Fimbres had described a *pitoreal* doing while the tiny woodpeckers protested. This was one of the few encouraging signs we saw on the entire expedition. But we also saw some dead pines that were untouched by woodpeckers. If there had been any imperial woodpeckers nearby, surely they would have foraged on them.

We decided to take a break and cook some food on top of a rocky promontory at the end of the mesa. We gathered pine limbs as well as small twigs and dry pine needles to get the fire going, and soon had a roaring blaze. Rafael had brought along a can of frijoles, and I had a stack of purple tortillas in my pack that his wife had made before we left that morning. He popped the can open slightly and stuck it right in the fire.

We sat basking in the warm Sierra Madre sun, eating until all the food was gone, and then lay down for an all-too-brief siesta. Our reveries were suddenly broken by the loud cackle of parrots as three military macaws—the first Martjan and I had ever seen—flew across the barranca and cruised along the far canyon wall giving us plenty of great views with our binoculars before they disappeared. This was shortly before two in the afternoon, and we had already reached our farthest point for the day. Now we had only the long trek back to camp to look forward to and, as usual, it would be a hard one. To reach the spot where we ate lunch, we had dropped down to just above seven thousand feet in altitude, and our camp was well above nine thousand feet.

We stopped to go through the double-knock protocol at three o'clock, and I was grateful to have a chance to catch my breath. I knew it would the last time for the day. As Martjan pounded on the box yet again, *BAM-bam*, and waited for a response, Oscar and Manuel started talking loudly in the background. The same thing had happened earlier in the day as the two of them spoke with Rafael.

"Keep silent!" he had snapped, which shut Rafael up for the rest of the day, but Oscar and Manuel could not seem to keep quiet for more than two or three minutes at a time anymore. They'd obviously given up on the *pitoreal*. This time Martjan exploded, dressing them down sternly. They looked crushed. Rafael just looked away, his face inscrutable as ever. Martjan later apologized.

"You know, I don't believe any more than you do that there are any imperial woodpeckers here," he said. "But we've gone to a lot

233

of trouble and expense and faced many dangers to get here, so we must take what we are doing seriously."

An hour later three flocks of thick-billed parrots, perhaps numbering as many as forty birds, flew over, but I felt so sick, I didn't even lift my binoculars to watch them. I took a few steps more and spotted an empty box of .22 rifle shells, which threw me into a deep funk. Even in this most remote of places there was no sanctuary, no place for the *pitoreales* to avoid being shot or poisoned or having their habitat obliterated.

It was five thirty when we finally reached El Hornito, and I was as physically spent as I've ever been in my life—worse than the day before; even worse than the day I blacked out—and I still had the same killer hike in front of me that had done me in a day earlier, a 330-meter altitude ascent in two kilometers yet to conquer.

By the time I reached the last slope, I was so drenched in sweat I looked like I'd just plunged into a river. Every step filled me with pain. I'd already told everyone to go ahead without me, and staggered on alone, stopping every ten feet, holding on to convenient trees as I struggled to catch my breath. When I reached a point just thirty feet below the level of the camp, I rushed the rest of the way up in one burst, pushing myself beyond all limits, then collapsed onto a rock, panting and nearly passing out again. I finally made myself go to my tent and change out of my sweat-drenched clothes. I hit the sack by eight o'clock.

There was no way I had another trek like this left in me on this expedition.

◆　◆　◆

The dawn broke crisp and clear, but for once we slept in for a couple of hours. We had decided to postpone the last major trek until the next morning and rest. I still felt awful. Martjan encouraged

Oscar and Manuel to go with Rafael to a thick-billed parrot nest tree he had mentioned the day before when we saw the flocks of them fly past. Martjan was going to hike around alone all day with his sound-recording equipment and camera. He said not to expect him back until dark. At seven thirty, everyone put on their packs and prepared to leave—except me. I was tempted to go along with Rafael, Oscar, and Manuel, because it would be easier than the trek we had taken the day before. But I had learned to distrust these Tepehuán supermen when estimating the time, distance, and level of hardship of a journey. I decided to stay in camp all day doing various chores.

I gathered firewood on and off throughout the day to keep the blaze going, tidied the camp, and refilled our two large five-gallon water bottles down the trail at the spring. But mostly I sat on a folding chair in the warm sunlight. I just wanted to survive the expedition and get back to my family. I had set my sights homeward.

◆ ◆ ◆

Rafael, Oscar, and Manuel trudged back into camp about five thirty in the afternoon. Only Rafael looked fresh. The other two were as thoroughly thrashed as I'd ever seen them, and Oscar was limping, having strained his Achilles tendon; Manuel's cold was much worse, so he immediately went to sleep in the back of the truck.

Martjan strode back to camp well past sundown, just as it was getting completely dark. We ate a simple meal of frijoles and tortillas, and Martjan, Oscar, and I huddled around the campfire for a couple more hours. The temperature outside was plummeting, and we all wore our winter coats and fleece hats with headlights strapped on top, turning them on only when we needed to see what we were doing—to stir the frijoles or heat up another of the tortillas Rafael's wife had made. But mostly we just sat around in the dark, talking.

Oscar told us about their long, brutal hike that day. Rafael had walked them past two poppy plantations, about ten-by-twenty yards each in size. One of them was probably the patch we had looked down on that first day with Antonio. The first was unattended, with plants too small to harvest. But at the second patch, the opium poppy plants were nearly mature, and a young Tepehuán, barely older than Manuel, was watering them with a black plastic hose, gravity fed from a spring. The boy was friendly, and the four of them sat together for a while, talking and smoking Pall Mall cigarettes as the sun slowly warmed up the chill morning air.

When I heard this story, I was glad I didn't go on the hike with them. It's one thing to have a couple of young Mexicans walk past your opium poppy patch and quite another for a gringo with a camera to do the same. But even though Oscar and Manuel had a pleasant time with the young Tepehuán, I wondered what would happen when he went back and told his father, his employer, or whoever else owned the poppy field. Oscar and Manuel probably told the boy where we were camped, and we would be easy to find if anyone came looking for us.

The only thing we had going for us was the goodwill of Carlos. We were depending on him to get us out of the mountains safely. He had told us to go back to Durango one day earlier than we'd planned and said he would escort us. But we had run into Carlos, driving the other way as we were on our way to Taxicaringa, and he asked us when we were leaving, as though he had forgotten. We reminded him, but our plans suddenly seemed sketchy. In Mexico, things are forgotten. There was a good chance we would have to drive out of the mountains alone on Friday, and the thought terrified me.

The stars shone bright in a clear sky that evening, and a bone-chilling cold descended. We had only one more night to go until Friday. It felt like a long time.

The skies clouded before dawn, and it started feeling less cold. I could easily have gone to sleep at that point, but then I heard Martjan snapping twigs to kindle the morning fire, so I put on my coat, fleece hat, and headlamp, and walked outside. It was calm, just the slightest breath of wind, and the world was silent. Oscar got up a minute later, and the three of us stood around the fire, trying to warm up. Manuel still slept soundly in the back of the truck.

"So, what about today's hike?" asked Martjan.

I glanced down at the fire and was silent for moment.

"I can't do it," I said finally. "I don't have one more long trek in me." I looked at him. "I'd only hold everyone up."

Martjan nodded. Then Oscar said he wasn't going either. His ankle was still bothering him. Martjan grimaced for an instant, then went to the back of the truck and spoke with Manuel, who told him that he, too, would be staying in camp. He had a bad cold and felt awful.

We all were at the end of our ropes, and only Martjan had the willpower and determination to press ahead. Rafael walked into camp a short time later, carrying his machete and a hand-woven bag full of fresh tortillas. Martjan quietly shouldered his backpack, the double-knock apparatus sticking out of the top, and slung his camera bag bandolero-style across his back. I wished him luck. No one deserved to see a *pitoreal* more than he. Then the two of them walked off down the steep trail, vanishing in the predawn darkness.

◆　◆　◆

That afternoon, a Tepehuán man wearing a white straw hat and a colorful woven shoulder bag walked past, with the obligatory machete in his hand. He was very old, with most of his teeth missing, and led three mules, a couple of them packed high with belongings and the other ridden by a Tepehuán woman and some young children. I'm not sure if they were his children or perhaps grandchildren. He stopped to say *buenas tardes* and asked if we would give him a cigarette. Oscar and Manuel had been inside the back of the truck all day, playing cards and listening to Mexican music CDs, but I asked them to come outside. Oscar handed the man a Pall Mall, and we had a conversation while he smoked, inhaling deeply from the cigarette. He said they had just walked all the way up from Taxicaringa and still had a long way to go. Apparently he had heard about us. He asked if we were the men looking for *pájaros* (birds) and then mentioned the *pitoreal*. He said he had often seen them around there, though not for at least fifty years. He kept saying how big the birds were, and he broke off a stick almost four inches in length and held it up to show me the size of their bills. The birds had been hunted with .22 rifles, he said. After smoking the cigarette down to a tiny nub, he snuffed out the butt and then strode off down the road to catch up with the woman and the children.

Rafael walked into camp shortly after six o'clock, and for the first time, he seemed tired. He had Martjan's double-knock box stuffed into his little woven backpack and was carrying the double-knock striker in one hand and his trusty machete in the other. He leaned the apparatus against the tree and stood with us for a while beside the fire, warming his hands. He told us Martjan was still looking for *pájaros*.

After Rafael left, I picked up Martjan's double knocker and held it over the fire. "No mas *bam-bam!*" I said, with a wild look in my eyes. Oscar and Manuel stared at me in astonishment. I smiled and tossed the double knocker back over by the tree, and we all burst out laughing.

By the time Martjan strode into camp an hour later, the night was already pitch-black. He told us it had been a tough hike.

"Rafael lost the trail and spent two hours hacking a new path through the undergrowth with his machete," he said. But Martjan was pleased with what he had seen. It was similar to the other places we had explored but had never been grazed by burros because there was no water for them to drink there. Consequently, it had a complete understory of grasses and flowers and even more large pines than the other places. They also found some recently dead large pines, but there were no signs of bark scaling and no large cavities—and no response to the double knocker. This area clearly had the highest probability of having imperial woodpeckers, but there were absolutely no signs of them. They seemed to be entirely absent from here and all the other places we checked—and perhaps from the whole region. And there were none of the tantalizing reports or rumors like those I had heard in the northern Sierra Madre Occidental. Here they are most likely gone.

Martjan said he had a spectacular eye-level flyby of a pair of military macaws and had seen some birds that were new for the expedition—a zone-tailed hawk and a red-naped sapsucker. He and Rafael had been able to look from their vantage point at the end of the ridge and see all the way down to the village of Taxicaringa. Martjan let Rafael look through his binoculars to see the people far below.

Oscar, Manuel, and I had already eaten dinner, but there were plenty of leftovers for Martjan. After he finished his meal, we headed to Rafael's rancho to show him the pictures and the film of Bill Rhein's 1956 expedition. Rafael's entire family was sitting about thirty feet from the front of his cabin, down a slight incline, huddled around a blazing bonfire trying to keep warm. They greeted us eagerly and ushered us into the kitchen of their simple, well-kept casa with its dirt floor and pine-board walls. A fire blazed brightly in the metal stove, the only illumination besides our headlamps.

We finally got to meet Rafael's wife, who looked like she might give birth to their seventh child at any moment. She wore her long black hair in a loose braid that hung down the center of her back. The children ranged in age from a toddler—a tiny boy with a dirty face who kept climbing onto his mother's lap to be nursed—to a teenage boy, perhaps fourteen or fifteen years old. They were all sooty from huddling before blazing pinewood fires to keep warm. People rarely bathe here because it's so difficult.

Martjan handed out eight-by-ten prints of Dick Heintzelman's pictures from the Rhein expedition and also some imperial woodpecker illustrations. And then it was time for the main event, watching the 1956 film. Everyone gazed with rapt attention at Martjan's computer screen as he spoke about the imperial woodpecker and said that the film had been made right in this area, near Guacamayita, and was the only photographic evidence ever recorded of the bird.

Before we left, we gave Rafael six hundred pesos—the equivalent of about fifty US dollars—and he seemed well pleased. He said he planned to walk to Guacamayita with his mules to buy some supplies.

We said good night and walked back to camp. Sometime in the early morning hours I started having that recurrent dream again. I was walking through a pine forest deep in the Sierra, and I heard the loud toots of a *pitoreal*. But this time the dream was different. Instead of moving quickly toward the sound and finally seeing an imperial woodpecker—and encountering the gunman—I turned away and ran as fast as I could to escape the bird's alluring call. And then I woke up. This time I was not drenched in sweat or thrashing around and calling out in terror. Amazingly, I felt good, refreshed. A whiskered screech owl was calling loudly from a tree somewhere just above my tent, and although it didn't sound like a *pitoreal*, I suspect it may have triggered my dream. I felt so happy and relieved that I drifted immediately into a deep, soothing slumber that lasted for the rest of the night. Whatever the next day might bring, at that moment I was fully at peace.

◆　◆　◆

At 6:30 a.m., Rafael and his two eldest sons had already started a blazing fire. They stood over it, rubbing their hands together to warm them. It had been a brutally cold night, and all of the standing water in the various potholes and depressions had frozen as thick as sheets of plate glass. We stood together beside the fire, eating cereal in small plastic cups, and then as the sky began lightening in the east, we got down to the task of breaking camp. I packed away all of my gear and put it in the back of the truck, then started taking down my dome tent. By eight o'clock, we were ready to leave. We said good-bye to Rafael and his sons and gave them most of our remaining food and camping supplies. They were still warming themselves at our fire as we pulled away into the dark forest. We all waved.

We still had to stop at our old adobe casa in Las Coloradas, where we had left our two drums of gasoline. I was a little worried that gas would splash all over the gear we were taking home with us. I could just imagine the faces of the security screeners at the airport as we handed them our bags, reeking of gasoline. I put my pack into a plastic trash bag I had brought along to help protect it from dust, grime, and gasoline, and we tried to put Martjan's gear as far away as possible from the drums.

If everything went as planned, we would meet Carlos and Julián there at ten and drive again in a convoy of three vehicles, which would still be dangerous, but far better than going alone.

The four of us crammed into the front seat (it was too smelly and toxic for anyone to ride with the gas drums). "Amigos," I said, and we laughed. We would just have to ride this way until Guacamayita, then one or two of us could ride in the forestry truck, we thought. When we arrived at Guacamayita, however, the village seemed deserted. The tiny, one-room school was in session, but the dirt streets were empty. We went to Carlos's cabin, but neither he nor his mother nor anyone else we knew was at home. We finally ran into a boy of about fifteen who suggested we talk to "the Judge" and took us to see him. We had met the man back on the day we arrived at Guacamayita, and he had gone to Los Pilares with us, though I had visions of the sinister character of that name in Cormac McCarthy's chilling novel about nineteenth-century Mexico, *Blood Meridian*.

The Judge seemed blasé about our concerns. He said Carlos had been due back two days earlier but hadn't shown up. And he hadn't seen or heard about anyone from the forestry unit coming here. He supposed we would have to drive to Durango by ourselves.

"Is it safe? Carlos told us not to drive back unescorted."

"Along the road, everything is quiet," he said. "The only thing that happened is that a few houses were burned down."

We were dumbfounded. "You really think we'll be able to get there safely?"

He shrugged. "You will get there at best," he said.

He yawned and seemed bored by our travails. I'm sure he was thinking, *Why not just get on the road and stop pestering me?* He was a portly man with a bushy gray moustache and a big belly that hung over his belt. We thanked him, shook his hand, and walked back to the truck.

At this point I thought: *We've got a fifty-fifty chance of running into some kind of dangerous situation on the long road back to Durango.* The road was full of potholes and huge exposed rocks. In some places, you could drive only three or four miles per hour—not as fast as most people can walk. It would be so easy to stage an ambush. Some bandits or *narcotraficantes* could just step out from behind a tree, holding AK-47s to our windshield, and all we could do is surrender and let them do as they pleased. We all knew that.

I took the memory cards from my cameras and my digital voice recorder and put them in the hip pocket of my jeans. I also stuck my notebook of the expedition and my passport into the pocket of the old coat I was wearing. I figured if some garden-variety highwaymen stopped us they might just take the truck and everything in it and leave us on the road, waiting for someone to come along and help us. If that happened, at least I would still have all of my travel documents, notes, and photographs, so my trip would not be a waste.

But I also had a terrible thought deep within me that if things went really bad—if the worst possible thing happened—my body would be identifiable from my passport, and my wife might receive my notes, recordings, and photographs with my personal effects. Maybe she could finish this book for me. It was a grim fantasy, and I couldn't get it out of my thoughts as we drove slowly through the bleak countryside. I went over my life in my mind again and again and felt many regrets. I thought of my wife and our many years together, sorry that I hadn't said how much she means to me and regretting that I wouldn't be able to watch my children grow into adulthood.

We rode in silence for a long time, all of us deep in thought, and were shocked when the first vehicle came around a corner ahead. It was a huge, old flatbed truck with a bunch of Tepehuanes huddled like refugees on the back—old men, women, and children with blankets wrapped around them against the cold. They looked scared. The truck stopped alongside us, and the woman riding in the passenger seat bent across the driver to speak with us. She said the road ahead was dangerous and to be very careful. Then, before they drove off, she said, "God may help you," and crossed herself.

We drove on and finally arrived at the scruffy little village of Las Espinas, where we had stopped with Carlos that first day in the mountains and also where we had bought flour a few days earlier at the tiny wooden shed. Martjan suggested stopping to pick up a few things. We were all a little surprised by this at first, because we were in such a hurry to get away from the Sierra. But then: Why not? And somehow it broke the tension.

It took a few minutes to find someone, but finally a young woman unlocked the door and removed the plywood board cover-

Several Tepehuanes huddle like refugees on the back of a flatbed truck, fleeing the violence lower down in the mountains. (*Photo by Tim Gallagher*)

ing the front. She seemed nervous and kept glancing around to see if anyone else was around. We didn't know what to make of it at the time. Martjan bought several packets of cookies and boxes of guava juice, the kind with a little straw attached that you poke through a hole on the top of the box.

"This is—how do you say it in English?—your last meal," said Martjan, handing me some cookies and juice. "Don't I get a last cigarette, too?" I said (even though I don't smoke), and we laughed.

We continued on, bouncing and grinding along that terrible road, trying to drive around all the potholes and protruding jagged rocks—and praying that the old Ford truck would not break down. It was unbearably slow going. In some places, we only drove one or two miles an hour for fear of blowing out a tire and getting stranded, helpless and alone. We dreaded every approaching blind corner, expecting an ambush any second. Finally, driving around a turn, we spotted a white pickup truck coming the other way toward us. The driver slowed almost to a stop, moving erratically for a moment, then continued driving toward us, moving as far to the other side of the road as he could get from us. When we finally drove past each other, I looked at the two men in the other truck, and they were visibly terrified—probably just the way we looked.

Martjan had his pocket GPS unit out, which he had used on our original drive up the mountain to track our route and establish waypoints, so now we were following the route in reverse. He had even marked the place where Carlos had said we were in the safe area, but we were long past that point now, heading deep into the no-man's-land where anything could happen. We did pass one large truck pulled over on the side of the road, but the driver wasn't in it, so we sped past as quickly as we could go on the bouncy road. Martjan kept picking up the GPS to see how much farther we had to go.

"We have twenty kilometers left until we reach the paved road, but that's if it were a straight line," said Martjan. "It might be closer to thirty or forty kilometers counting all the curves."

That was the slowest, most agonizing twenty kilometers of my life. When the road started to improve, and we finally were able to drive a little faster, we saw three freshly burned-out houses on the left side of the road. Now ghastly, they had been in perfect condition when we drove past them on the way up the mountains. Two of them had been cabins and were now just piles of blackened rubble, but the other had been much larger and more elaborate, made of stuccoed adobe painted light purple—now a gutted ruin with the roof caved in. We didn't dare stop but just kept pushing on, trying to reach the safety of the paved highway, where we could blast along at 80 miles an hour and get out of this scary place.

We looked at the GPS and saw that we were so close to the end of the dirt road that we finally dared hope that our ordeal might soon be over. And then it was there—the blacktop highway. Not a great road, but in many ways the nicest one we'd ever seen. I had saved my box of guava juice for just this moment, to celebrate our escape, and I poked the straw through the top and drank deeply of the sweet liquid. Oscar stuck a Mexican CD into the player in the dashboard, and we cheered, blasting down the highway, the four of us still crammed tightly together in the front bench seat of the truck—*cuatro amigos*.

We finally got a cell phone signal as we neared Durango City, but I could not get mine to make outgoing calls. I felt desperate to talk to my wife Rachel and hear her voice. Martjan got his phone to work, and he telephoned Utami, who was driving at the time and had to call him back a few minutes later. Then I borrowed Martjan's phone and left a message on Rachel's voicemail to call me back. As we were driving through the sweltering streets of central Durango—far hotter than it ever gets in the Sierra Madre—Rachel called me, and for the first time, I felt like I was out of danger, that everything would be fine.

Manuel drove past the Plaza de Armas and the old cathedral and turned right onto the street with the pay parking lot. We got a spot and opened up the back of the camper shell and were immediately knocked back by the reek of gasoline, which had leaked down the sides of the barrels and splashed over much of our equipment. The fumes were so strong it was amazing the whole thing hadn't exploded in a great fireball along the dirt road, leaving barely a trace of us. We pulled out our gear, leaving the Pronatura equipment and gas drums in the truck, with the screened windows open. The parking lot was guarded around the clock, so we hoped everything would be safe.

Like a ragged band of happy survivors, we made our way through the blazing streets of Durango—with packs on our backs and equipment slung around our necks, dragging wheeled duffels behind us but smiling broadly at every passerby.

Martjan and I checked in back at the old hotel, got our same room (number 218), and dragged our things inside. Later, we hit the streets to get some good Mexican food at the tortas shop where Martjan and I had eaten when we first arrived in Durango. The food was great.

◆ ◆ ◆

Martjan had spoken briefly with Julián on the telephone and arranged for us to meet him the next morning and have breakfast together. It was nearly eight o'clock and sunny as we walked across the Plaza de Armas looking for Julián. We finally spotted him a second before he saw us. He rushed toward us, his face a mix of intense emotions: anger, sorrow, and above all relief. And when he got to us he embraced each of us tightly. His thoughts spilled out in a torrent: how he would never have forgiven himself if anything had happened to us; how sorry he was that he encouraged us initially, saying that the area was safe; and how much he had wanted us to abandon our expedition that night in the plaza two weeks earlier. He told us a rising tide of violence had swept into the area days before we arrived and was just starting to crest as we went into the Sierra Madre. He felt that because he had encouraged us earlier, he had to help us get there, but he didn't want to do it. He said on Thursday a man had been abducted in Las Espinas—the village where we bought the cookies a day later on our journey out of the mountains and the place Carlos had said was safe. He had been grabbed at random and held for a ransom of 10,000 pesos—about $800, which the Tepehuán villagers had all pitched in to raise—a fortune for them.

No wonder everything had seemed so quiet and strange there yesterday. What would happen the next time someone was abducted and no one had any money to spare for a ransom? The whole society seemed to be breaking down. Julián knew about the burned houses and had wanted to get in touch with us somehow to tell us not to attempt to drive out that way. Even going the other route, crossing through part of the Zetas' land, would probably have been safer, he said. He could not get away to meet us, then heard that Carlos could not escort us from Guacamayita, and he was horrified. He said on Thursday night he and his wife got down on their knees and prayed to God for our safety. I choked up several times as we stood together talking and later as we ate breakfast.

Before we bid him good-bye, Julián handed Martjan and me each a hand-woven Tepehuán bag, like the one Rafael had carried on his back to hold tortillas and other supplies. Then we hugged again and walked our separate ways across the Plaza de Armas. We were safe. In two days we would be landing in Houston, a world away from here, and it could not be soon enough.

EPILOGUE

Vaya con Dios, Pitoreal

I often think back to my final night in the Sierra Madre—the last time I had that terrifying dream about encountering an imperial woodpecker . . . and experiencing my own violent death. The Durango expedition was the fifth time in the space of a year that I'd been in Mexico, chasing the ghost of the *pitoreal*—a fading mirage that seemed always just over the horizon. What was different from the other times I'd had the dream was that for the first time I ran away as fast as I could to escape the bird's alluring call. Perhaps my subconscious was sending a message I was too blind to see in my waking hours. Perhaps I finally realized that all I really wanted to do was to get back to my wife and children and stop this mad quest.

There was a point during the latter part of the Durango expedition when Martjan and I had sat by the campfire discussing some of the recent possible *pitoreal* sightings I had uncovered during my interviews in the mountains of Chihuahua. At least three of them in the Chuhuichupa area seemed believable and intriguing, and I didn't have a chance to check the area adequately. We had looked at a couple of places near there on Google Earth before we left for Durango, and the habitat looked good. As we spoke, the thought of exploring that area, searching it thoroughly for imperial woodpeckers, suddenly seemed so imperative. My heart beat faster as I envisioned the expedition in my mind. We could cobble together a couple of small grants. We could live on the cheap—frijoles and tortillas. And then it dawned on me with a jolt: there we would be again, putting ourselves in harm's way for this rare and noble bird that may no longer exist. Maybe this is how it is with gamblers or all of those treasure hunters and prospectors who have scoured these mountains from top to bottom over the decades if not centuries—another form of gold fever. Then I knew it was time to pass the baton of searching for the imperial woodpecker to others. Martjan realized that, too.

I hope other searchers will someday pick up where we left off, but I must give this one cautionary note to anyone who wishes to take up this mantle: you stand a far better chance of getting killed in the Sierra Madre now than of ever seeing a *pitoreal*.

Afterword

Since I completed this manuscript, I'm happy to report some recent hopeful signs that the current state of affairs in Mexico, particularly the country's relationship with its natural environment, may be improving.

The people of Cherán, a mountain town in the state of Michoacán (in the historical range of the imperial woodpecker) with a population of sixteen thousand, have risen up against the drug-cartel-backed loggers who had been illegally clear-cutting their communal forest, destroying thousands of acres of woodlands. For more than three years, local residents—made up mostly of indigenous Purépechas—had been subjected to murder, rape, kidnapping, and extortion by the loggers and drug traffickers. Frustrated by the lack of protection from the police and the civil government, the populace took matters into their own hands in April 2011, forcing several loggers out of their trucks and burning their vehicles. They then seized control of the police station, taking the weapons for their own protection and disbanding the police department. Law and order is now in the hands of the people of Cherán, who have kept the entrances to the town blockaded for more than a year, keeping out illegal loggers, drug traffickers, and other dangerous outsiders. Their efforts seem to be working: the crime rate has plummeted and the destruction of the surrounding forest has been halted. More of this kind of response may occur in the towns and villages of the Sierra Madre, dangerous though it is for the citizens themselves.

On the environmental front, organizations such as Pronatura, World Wildlife Fund Mexico, and others have been working to preserve vital habitats in the country. In a recent success story, illegal logging has been almost entirely eliminated in the monarch butterfly wintering areas in the mountaintop forests west of Mexico City, thanks to government antilogging patrols and education efforts encouraging local residents to plant trees and support ecotourism.

Mexico has also recently had a change in government, with Enrique Peña Nieto replacing Felipe Calderón as president in December 2012. It remains to be seen how the new national leadership will affect the dire situation in the country. But Peña Nieto has pledged to change the existing law enforcement strategy of targeting high-profile drug lords and cartels and instead make an all-out effort to quell the rape, murder, kidnapping, extortion, and shoot-outs that are harming so many Mexicans from all walks of life. To date, more than fifty thousand Mexicans have died in the drug war, with little to show for it. If his efforts to reduce the level of violence and reestablish law and order in Mexico succeed, it will vastly improve the chances of bringing meaningful conservation initiatives to the remotest regions of the Sierra Madre and across the country.

Acknowledgments

I owe a deep debt of gratitude to the many people who helped me with this book. I especially thank Martjan Lammertink, a scientist, explorer, and friend, whose deep interest in the imperial and ivory-billed woodpeckers stretches back to childhood. Martjan generously shared his knowledge of the imperial woodpecker and his many contacts with me. We spoke often as I worked on this project, and we traveled together during my final and most dangerous expedition—a journey through the high-mountain drug lands of Durango.

I thank John Hatch, who guided me on most of my forays into the Sierra Madre Occidental, helping me figure out which places were worth exploring, tracking down leads, arranging interviews, and serving as a translator. Without his able assistance, this project would have been impossible.

I also thank my other Mexican friends, Nelda and Efraín Villa and Elvin Whetten, for their help and hospitality; Julián Bautista, for introducing me to key people in the Guacamayita area; and Oscar Paz and Manuel Escarcega, for their hard work on the Durango expedition.

I am grateful to journalist Paul Salopek. Even though I didn't know him when I began my quest, Paul was willing to meet with me and provided an enormous amount of help and encouragement, suggesting people to interview and places to visit, and we still keep in touch.

I thank David Allen, who shared his memories of the imperial woodpecker he saw during his father's 1946 expedition and of his subsequent expedition in the 1970s, and gave me his "treasure map." He was an inspiration to me.

ACKNOWLEDGMENTS

I also thank everyone who let me interview them for this book. For me, the most fascinating part of the reporting process was to hear firsthand the stories of people who had seen living imperial woodpeckers. Sadly, they may be the final eyewitnesses of the bird's existence.

I am indebted to my agent, Russ Galen, for his advice and encouragement throughout this project. Without his help, this book would never have been written.

I thank everyone at Simon & Schuster who helped with this book, especially senior editor Leslie Meredith, who took on the project and guided me through several rewrites of my manuscript; associate editor Donna Loffredo; and senior production editor Mara Lurie.

Above all, I thank everyone who helped my wife, Rachel, and me survive the most difficult year of our lives—a time when we lost both of our mothers followed by the worst loss of all, the sudden death of our son Jack, just two months short of his eighteenth birthday. We could not have made it through this difficult time without the love of our daughters Railey, Clara, and Gwen; my sisters Maureen and Janet; Rachel's sisters Anne and Amy; and the rest of our extended family. I'm eternally grateful to my friend Bobby Harrison for coming here from Alabama at a moment's notice to attend my son's funeral and provide emotional support during the depths of my grief. I thank my friends at the Cornell Lab of Ornithology, and indeed the entire university, for their understanding and compassion during this difficult time. I will also always remember the outpouring of emotional support we received from the people of Freeville and Dryden, New York, who embraced us as family.

Selected Bibliography

Allen, Arthur A. 1951. *Stalking Birds with Color Camera*. Washington, D.C.: National Geographic Society.

Bowden, Charles. 2010. *Murder City: Ciudad Juárez and the Global Economy's New Killing Fields*. New York: Nation Books.

Debo, Angio. 1976. *Geronimo: The Man, His Time, His Place*. Norman, Oklahoma: University of Oklahoma Press.

Fitzpatrick, John, Martjan Lammertink, Tim W. Gallagher, et al. 2005. "Ivory-billed Woodpecker (*Campephilus principalis*) Persists in North America." *Science* 308: 1460–62.

Forbes, William. 2004. "Revisiting Aldo Leopold's 'Perfect' Land Health: Conservation and Development in Mexico's Rio Gavilan." Denton, Texas: UNT Digital Library.

Gallagher, Tim. 2005. *The Grail Bird*. New York: Houghton Mifflin.

———. 2011. "Return to Durango." *Living Bird* 30 (4): 16–25.

Geronimo. 1906. *Geronimo's Story of his Life, as told to Stephen Melvil Barrett*. New York: Duffield & Company.

Goldman, Edward Alphonso. 1951. *Biological Investigations in Mexico*. Washington, D.C.: Smithsonian Institution.

Goodwin, Grenville, and Neil Goodwin. 2000. *The Apache Diaries: A Father-Son Journey*. Lincoln, Nebraska: University of Nebraska Press.

Grant, Richard. 2008. *God's Middle Finger: Into the Lawless Heart of the Sierra Madre*. New York: Free Press.

Guzmán, M. L. 1975. *Memoirs of Pancho Villa*. Austin, Texas: University of Texas Press.

Hatch, E. LeRoy. 2003. *Médico: My Life as a Country Doctor in Mexico*. Mesa, Arizona: Jeanne J. Hatch.

Ingstad, Helge. 2004. *The Apache Indians: In Search of the Missing Tribe*. Lincoln, Nebraska: University of Nebraska Press.

Katz, Friedrich. 1998. *The Life and Times of Pancho Villa*. Stanford, California: Stanford University Press.

Lammertink, Martjan. 1992. "Search for Ivory-billed Woodpecker in Cuba." *Dutch Birding* 14: 170–73.

———. 1995. "No more hope for the Ivory-billed Woodpecker." *Cotinga* 3: 45–47.

———. 1996. "The Lost Empire of the Imperial Woodpecker." *World Birdwatch* 18:8–12.

———, A. R. Estrada. 1995. "Status of the Ivory-billed Woodpecker in Cuba: almost certainly extinct." *Bird Conservation International* 5: 53–59.

———, J. A. Rojas Tome, F. M. Casillas-Orona, and R. L. Otto. 1996. "Status and conservation of old-growth forest and endemic birds in the pine-oak zone of the Sierra Madre Occidental, Mexico." *Verslagen en Technische Gegevens* 69:1–89.

———, Tim Gallagher, et al. 2011. "Film Footage of the Probably Extinct Imperial Woodpecker." *The Auk* 128 (4): 671–77.

Leopold, Aldo. 1949. *A Sand County Almanac and Sketches Here and There.* New York: Oxford University Press.

———. 1953. *Round River.* New York: Oxford University Press.

Leopold, A. Starker. 1949. "Adios, Gavilan." *Pacific Discovery* 2 (1): 4–13.

———. 1959. *Wildlife of Mexico.* Berkeley: University of California Press.

Lumholtz, Carl. 1902. *Unknown Mexico*, 2 vols. New York: Charles Scribners Sons.

Marshall, Joe T. 1957. *Birds of the Pine-oak Woodland in Southern Arizona and Adjacent Mexico.* Berkeley, California: Cooper Ornithological Society.

Meed, Douglas V. 1993. *They Never Surrendered: Bronco Apaches of the Sierra Madres 1890–1935.* Tucson, Arizona: Westernlore.

Mendenhall, Matt. 2005. "Old Friend Missing." *Birder's World.* December 2005.

Nelson, E. W. 1898. "The Imperial Ivory-billed Woodpecker, *Campephilus imperialis* (Gould)." *The Auk* 15 (3): 216–23.

Romney, Thomas C. 1938. *The Mormon Colonies in Mexico.* Salt Lake City, Utah: Deseret Book Company.

Sauer, Gordon C., ed. 1898. *John Gould: The Bird Man; Correspondence through 1838.* Mansfield Center, Connecticut: Maurizio Martino Publisher.

Snyder, Noel F. R., David E. Brown, and Kevin B. Clark. 2009. *The Travails of Two Woodpeckers.* Albuquerque, New Mexico: University of New Mexico Press.

Tanner, James T. 1964. "The Decline and Present Status of the Imperial Woodpecker of Mexico." *The Auk* 81 (1): 74–81.

Traven, B. 1935. *The Treasure of the Sierra Madre.* New York: Alfred A. Knopf.

Whetten, LaVon Brown. 2010. *Colonia Juárez: Commemorating 125 Years of the Mormon Colonies in Mexico.* Bloomington, Indiana: Author-House.

Index

ABOUT THE AUTHOR

Tim Gallagher is an award-winning author, wildlife photographer, and magazine editor. He is currently editor in chief of *Living Bird*, the flagship publication of the Cornell Lab of Ornithology. In the 1970s he worked with the Santa Cruz Predatory Bird Research Group—an affiliate of the Peregrine Fund—helping their efforts to save the peregrine falcon and other threatened species. Gallagher also spent several years traveling across the South, interviewing people who claimed to have seen the legendary ivory-billed woodpecker, and then had a sighting of this sought-after bird. This sighting—the first time since 1944 that two qualified observers had positively identified an ivory-billed woodpecker in the United States—quickly led to the largest search ever launched to find a rare bird and ultimately to the announcement on April 28, 2005, of the rediscovery of the species. His book *The Grail Bird* is about this rediscovery, *Parts Unknown* about his travels in search of birds and wild places, and *Falcon Fever* about his lifelong interest in birds of prey and falconry.